P9-DEA-001

Understanding women in distress

Understanding women in distress

Pamela Ashurst and Zaida Hall

With contributions from
George Christie
Gill Gorell-Barnes
Jane Knowles
Mike Pawson
Dinora Pines

Tavistock/Routledge
London and New York

First Published in 1989 by Routledge
11 New Fetter Lane, London EC4P 4EE
29 West 35th Street, New York, NY 10001

Typeset by Laserscript Ltd, Mitcham, Surrey
Printed and bound in Great Britain by
MacKays of Chatham PLC, Chatham, Kent

British Library Cataloguing in Publication Data

Ashurst, Pamela,
Understanding women in distress
1. Women. Psychotherapy
I. Title II. Hall, Zaida,
616.89'1

ISBN 0-415-01832-3
ISBN 0-415-01833-1 Pbk

Library of Congress Cataloging-in-Publication Data

Ashurst, Pamela,
Understanding Women in distress/Pamela Ashurst and Zaida Hall
with contributions from George Christie . . . [et al.].
p. cm.
Bibliography: p.
Includes index.
1. Women — Mental Health. 2. Women — Psychology. 3. Depression, Mental. 4. Stress (Psychology) I. Hall, Zaida, 1925- .
II. Title.
[DNLM: 1. Genital Diseases, Female — psychology. 2. Identification (Psychology) 3. Life Changes Events. 4. Mothers — psychology. 5. Stress, Psychological. 6. Women — psychology. HQ 1206 A829u]
RC451.4.W6A84 1989
616.89'0088042 — dc19
DNLM/DLC
for Library of Congress 89-3569
CIP

ISBN 0-415-01832-3 — ISBN 0-415 01833-1 (pbk.)

For our husbands and our sons

We may safely assert that the knowledge that men can acquire of women, even as they have been and are, without reference to what they might be, is wretchedly imperfect and superficial and will always be so until women themselves have told all that they have to tell.

John Stuart Mill

Contents

Authors and contributors

Authors

Pamela Ashurst M.B., Ch.B., F.R.C.Psych. Consultant Psychotherapist, Royal South Hants Hospital, Southampton. Honorary Clinical Teacher, Southampton Medical School. She is an Examiner of the Royal College of Psychiatrists, and is active in Psychotherapy training, in women's affairs, and in public education. She has a particular interest in brief psychotherapy and has specialised in the treatment of grief and patients with cancer.

Zaida Hall D.M., F.R.C.P., F.R.C.Psych. Consultant Psychotherapist, Department of Psychotherapy, Royal South Hants Hospital, Southampton. Consultant Psychiatrist to the University of Southampton. Honorary Clinical Teacher, Southampton Medical School. Consultant Psychiatrist at Winchester Assessment Centre for adolescent girls, until 1985. She has specialised in the treatment of adult women victims of childhood sexual and psychological abuse.

Contributors

Dinora Pines MB, BS. Training Analyst of the British Society of Psychoanalysis. She has written many papers on pregnancy and female sexuality.

George Christie FRANZCP, MRCPsych. Consultant Psychiatrist and Psychotherapist, Melbourne, Australia and Member of the Australian Psychoanalytic Society.

Mike Pawson, FRCOG. Honorary Consultant and Senior Lecturer in Obstetrics and Gynaecology, Charing Cross Hospital, London.

Gill Gorell-Barnes MA, MSc. Senior Social Worker at the Tavistock Clinic. Director of Training at the Institute of Family Therapy, London. She is currently engaged on a Stepfamily Research Project.

Jane Knowles MB, BS, MRCPsych. Consultant Psychotherapist, West Berkshire. She has a special interest in the psychology of women.

Foreword

This important book is based on the authors' extensive personal experience of helping women in distress. As befits a work written by professionals, the aim is to help the reader to understand, not to pass judgement. Nor do the authors attempt an extensive assessment of the 'body of knowledge' on any particular topic. Theirs is a personal view, and the width and depth of their experience is vividly reflected in their writing, which conveys their accumulated wisdom with refreshing clarity. They bring their own insights and interpretations to the many predicaments – some of them new, many of them very old – which women are now encountering.

This book will be valuable, not only to professionals, but to all those who seek to understand more about their fellow human beings and about themselves. I have learnt much from reading it.

Dr J.L.T. Birley,
President,
The Royal College of Psychiatrists

Introduction

Over the years we have been made aware that many women have chosen to consult us as psychotherapists specifically because we are women. They have expected us to understand some of the experiences that they have felt to be of fundamental importance to them as women, and that have been associated with considerable distress, sometimes leading to prolonged periods of psychiatric care. Friends and family may have given support and understanding; but when such distress is sufficient for a woman to consult her doctor, she is defining herself as a patient and implicitly and explicitly asking for help that is not otherwise available to her.

We had both been interested for some years in the special ingredients of women's distress: the feminine identity and the mothering urge, and how their absence, their frustration, or their lack of fulfilment had produced psychopathology in our patients. We had seen the pain caused by a failure to conceive, or by the loss of the conceived foetus through a stillbirth or by the death of a child; the sometimes almost pathological strength of the maternal urge in a threatened miscarriage; and the anguish when a patient lost the physical attributes of femininity through a mastectomy, a sterilization, or a hysterectomy. We had explored with our patients the hidden meanings of artificial insemination by husband or donor. We had noted how delinquent adolescent girls leap into sexual activity and pregnancy for reasons deriving from their deprived or abused childhoods; and had observed the uncertainty and confusion shown by some patients with regard to their feminine identity, and their difficulty in thinking of themselves as potentially good mothers.

We decided, therefore, to explore more deeply these aspects of women's distress. What was the essence of this special feminine identity and this mothering urge? How had they developed and how did they affect women's lives?

Hidden behind seemingly inexplicable symptoms in women patients lie painful traumatic experiences in the recent or distant past, which relate to the patient's image of herself as a women or as a mother . Once these experiences are brought to light, she can, perhaps for the first time, express her sadness, rage, humiliation, or despair, understand the meaning of her symptoms, and begin to overcome them. These traumatic experiences are not divulged, or the emotions are not expressed, because the patient does not realize, or does not expect others to realize their importance; and the doctor or other professional either does not enquire about them or disregards or makes little of them, leaving the distress to persist, sometimes for years.

Women are usually more in touch with their emotions than men, while most men, partly due to upbringing, shy away from theirs. Because women usually complain and consult about their neurotic symptoms more than men do, male doctors tend to become bored, exasperated, or defeated by the many problems and difficulties of women. Although 38 per cent of doctors in Britain are women, most women patients consult doctors who are men, and most senior medical posts are held by men. Women have had minimal influence on planning, policy, research, and decision-making in the health-care field, and relatively little attention has been given to the specific health problems of women – particularly to the psychological aspects.

How can men be helped to understand the causes of distress in women? They cannot experience menstruation, pregnancy, childbirth, or suckling; they cannot know what it is to be female. Yet it is possible that they might, by an act of creative empathy, imagine what it is to be a woman, with breasts, a vagina, a period. By recognizing those special aspects of womanhood, they may comprehend how disorders associated with them lead to the distress for which she seeks help.

There are, of course, areas in which men can suffer distress that specifically affects their manhood, for example, impotence, infertility, sexual assault, damage to genitals from vasectomy, or failure of development of masculine sexual characteristics. There are also the general areas of power and status where men suffer injury to their image of themselves as men – the loss of a job, unemployment, demotion, and public humiliation or failure of any kind. And men share with women shame or hurt at disfigurement, disability, rejection, bereavement, or divorce. Much of what we say of such situations will apply equally to men.

It is difficult for a man to comprehend the way a woman feels, just as, no doubt, it is difficult for a woman fully to understand the drives and impulses, and the bruises to masculine identity that a man may experience. But men's specific ills and the difficulties resulting from loss of power or status are generally well understood, whereas the significance of traumas involving women *because* they are women, are only beginning to be understood and are often ignored. We recognize that neither sex can fully understand what it is to be the other, but hope that our book may at least contribute towards a better understanding of the female predicament.

Our women patients tell us of the ways in which doctors can be insensitive to their anxiety and distress. They are well-meaning and concerned to cure their patients and to save their lives, but because of embarrassment, lack of time, or lack of perception, they can say things that they would surely regret if they understood how much hurt they caused. For example, a patient who asked for a prosthesis to replace a breast lost by mastectomy was told, 'You are so small, it's hardly worth bothering'; and a young woman after a stillbirth was told, 'Never mind, there are plenty more where that came from'.

There is much evidence that women are constitutionally stronger than men, and in every age group women outlive their male contemporaries. Advances in contraception and obstetric practice have reduced the hazards of pregnany and childbirth, giving women a greater life expectancy. Despite this healthy physical outlook, a woman's psychological vulnerability increases at key points during her lifetime. The significance of certain developmental stages and life events needs to be understood from the woman's point of view if she is to be helped.

Single women show less tendency to develop mental illness than unmarried men. Marriage, however, seems to increase a woman's vulnerability, for married women are more likely than married men to become psychiatric casualties. Separation, divorce, and widowhood all bring further problems, but the return to unmarried status for women is seldom accompanied by improved prospects of mental health. The admission and readmission rates of women to mental hospitals at all ages substantially exceeds that of men, and women's longevity means that this tendency increases with age. Women are more likely to be treated for neurotic disorders, to be prescribed tranquilizers and antidepressants, and to suffer from complaints that are generally regarded as being psychosomatic.

This book is based on our personal and extensive clinical experience of both men and women. We have only included material with which we are daily familiar; it is therefore not comprehensive. Four chapters have been contributed by other colleagues, all of whom are experts in their own field. We are grateful to them, as we are to Dr Jim Birley for his kindness in writing the foreword.

Chapter 1 gives an account of how distress is caused and is translated into symptoms; and how it can be relieved by psychotherapy. The remainder of Part One is devoted to the consideration of the biological, familial, and social influences and the psychological factors promoting the development of a woman's identity throughout the various stages of her life experience as daughter, adolescent, young woman, wife, and mother. The factors promoting or militating against satisfactory bonding between mother and child, and the consequences of its failure – leading to rejection, unhappiness, and psychopathology – are dealt with in some detail. Part Two describes the various deviations from and failures of this normal development and the life traumas that threaten feminine identity. We have so ordered the chapters that they more or less reflect the sequence of events in a woman's life cycle, in order that various traumatic aspects of a woman's life experience can be clarified and explored. This division is inevitably artificial, leading to some overlap and repetition, in order that each chapter can stand alone.

Throughout this book we have tried to illustrate our theme with clinical examples from our practice. We have simplified our patients' stories in order to make them clearer to the reader. So often a patient's history has contained many successive traumas, each contributing to her being overwhelmed by life events and to the development of her symptoms. We have altered the names, situations, and other details in order to make them anonymous to the reader and to preserve confidentiality. Our patients may recognize themselves in these pages; we hope that we have made it impossible for anyone else to recognize them individually, but we believe that our readers will find many of these stories familiar.

For ease of reading we have used the masculine pronoun to indicate infants of both sexes, boys and girls, and men and women. Where we use the feminine pronoun we refer only to females. We have listed key references at the end of the book in order to avoid encumbering the text. Suggestions for further reading and some useful addresses are given at the end of several chapters.

We have been privileged to share most intimate and moving confidences from women of all ages, from girlhood into old age, and to accompany them on painful and revealing journeys into their past experiences, often exploring tragedy unremarked when it actually occurred. We have been concerned with failures of emotional and psychological understanding. We have shared our patients' joy and satisfaction when they have achieved renewed health and creative purpose as a result of understanding and integrating their experiences. Release from the burden of suffering is not a denial of the experience; it frees the woman to put aside the past, and to make her future more rewarding and creative.

This book is planned to be readable and easily understood, so that it is accessible to a lay audience. We hope, nevertheless, that doctors, medical students, and other professional caregivers will acknowledge it as a serious attempt to promote good psychiatric practice. The recognition and understanding of distress in women patients enables more effective help to be offered at an early stage.

We have been helped by many friends and colleagues who have generously shared their experience with us and who have encouraged us in the preparation of this book. We are unable to thank them all individually but we would like to mention Carol Kennedy, Dorothy Moore, Ailsa Royston, Andrea Pound, and Estela Welldon. We also wish to thank our colleagues in the Department and our generations of trainee psychotherapists. Our hospital librarian Bobby Noyes and her staff have helped us willingly with many queries and references. We acknowledge with gratitude the support of Jill Hatfield, our Department secretary, and her constant kindness and help both on the telephone and in person to our patients and to ourselves. We thank Leona Hope and Jane Trask for their patience in typing this manuscript. We are grateful to our families, especially our husbands, for their forebearance and encouragement during the writing of this book.

Not least, we wish to record our gratitude to those women, our patients, from whom we have learned so much. We hope that this book will contribute to the fuller understanding of all women in distress.

Part One

Womanhood

Chapter one

Understanding distress

The development and relief of symptoms

Below the surface-stream, shallow and light,
Of what we *say* we feel – below the stream,
As light, of what we *think* we feel – there flows
With noiseless current strong, obscure and deep,
The central stream of what we feel indeed.

Matthew Arnold

Distress is the experience by which we signify that all is not well with our world. It may be life-saving or life-threatening. We express it in many different ways, determined largely by our previous experience, all of which indicate a state of 'dis-ease' with our bodies, with our environment, and with other people. Health is that state of equilibrium that we enjoy when we thrive in the context in which we live. Illness, or dis-ease, represents a deviation from that healthy equilibrium.

People consult their doctors in order to seek an explanation for symptoms or experiences that they identify as sickness or disease. Such symptoms may have developed recently or may have been present for a long time, but the act of consulting a doctor defines the person concerned as a patient.

Distress or mental pain manifests itself in physical or mental symptoms or experiences. We may use psychological language to try to describe the experiences, but whether we have bodily or psychological symptoms, we probably experience them cerebrally as a mind–body continuum. Language gives a poor approximation of what we are experiencing but is essential if we are to communicate our distress. The psychotherapist does not try to classify or label a patients' symptoms with a diagnosis in order to give treatment, but accepts the existential description of the distress as the actual disease, and addresses that.

When we are healthy we experience ourselves as being in control of our bodies and thus of our immediate world. When we are sick we fear loss of control, and our very existence seems threatened. Putting the experience of distress into words to another person who listens and hears brings some relief to the patient. It gives him the possibility of control over it. The task of the doctor is to make sense of the symptoms and signs of which the patient complains, providing an explanation and thereby reassuring him that the situation is comprehensible, that his symptoms can be understood and treated or managed, or will recover spontaneously. Such explanation and reassurance is a major part of the healing offered by the physician and a necessary accompaniment of any form of treatment.

For the psychotherapist, explaining and making sense of the patient's predicament is one of the most potent tools in therapy. Language is thus the vehicle for the practice of psychotherapy, which consists of the mutual exploration by patient and therapist of the underlying causes of his distress. The therapist is like a sherpa or mountain guide who knows something of the terrain and is more familiar with it than the person he is guiding. The sherpa cannot, however, take the steps for the traveller or stop him from experiencing some further pain on the way; but he can, by his presence, support and reassure, and take away the loneliness and terror of the journey.

How stress causes symptoms

Somewhat surprisingly, the explanation of how mental and physical symptoms arise as a result of the stresses of life experience is an endeavour rarely attempted in textbooks on psychiatry or psychotherapy; the emphasis is usually on unravelling the causation in past experience rather than on following the effect of the cause, or the multiple causes or stresses, on the individual through to the production of symptoms. The term 'stress' is often misused, being taken to refer to the disease itself – 'I'm suffering from stress' – as well as to the cause of the disease. Our explanation of the chain of events – stress → distress → symptoms – can only provide a theoretical model of the process based on our experience as psychotherapists and supervisors of trainee therapists, in individual, group, marital, and family therapy over twenty years.

Identity

The key structure in this pathway is our concept of self or identity. We are conscious of our body image, the way in which we appear to ourselves and others. We use our role and the immediate environment both as an expression and an extension of our identity. Our clothes express the sort of person we feel we are. An adolescent's room with its posters represents so vividly what he feels to be his personality that any attempt to alter it or tidy it by his mother is felt as an assault upon his person. A woman's house or a man's car may be experienced as similar extensions of the self, vehemently defended against attack.

Identity is not static; it is constantly altered by the reflections back from the other people in our lives. That is, in fact, the way in which our identity is first formed, as we discuss in greater detail in Chapter 3. The closer the family relationship, the greater the effect, strengthening or weakening our identity. We are less influenced by friends, and even less by acquaintances, unless they occupy positions of importance for us – for instance the boss, or the form teacher, or the special friend; though the effect of the peer group can be enhancing or belittling. It is this reflective quality known as 'mirroring' that can make group therapy so healing, each member 'discovering himself' from the reflections of the other members.

The most important reflections are therefore in the immediate family – mother, father, siblings, partner or spouse, or child. For a student it might be the other students with whom he shares a house. Outside this closed circle is the wider environment, which also exerts an influence on identity.

But a person's identity does not only exist in the present: it extends to the future, with expectations and aims. A middle-aged woman whose husband dies experiences not only the pain of his absence *now* but apprehension about her future. It is threatening to her identity not to be able to envisage how her life will continue as a widow. University students are often less anxious about the final examinations than about what they will be doing and where they will be living *after* graduation. Losing a job may have grave implications for the future. Life-threatening illness brings with it not only fears of incapacity and of possible death, but also fears for the future of the family left behind.

Individual identity depends not only on the present and the future but also on the past or what is thought to the the past. A discovery that one's origins were not exactly what one had always assumed can be profoundly unsettling.

> A young woman was told by her mother on the day of her father's death, when she was 10 years old, that her father was not really her father, and that her mother had married him while pregnant by another man. Her identity was thus doubly assaulted by the death of her father and by the loss of his being her true father. Who *was* she then? This immense discontinuity to her concept of herself was more disturbing because the loved father was no longer there to comfort and reassure her.

Revelations about the past are often made by relatives and neighbours to young people reaching adolescence, increasing the usual emotional turmoil experienced at that age. Then parents, relatives, and social workers are surprised at the resulting acting-out behaviour – disobedience at home, disruption at school, and acceptance of deviant peer-group values.

> An adolescent girl was upset to discover that the person she had supposed to be her mother was not in fact her mother but her *grandmother*, and that her true mother was the rather tiresome older sister now married, with her own children, who had never bothered with her. (The girl had been an illegitimate baby and her grandmother had brought her up as her own child.) Her identity was threatened by this discovery, and her behaviour became disturbed.

How is this identity formed? It has been assumed that the infant's concept of self has its beginnings after birth, but it is by no means certain that some dim awareness of his presence in the womb does not contribute to his concept. Whether or not this is so, the moment of conception has special significance for the parents, and later for the child, as it is at that instant that the inheritance of the 'good' or 'bad' blood – or, if one is more sophisticated, the 'good' or 'bad' genes – occurs. The family members' view of the inherited characteristics can influence their upbringing of the child. If they expect the child to be bearing the bad inheritance, they will reflect back the child's identity accordingly.

> For instance, some adoptive parents were being interviewed about their adopted teenage daughter's shoplifting. Because her natural mother had been unmarried when the daughter had been born, they assumed that she was 'a bad lot' and cited the daughter's stealing of toffees as a young child as evidence of her inherited badness, and would not be convinced otherwise. It was, in fact, their lack of love towards her and constant 'picking on her' that drove her in adolescence to delinquent behaviour; she acted in the way she was expected to.

Those who wish to make a child develop a particular attribute must see the potential for its development in the child and must somehow communicate this to him. This trust in a child's ability to learn or to behave in a certain way is likely to produce the required result, whereas constant criticism is counterproductive. Indeed, this trust of a persons' potential and acceptance and valuing of what he is *at that moment*, is also one of the most useful tools of the psychotherapist in what is predominantly the learning experience of therapy.

The influence of the mother or the primary carer is of paramount importance to the infant. She needs to be, in Winnicott's terms (1960) the 'good enough mother', responding readily to her child's needs at first, but later, as she senses he is ready to cope with some frustration, responding less readily. From her smiling face and the way she handles him, mirroring back to him what a marvellous person she finds him, he will slowly begin to develop some concept of himself as a person and, moreover, as an acceptable person.

With the dawning understanding of himself as a separate person from his mother, the infant begins to focus on the father, and, in the oedipal triad, his own position in relation to his parents influences his sexuality. These early influences are discussed further in Chapter 3.

The rivalries between siblings for the parents' attention and affection, and the increasing influence of the world outside the family – the playgroup and school – characterize the period from toddlerhood to adolescence. Puberty has a profound effect on the individual's self-image, with the great change in body size and shape, and in boys' strength, with the hormonal changes, and with the developing sexuality. In addition there are all the social changes inherent in the move to secondary schooling – increase in the size of buildings, in the number and size of the other pupils, and in opportunities for the more grown-up excitements of smoking, graffiti, bullying, sex, drinking, drugs, and delinquency. If the home life is deprived and there is no security at home or at school, the emerging identity is profoundly threatened. With enough stability and security in home and school, however, the adolescent can undertake the tasks of becoming independent of parents and of discovering sexual identity, choice of career, and religious and political values (Erikson, 1959). These tasks take time, and the identity is not fully formed – that is adolescence is not ended – until somewhere between the ages of 18 and 23.

Everyone carries an internal image of one or both parents, often highly critical, sometimes approving. Good images are enabling, whereas critical ones are usually disabling. Even in adulthood many people have not been able fully to free themselves from the controlling standards of their parents, continuing either to adhere to them slavishly or to rebel against them on principle. This is a hallmark of adolescence, and the establishment of one's own values and opinions is evidence of autonomy and emotional maturity. In order to try to escape them, some people put *physical* distance (sometimes thousands of miles) between themselves and their parents, but clearly have not been able to achieve *emotional* distance.

Even though identity has been formed, it is not fixed and must constantly be adjusted to changing life circumstances if the individual is to remain free from dis-ease. The self-image has to weather the more-or-less inevitable storms that come with the finding of a partner, the advent of children, the establishment of a career, the realization of limitations on achievement, and the abandonment of adolescent dreams of fame and success; and, at a later stage, to come to terms with children leaving home, the waning of power with retirement, and the increasing physical, and often mental, disabilities of old age. There are also the chance storms such as moving house, illness in oneself or in others, loss of a job, or bereavement. If an individual has had good-enough parenting, he will be robust enough to weather these storms, especially if there is enough support during the crisis from spouse, parent, child, friend, teacher, priest, or counsellor.

A person jogs along in relative balance or coherence in his identity, until a trauma or stress occurs. All change is stressful, even those changes that are welcome and freely chosen such as promotion, moving house, marriage, or parenthood. Change that is unsought and unwelcome is obviously more stressful. The stress may be acute, as in sudden bereavement or sudden illness. It may be chronic, as when an employee is constantly picked on by a superior, or one spouse is constantly nagged and denigrated by the other. Or it may be intermittent, as for instance the experience of worrying about an exam, or an unwanted pregnancy, when it may be forgotten at intervals, but as time progresses the dreaded event looms larger.

Our concept of self depends on many factors, but perhaps a sense of mastery, of being in control of one's environment, including one's body, is crucial. We all fear being out of control, 'losing control', and linked with this is the fear of losing one's authenticity, of 'not being'. Lack of constancy and consistency may threaten our very sense of being, as Kafka portrayed it in *The Trial* when all the familiar landmarks and values in the man's life were inexplicably and terrifyingly altered (Kafka, 1977). Stress threatens all aspects of the self, particularly those of continuity and the sense of mastery of life, and it thus provokes powerful emotions in response. These include anxiety, despondency, despair, hate, rage, sexual feelings, and love. If the stress is too great or there are many cumulative stresses, especially if the identity is not basically robust (which probably derives from the early mother-child relationship), the individual feels threatened and unable to cope. It is at this point that distress is expressed by symptoms. An individual can seemingly take many stresses in his stride, only to 'break down' (i.e. to produce symptoms of distress) as a result of a final relatively minor trauma. Unless a careful history is taken, the preceding traumatic life events are unrecognized as sources of anguish.

> The patient often fails to recognize the importance of earlier traumatic events. A woman who had been agoraphobic for many years was surprised when a therapist connected it to the time fifteen years earlier when she had been raped.
>
> A first-year University student with severe identity problems

relating to the break-up of his parents' marriage, was lonely and depressed in the strange environment. He felt under continuous pressure because he had to share a room with two others. He finally broke down in tears when a coffee-vending machine poured the coffee but failed to provide the cup to catch it in.

The emotional turmoil resulting from stress – with mental and physical symptoms of sleeplessness, irritability, lack of appetite, overeating, and so on – is an entirely normal reaction. If the emotions can be expressed in some way, the turmoil eventually lessens. If there is no trusted person available at the time, then at least feelings can be expressed in solitude, for instance by weeping alone, by pummelling the pillow, or by furiously digging the garden. Or the feelings may be given vent in poetry, in a diary, or by writing a book. If the emotions, for whatever reason, cannot be expressed at the time, they can be shared perhaps years later in psychotherapy, when sufficient trust in the therapist has been built up.

It is probably the adequate recognition and expression of one's emotions, preferably to another person, that determines whether there can be a healthy outcome of crises, with the individual growing and becoming stronger. Then the sense of authenticity, self-esteem, and self-confidence increases. Alternatively, no growth may occur and the individual remains as he was. If the feelings are not expressed in any way, weakening of identity may occur. If this path is taken with successive stresses, the individual may end up with disabling mental or physical symptoms needing psychiatric or psychotherapeutic help.

Emotions may be so powerful that a person may unconsciously feel that their heat will cause a conflagration. Or that the tide of them will swamp him and he will drown – as Alice did in her tears. A girl may feel that her emotions will be so out of her control that she stops eating in an attempt to control them. The strength of feelings, particularly hate or rage may make a person fear he will 'go beserk', with fantasies of being carted off to prison or to a padded cell. This fear of 'going mad' is quite common. Whatever the fantasy, the individual may feel his emotions to be so out of control that they will annihilate him completely, so that he ceases to exist. This is a more terrifying concept for the self than that of dying, when there may be religious or other reasons for assuming some continuity in the afterlife. Emotions must therefore be forcefully defended against or controlled, not only to prevent the self from bearing the pain, but to protect other loved persons from their destructive effects. This 'defence' is the neurosis, the symptoms of which can become more threatening than the feelings produced by the original trauma.

There are many unconscious ways of defending against emotions.

They can be suppressed, so that the feelings are not recognized as they arise; many abused children use this numbing mechanism in order to survive. Alcohol and drugs may also be used to suppress feelings. The individual may try to control the unconscious inner feelings by obsessive–compulsive behaviour – endlessly checking gas taps to prevent explosion, checking water taps to prevent flooding, or keeping everything in the outer world in control by excessive tidiness, thus defending against inner chaos. The obsessively houseproud woman and the martinet of a teacher fall into this latter category.

Alternatively, the individual may unconsciously 'act out' his emotions instead of daring to experience them – the behaviour of the young husband, forced to abandon football on television by his wife's silent reproach over the washing-up, who 'accidentally' drops a precious plate; the adolescent who slams the door when scolded by his mother, instead of hitting her; and the wife who develops a headache at bedtime. Much addictive and delinquent behaviour is a form of acting out, often with symbolic meaning.

The strand of symptoms 'chosen' by the patient to express his neurosis will be drawn from the many threads of his past experiences and from his present fantasies.

> An adolescent girl shoplifted expensive tins of Chinese food she did not really want. Her divorced young mother was about to marry a younger man of whom the girl was jealous. The girl had recently managed to give up cannabis and 'speed', and she felt orally deprived by losing the comfort of the drugs and of her mother's food/milk. Without understanding why, she stole the most unusual and expensive examples of oral satisfaction in the supermarket, although in fact she preferred fish and chips and ice cream.
>
> The housewife whose back 'went' when her invalid mother came to be nursed felt this extra stress was literally 'breaking her back'. Her symptom symbolized her inability to bear the burden, although consciously she could not register her protest.

The turbulent feelings are often suppressed, displaced, or projected, and only anxiety is experienced, with its various mental and physical symptoms. This may be accompanied by anger and rage that some people, partly because of their upbringing, find particularly difficult to acknowledge. It is the underlying cause of much phobic anxiety and of panic attacks.

The Psychotherapies

Once the various defences against powerful emotions have crystallized into neurotic behaviour and neurotic ways of reacting in relationships, habits have been formed that perpetuate themselves. Behaviour therapy aims to replace these bad habits of thinking and behaving with new, more rewarding habits. It does this by 'applied commonsense', with both therapist and patient together deciding on goals and assigning tasks or homework. Encouragement is given openly, and together they explore any reason for failure to complete the tasks. Avoidance of anxiety-provoking situations and thoughts merely increases and prolongs the anxiety whereas confrontation diminishes it. Suppression of anxiety by the use of alcohol, soft or hard drugs, or tranquillizers merely postpones the anxiety temporarily, whereas if it is tolerated, it will decrease. Gradually increased exposure to the feared situation will increase the patient's confidence and diminish anxiety. A behavioural approach is particularly helpful in dealing with circumscribed problems.

Where the symptoms have their origins in early childhood or affect the whole personality, psychodynamic psychotherapy is indicated. The primary aim of this is to unearth the underlying cause of the suppressed emotions and to enable these to be expressed. For this to happen, a trusting relationship has to be built up with the therapist who symbolically provides the good parenting that was missed. The therapist conveys his acceptance of the patient, with all his despair and rage and failure, conveying the assurance that mental pain can be tolerated, and that neither he nor the patient will be annihilated. The trust between them enables memories and emotions, hitherto blocked off, to float up from the unconscious; they can then be re-experienced in the safety of the therapeutic relationship. The memories cannot be totally wiped out, but their intensity and their capacity to disturb the patient are reduced, and the symptoms they evoked recede or disappear. Instead of believing that he has inexplicable symptoms that disturb and alarm him and that he may be going mad, he finds reasons that make sense of his predicament in the totality of his life situation. The patient is freed from the limitations imposed by distorted perceptions in personal relationships, and can thus make free choices, and resolve the conflicts that have entangled and entrapped him. His relationships can become more open, more positive, and more rewarding. His whole life can be transformed. A patient wrote: 'The therapy produced such an improvement in the quality of my life . . . symptoms and difficulties that had been troubling me for many years have disappeared and I am now able to live my life more fully.'

As will be seen from the many clinical examples throughout this book, distress in women may show itself in many forms and psychopathologies. Although certain generalizations hold true for the types of responses that women experience when subject to certain traumas, the *specific* symptoms that a woman will develop will depend on her personality and her life situation, on early life experiences, and the current context of her life and relationships, as well as on the particular significance of the stress that has overwhelmed her.

Many of the women who have consulted us have been subject to several major traumas or losses, and it is the cumulative effect of these blows, their interaction and their consequences that has overwhelmed their natural resilience and turned them into psychiatric casualties. Such women may be labelled inadequate, hysterical, personality-disordered, or mentally ill because the significance of their experiences has not been fully comprehended.

Thus the application of a diagnostic label – anxiety, depression, anorexia – may have some importance in deciding on management and treatment, but without a fuller appreciation of the reason *why* each individual has become distressed, and *why* she manifests her distress in this particular way and at this particular time, treatment is at best unlikely to promote full recovery, and may be ineffectual or even downright harmful. We believe that many women have suffered as a result of the failure to comprehend the true nature of their distress, and that they have come to believe that their illness is too severe, or refractory, or complicated to respond to treatment, because this is the message that their doctors have given them. Throughout this book we describe many patients with apparently inexplicable symptoms who have recovered partially or completely once the underlying traumatic experience and accompanying powerful emotions were uncovered.

Further Reading

Buber, M. (1966) *I and Thou*, Edinburgh: T & T. Clark.
Erikson, E.H. (1965) *Childhood and Society*, London: Penguin Books.
Storr, A. (1979) *The Art of Psychotherapy*, London: Secker & Warburg.
Winnicott, D. (1971) *Playing and Reality* London: Tavistock Publications.

Chapter two

Women's role and identity

Biological and sociological influences

Why can't a woman be more like a man?

My Fair Lady

Feminine identity is a complex and elusive concept. How far do roles and attributes of gender – maleness and femaleness – depend on biological sex, and how far on social and cultural factors, on society's views of what an average, or ideal, man or woman should be at each point in history?

Social factors affecting identity

A woman's biology is her destiny. Child-bearing and child-rearing have occupied her energies, limited her mobility, and restricted her capacity for other social and creative activities. She has inevitably a greater investment in the children that she bears than any man can have. She gives shelter and nourishment to the fertilized ovum. Without this provision of growth space within her own body, her baby cannot grow, develop, and finally be born, to commence the separate existence in the outside world that is necessary for the continuation of the human species. Once outside the mother's womb, parenting functions can, and may, be provided by any individual or group of individuals of either sex, as long as food, warmth, and protection is sufficient to meet the needs of the infant for survival. Different cultures, climes, and races have made social arrangements of various sorts to ensure that these fundamental needs are met.

Since a man could father many children, his immortality would best be served by impregnating and fertilizing the ova of many women. For a woman, the potential total number of her children would be limited by her own biological clock, by the rhythms of her menstrual cycle, and by pregnancy and lactation. A social and personal relationship with a mate that afforded rest, food, and protection was most likely to ensure her survival and her immortality through the successful bearing and rearing of her offspring. On reaching sexual maturity, they would in their turn reproduce. So it was that men were free to hunt, to fight, to be nomadic and polygamous, but women needed to be more rooted in conditions conducive to raising and feeding their young.

Anthropologists are agreed that, with some exceptions such as the matriarchy of Minoan Crete, women have always been in some degree subordinate to men, even in the earliest egalitarian societies (Bridenthal and Koonz, 1977). This may have been because men, already dominant because of superior muscular power and freedom from child-rearing, wanted to bequeath their property and status to their descendants. Here, a powerful difference between the sexes became important. A woman knew that a child she had borne carried her blood, whereas a man could not be certain who were his children. He could only ensure that a woman was carrying his child by exerting proprietorial rights over her. From this solution to their social dilemma arose the situation of women as chattels and the objects of men's possession, which has persisted, in various forms, throughout different ages, continents, and cultures, until this century.

In the Middle Ages in Europe women were seen as two polar opposites: the idealized Virgin, passive, maternal, and nonsexual, and the wicked woman, Eve, the harlot. Men placed the responsibility for sexuality in women. Rather than seeing themselves as lustful towards women, they considered women to be sexually seductive towards men. Women were thought to be natural fornicators and deceivers, with an insatiable sexual appetite. For these reasons, as well as in order to be certain of the paternity of their offspring, women had to be subjugated by their husbands, with the approval of the Church (Duby, 1981).

In the west, particularly from the Middle Ages until the seventeenth century, many women were accused of being witches. The accusation of witchcraft was partly a reflection of men's fear of a woman's independence, both sexual and economic. Witches were persecuted in the name of Christianity for their Satan-orientated sexuality. It was believed that by witchcraft a woman could cause harm – *malefacium* – such as making milk go sour, cows infertile, women barren, and men impotent. She could bring on illness and death, and ruin crops by inclement weather. She could appear as a cat or fly in the night on a broomstick. Her blood was considered to be both powerful and dangerous; possibly this related to her menstrual flow, a particular symbol of femininity. Making a witch's blood flow placed her in your power (Warner, 1981), though it has also been suggested that her mode of execution had to be by burning in order to avoid contamination from her blood (Shuttle and Redgrove, 1978).

The Islamic practice of hiding women in the chador is a similar reflection of the medieval disposition to place sexual desire and enticement in women rather than in men.

In Medieval Britain, men made a clear distinction between their friends and their wives. Friends were for companionship, for intellectual stimulation, and for conversation and active pursuits. Wives were not expected to provide good fellowship, but to be good housekeepers or mistresses of their house. In Tyndale's translation of the New Testament into English in 1526, St Peter advised wives to 'be in subjection to your own husbands', and he urged the husbands to give ' honour unto the wife as unto the weaker vessel'. At the beginning of the seventeenth century, women were generally acknowledged not only to be physically weaker, but also morally, perhaps spiritually, and certainly intellectually inferior (Fraser, 1984). It was still generally supposed that women were ruled by the strength of their passions, which might override their weaker reason. Queen Elizabeth I described herself as having 'the body of a weak and feeble woman, but the heart and stomach of a king'. The Church's teaching was that women should bear children and that the estate of marriage was ordained for that purpose. Great-bellied women were the norm, and perpetual child-bearing was expected during the reproductive years of married women, although infant mortality was high and childbirth perilous for both mother and baby. Child-bearing was equated with grace, and infertility with sin.

Under the Common Law of England, when James I succeeded Elizabeth, no female had any rights at all. On marriage she passed from the guardianship of her father to the guardianship of her husband, and her property or dowry became the property of her husband. The traces of this legislation, reflecting society's view of the woman's proper position, have lingered on. Unmarried women bear their father's name, taking their husband's name on marriage. Universal suffrage was obtained earlier this century only after a long and sometimes bloody struggle. Until 1928, a woman was not allowed to buy property or to own a house. Adultery was grounds for a man to divorce his wife and for her to be deprived of her children. Even today there is gross inequality over taxation, which is only now being rectified, and in spite of legislation for equality, many women continue to underachieve, or to occupy lowly and low-paid jobs, which prevents them from achieving economic independence.

With World War Two, while the men were away fighting, women emerged from the home to become a powerful economic and productive force. This further disrupted the traditional basis of sex-role stereotypes and the division of power and labour. It has been reflected, not only in the Feminist movement, but also in subtle social changes and social pressures that are imperceptibly altering the world and women's place in it.

With the growing political emancipation of women and the freedom given by increased opportunities for education has come their biological emancipation through contraception and abortion. A woman can now take responsibility for her own fertility and choose not to be fettered by pregnancy and child care. The decrease in infant and child mortality has made it more unusual and therefore more painful to lose a child.

As recently as 1955, Anne Morrow Lindbergh could write in *Gift from the Sea*:

> Except for the child, woman's creation is so often invisible, especially today. We are working at an arrangement in form, of the myriad disparate details of housework, family routine and social life. It is a kind of intricate game of cat's cradle we manipulate on our fingers with invisible threads. How can one point to this constant tangle of household chores, errands, and fragments of human relationships, as a creation? It is hard even to think of it as purposeful activity, so much of it is automatic. Woman herself begins to feel like a telephone exchange or a laundromat.
>
> (Morrow Lindberg, 1985)

A woman's creativity was thus directed to home, family, and relationships. By the time she was not needed as a mother, there would be grandchildren to fill the gap. Now she can no longer rely on her children to provide her with grandchildren – and if they do, they may live half-way across the world. Previous generations of women have provided one another with support and comfort, not only through close relatives and extended family but with servants and neighbours and friends – a sisterhood. Child-rearing and laundering, for example, were communal activities. Interdependence was the key to survival. Isolation and lack of support have now combined with other social pressures to make the experience of motherhood potentially the most lonely and unsupported period of a woman's life. She becomes, for the first time, responsible for another being – a baby – incapable of independent existence. She is likely to have given up her job and to have lost the routine and companionship of her previous work, quite apart from the paypacket that reinforced her 'value' to society and that gave her some economic independence. Materially, socially, physically, physiologically, and, above all, emotionally and psychologically, she faces immense change.

Women are no longer satisfied with the roles of housewife and mother but want fulfilment in other spheres. We see today, therefore, the traditional roles fundamentally altered or reversed, with the new freedoms resulting in new confusions and doubts. The tyranny of continuous child-bearing from uncontrollable fertility has ended. The woman is no longer restricted to being a homemaker, providing for her husband's needs and bringing up the children, but finds herself doing all these things and trying to hold down a job competitively with men. When the two roles conflict, she may feel guilty and frustrated, succeeding in neither role. When, as often happens nowadays, she finds herself bringing up the children alone, trying to be both mother and father, both provider and nurturer, she may resent the overwhelming demands and long to be 'the little woman', provided for and cherished by a powerful man.

In the past she could expect her husband to provide financially for the family's needs. At marriage, the young couple left their parental homes to live independently in their own home. He would be expected to have a job. She would often give up her job then, especially if the marriage was precipitated by pregnancy. Sexual activity would have begun, either shortly before or at the time of marriage. Now women often see their career rather than marriage as a fulfilling goal, and either postpone marriage or, having married, postpone having a child for some years. Living alone is not such a frightening prospect as it was for either sex. Many couples will have lived together in a sexual relationship and parted before their marriage to new partners. The disruption of a marriage may nowadays be seen as less of a major disaster than it once was.

Frequent divorce has altered the pattern of society. In the United States, for instance, about half of all marriages will end in divorce, though most of the partners will soon remarry, taking on stepchildren and producing half-siblings for the children from their first marriages. The effects on the children are profound; not only will they have step- and half-siblings to cope with, but many will effectively lose one parent (usually the father) and may also lose other loved relatives and friends of that parent (Furstenberg and Spanier, 1987). The extended family of previous spouses and in-laws and stepchildren makes for endless difficulties for the new couple, in terms of time, and energy, and emotions. If a woman is also working outside the home, she may end up being both physically and emotionally exhausted.

Women have exacerbated these social and economic changes by rebelling against male domination. Feminists have rejected men by seeing them as dangerous, to be fought against; or have excluded men, as at the Women's Peace Camp at Greenham Common demonstrating against the US Air Force Missile Base. This occurred at a time when society was placing great emphasis on success in heterosexual activity, epitomized by the work of Masters and Johnson, and the Hite report. But anti-male invective has been fuelled by the increasing knowledge about incestuous assaults on young girls and media reports of rape.

Feminine identity

A woman's identity is, therefore, much influenced by the role allocated to her by society, whether she accepts this or rebels against it. But what is the essence of feminine identity, and how does it differ from masculine identity?

Is the truly female identity the opposite equivalent of the active macho, potent, male image: submissive, receptive, containing, and nurturing? Freud (1924) considered that activity was essentially masculine and passivity essentially feminine, though he recognized that both components occur in both sexes. In his view, potency and passive receptivity are the two distinguishing gender attributes, which suggests that the negative aspects would be impotence in a man and frigidity in a woman. But we believe that, in many ways, the true feminine equivalent of male potency is fertility, the ability to conceive and bear a child. A woman who cannot do this feels a profound sense of failure; indeed an impotence, which is seldom produced simply by a failure to respond sexually.

Yet what about the receptiveness, the holding and nurturing aspects? Freud (1931) believed that the young girl was not even unconsciously aware of her vagina until puberty, when, as he wrote, she moved from the clitoral to the vaginal stage. The penis, therefore, became the coveted organ, giving superiority to its possessors and inferiority to those without it. No mention was made of breasts as appendages that the girl would grow up to possess, outward indicators of her womb and mothering ability. He seems not to have seriously considered that girls may value their femininity and potential motherhood, just as boys may value their masculine virility and potency.

Men's subjugation and persecution of women, and their preference for male society, seems to imply either envy or fear of women. Fear would hardly be surprising, considering that in the nursery men are very much at the mercy of all-powerful and controlling women. But there may also be unconscious envy; some men even consciously envy the capacity to bear a child.

The symbol of femininity from the masculine point of view seems then not to be, as Freud thought, the absence of a penis, but the presence of the womb. For a woman, too, the womb is the vital organ, though she can feel feminine with her whole body, especially with her arms and her lap. How then do women view the womb? Simone de Beauvoir (1953; 1972) wrote of the feminine sex organ as being mysterious, concealed, 'with a secret and perilous life of its own'. Joan Raphael-Leff (1980) has called it

> the secret chamber that is the centre of life. It lies dormant, fallow, and unknowable during all the years of her childhood until, in

> adolescence, it awakens, sending monthly reminders of its existence, waiting empty and unfulfilled. Then the void is filled and closes around a fertilised seed of future life. Whatever its fate, the process is irreversible.
>
> (Raphael-Leff, 1980)

The basic factor is her reproductive function, and throughout her reproductive years she is subject to the relentless inevitability of her menstrual flow or of the forty weeks' build-up to labour; and if she suckles, the recurrent cycle of filling breasts and baby's demand. She is thus governed by a rhythm she cannot avoid, from the first menstrual period, whether greeted with pride or dismay, to the menopause, signalling the inexorable ending of her reproductive function. Whatever she makes of her life in terms of intellectual, artistic, or spiritual development, she must submit to the domination of this rhythmic pattern.

This subordination of the body to the domination of the menstrual cycle is resented by many women. The flow itself may be perceived as 'the curse' – ugly, smelly, and shameful, with the fear of telltale evidence to others. As Simone de Beauvoir (1953) says: 'the event always seems to her repugnant and humiliating ... the monthly uncleanness makes her inclined to feel disgust and fear'. The domestic words used to describe it show how it is looked upon as abnormal – 'she's poorly', 'she's unwell', 'I've got the curse'. The heavy pain beforehand makes the woman feel bloated, weighted down with the engorged pelvic mass. The griping pains at the onset may severely incapacitate her. Almost worse than all this is the preceding week's depression, seemingly miraculously lifted with the onset of the flow. Women vary in how they view these ordeals – some seem not to be affected by them, while others feel life is hardly worth living for two weeks out of the four-week cycle. Anorexia nervosa is one way out, by regression to the prepubertal state.

> Another extreme way of avoiding the ordeal was attempted by a 20-year-old-woman patient of ours who suffered so much that she demanded a hysterectomy from GPs, obstetricians, and psychiatrists, threatening to end her life if they would not recommend it. It was difficult to withstand her threats; her doctors felt as if they were held at gunpoint by her, and no doubt this is what she felt herself.

Joan Raphael-Leff's 'secret chamber' (1980) clearly refers to the womb. But it is probably fantasized by both men and women, ignorant of anatomy, as one chamber, womb and vagina in continuum, into which a man penetrates and from which a child or menstrual fluid emerges.

How does a woman think of this secret chamber? Is it a good place inside her, of which she is proud; and because it is good, then the outward indications of it are good, as Renoir's *Bather* clearly feels – her feminine curves, her breasts, her genitalia – and the further extensions of these, the way she dresses, her walk, and movements, and behaviour? If so, she will be able to put up with the difficulties and discomfort of menstruation. She will feel that her womb/vagina will be a good place for a man to be inside, and that he will be benefited by this, that his seed will grow well there. The chamber will be able to hold and care for the growing child.

But if the secret chamber is not a good place, then her feminine identity is awry. She will feel deep within herself that she is bad, a failure as a woman. Her periods become a source of pain and humiliation to her, and may dry up altogether. She will dislike her outward form, try to disguise it by dressing asexually, by undereating and becoming prepubertal again, as in anorexia, or by overeating so that her sexiness is hidden beneath a camouflage of flesh. Or she may so undervalue herself that she offers her sexuality to any man for brief affairs, to be used as a worthless sexual object.

Or feeling her womb/vagina is a bad place, she may be unable to enjoy sexual activity for fear of harming the man, or doubt her womb's ability to contain a foetus adequately and her own ability to be a good mother and nurturer of her child, even fearing she may harm him. This last fantasy may be expressed in terms of passing on to the child her own worthlessness and badness by making him anxious or depressed like herself, or by making him deformed.

A woman's identity, therefore, depends not only on society's view of her role, but on her own biological rhythm, with its intimations of her sexual and reproductive function and its inescapable control of her life.

Further reading

de Beauvoir, S. (1953; 1972) *The Second Sex*, London: Jonathan Cape; London: Penguin Books.

Erikson, E. H. (1968) *Identity Youth and Crisis*, New York: Norton & Co.

Fraser, A. (1984) *The Weaker Vessel*, London: Methuen.

Friedan, B. (1963) *The Feminine Mystique*, London: Pelican.

Morrow Lindbergh, A. (1955) *A Gift from the Sea*, London: Chatto & Windus.

Shuttle, P. and Redgrove, P. (1978), *The Wise Wound*, Glasgow: Paladin Books.

Chapter three

The development of feminine identity and sexuality

What lies behind us and what lies before us are tiny matters compared to what lies within us.

Ralph Waldo Emerson

While there are many factors that contribute to the development of identity, the critical one for both men and women is the early relationship with the mother. After birth the infant is only concerned with bodily comfort, hunger, and satiation. Gradually he becomes aware of his mother as a separate individual, learns to relate to her, and begins to explore his surroundings. As he first sits, then crawls and walks, he exults in his increasing mastery of his environment. In the second year, his capacity to differentiate himself from his mother brings with it a sense of his own vulnerability and helplessness, and he experiences fear of the unfamiliar and loneliness. Slowly he learns to tolerate his mother's absence, and by about three years of age is well on the way to becoming an independent individual with his own thoughts and experiences (Mahler, 1967).

Before gender identity develops for either sex, a child must form its primary basic identity, what Winnicott (1971) calls 'the true self', which he defines as the ability to experience oneself as an effective, emotional, and interpersonal agent. A baby learns trust and a sense of existing, of *being*, when his mother adapts sufficiently to his needs, is a 'good-enough' mother. The infant defines himself from the image he perceives reflected back from his mother's face, 'the glint in his mother's eye' (Kohut, 1978). If the mother cannot do this for the child, he begins to believe it is his fault, because he is not good enough. R.D. Laing (1970) described this in his book *Knots* about the tangles people get themselves into in their relationships:

My mother does not love me
    I feel bad

I feel bad because she does not love me
I am bad because I feel bad
I feel bad because I am bad
I am bad because she does not love me
She does not love me because I am bad.

Even if the mother has been able to adapt well enough to her infant's needs and he feels loved by her and is therefore able to develop a good self-image, Melanie Klein (1957) suggests that he may nevertheless experience rage and destructive urges towards her and the breast when his needs are not satisfied.

Although analysts have stressed the importance of the infant's oral relationship to the mother's breast, warmth and closeness to another person is as important to the infant as food. Bowlby (1969) argues from ethology that there is an in-built propensity for an infant to cling to or attach himself to a human being, which is independent of food but is essential for the protection and survival of the species. A man has the capacity, therefore, to be as effective a mother figure, or attachment figure, as a woman.

Gender identity was considered by Freud (1931) to develop in the oedipal phase from 2 to 5 years of age. During these years, both boys and girls compete with the parent of the same sex for the love and attention of the parent of the opposite sex, and both resolve the conflict to some extent by identification with the parent of the same sex, the girl with her mother, the boy with his father.

There is, however, an essential difference in this development between men and women. Since it has been mothers rather than fathers who have usually cared for infants, for both boys and girls the first object of gratification is the mother figure. As infants, both are in close symbiotic relationship with their mother, enjoying her breast and the intimacy of her body. The girl, because she is the same sex as her mother, may be the more merged with her. Yet while in the oedipal phase the boy remains attracted to his mother, and in adult life to women, the girl has to give up her close relationship with her mother in order to turn towards her father, and in adult life, to men.

Various theorists since Freud have used this contrasting development in girls and boys to explain many of the differences in behaviour between men and women.

Nancy Chodorow (1978) has speculated on the consequences of these early influences. She suggests that mothers, because they are the same gender as daughters and have themselves been girls, find it difficult to separate themselves from daughters, whom they see as images of themselves, and fantasize as being still part of themselves as they were when in the womb. But they perceive sons as separate, because sexually distinct from themselves. Fathers, on the other hand, not having been biologically involved in the pregnancy and birth, tend to treat children of both sexes in such a way that the children are aware of separateness from them. They bounce and tickle babies and generally excite them, whereas women quietly hold babies and calm them. Since daughters are particularly susceptible to threats of fusion with their mothers, their identities are more threatened by closeness to them than by closeness to their fathers.

Certainly women seem to know what other women are thinking, particularly mothers and daughters, whereas men seldom seem to know what women are thinking. This is one of the reasons women choose to live with men; they are free from intrusion into their thoughts. This threat of fusion with their mothers could account for the especial difficulties that adolescent girls experience with their mothers, with alternating closeness and hostility; and it could explain why anorexia, with the intense preoccupation with body image, is so much more common in girls than in boys.

Chodorow (1978) thinks that this tendency of girls to merge with their mothers explains why, unlike men, they are 'be-ers' rather than doers and are more interested in emotions and relationships than in outside activity and competition. She postulates that, because women are less able than men to regain in intercourse the original fusion with the mother, they will always be less involved sexually and more involved emotionally than men.

This certainly would account for the constant finding in sexual-dysfunction therapy that women feel that they never get enough affection from their partners, while men generally feel they don't get enough sex. It would also explain the close affectional bond and permanence of female homosexual partners and the relatively weak affectional bond and transient nature of most male homosexual pairing.

We are less persuaded by the views of Dorothy Dinnerstein (1976) who has also used the situation of the woman having 'to renounce her first love' – her mother – when she turns towards her father, to explain some facets of what she sees as woman's predicament. She considers that women are never so wholly heterosexual as men, their heterosexual jealousy is not so intense, and they are not so abandoned in sexual union as men. Yet she notes that men can fear woman's power, perceiving them to be demanding, insatiable, and dangerous, and can try to escape by joining the society of men, by subjugating women, and by trivializing sex.

On the other hand, Stoller (1968) suggests that the reason many men are aggressively masculine is because they fear femininity in themselves and overcompensate; they have had to fight in themselves the powerful influence of the mother that tends to make them effeminate.

Both Chodorow (1978) and Dinnerstein (1976) contend that these patterns of gender behaviour will continue until men play an equal or greater part in caring for young children – until 'fathering a child' becomes equated with 'mothering a child'.

There has been much recent psychological and social research in the United States on adolescents and young adults to discover the differences between the concept of self in men and in women (Josselson, 1987). Adolescent girls seem to value peer opinion and to be more aware of their body image than adolescent boys (Simmons 1987). Men seem to prize achievement and to want to put space between themselves and others, lest they be overtaken or put down. They are competitive and more able to exist on their own, caring less for the opinions of others, except in so far as they need approval in order to succeed. Women, on the other hand, need to exist in a network of family and friends, requiring their approval in preference to a personal sense of achievement in a career, which they tend to postpone until they have acquired a partner. They are emotionally dependent on parents or partners, both needing support and cherishing from the people with whom they are intimately connected and giving it in return.

Men value separateness and are threatened by intimacy, whereas women value connectedness and are threatened by separation. Thus, because of these attributes, men and women may be speaking different languages without realizing it (Gilligan, 1982). This analysis would explain why so often a marriage is threatened because a woman longs to share her unhappy emotions with a husband who dreads that intimacy and fears he will be inadequate to deal with it. Men, in general, find their intimacy in sex, whereas women so often feel they lose real intimacy once the talking and cuddling progresses to sexual activity.

Identification with her mother is an important factor in the development and enjoyment of femininity in a girl, despite her fears of her mother's power and the ambivalence of her wish to recapture the early closeness with her mother. A mother who is cold and withholding, uncertain of her own value as a woman, perhaps dominated by or dominating her husband, will not provide a good pattern of womanhood for her daughter to emulate. On the other hand, if the mother possesses a warm feminine personality and is perceived by the daughter as a successful sexual woman, it is likely that the daughter will develop a healthy feminine identity herself. If this identification has not occurred because the mother is seen as critical or destructive, it can be accomplished later in life, during the course of therapy, by identification with a female therapist. Mental illness, serious physical illness, or repeated absences of the mother can interfere with an infant's earliest image of himself. Many girls in childhood and adolescence find it difficult to continue to identify with mothers who, because of serious illness, particularly of the breast or womb, change physically and psychologically; and they feel their view of themselves threatened by the confusing reflection from the faulty maternal mirror.

> A depressed student had for some years had a strange feeling of a malevolent female presence behind a closed door, which she found very frightening. She passively accepted verbal and physical abuse from her boyfriend, as she was afraid he would kill himself if she left him. When she was aged 11 her mother had died from cancer after a long illness, during which her physical appearance had changed, and she had become querulous and fault-finding. After her death the father became depressed. It was clear that this girl had been repelled by her mother's change of appearance and personality and, unable to cope consciously with her ambivalence and guilt, she felt herself somehow to blame for her mother's death. Her unconscious fear of her destructive potential accounted for her passivity with her boyfriend, and her sense of responsibility for his wellbeing. She had suppressed her anger at the time of her mother's illness, and it now emerged as the 'malevolent female presence', which was also the sadly changed mother. The student's sense of identity had been seriously disturbed, but during the course of therapy she felt stronger, could stand up for her own values, and could acknowledge and express her anger to her boyfriend. He, in turn, became more tender towards her. The 'presence' became less intrusive and frightening, and her depression lifted.

Since the mother is the principal carer of a child, she will influence a daughter's view of her own sexuality by her own attitudes. If sexual matters are never discussed, sexual jokes never laughed at, if the television is turned off when explicit sexual embraces are enacted, and if the parents never hold hands, put an arm around one another or kiss, the child may come to feel that sexual warmth and arousal are bad things and strive to suppress them in herself, becoming guilty and ashamed of them. The extremes of such a repressive upbringing are exemplified in Lorca's play *The House of Bernarda Alba*, in which the dominant and controlling mother imposes a prison sentence of eight years' mourning for the father on her five daughters, whose only hope of escape was by a suitable marriage. No hint of levity or sexuality was allowed in that house.

The information about sexual matters that a daughter receives will also influence her, either indirectly through the family myths about sexuality, 'all men are beasts, only after one thing', or through the preparation she is given – or not given – for puberty, sex, pregnancy, and childbirth. Her first menstruation may be welcomed with pride that she is fully a woman, capable of child-bearing, but it may also be greeted with dismay and shame, particularly if she had not been warned about it beforehand.

> A university student who sought our help for frigidity towards her much-loved boyfriend had known nothing about menstruation as a child and had not been told about it by her mother. At 11 years old she was admitted to hospital for an urgent appendectomy, and three days later in the hospital bed she had her first period. It was not surprising that unconsciously she felt that a stealthy assault on her abdomen by a powerful man had caused bleeding from her womb.

The father's interest and approval can also confirm a girl's femininity and make her believe it is good. If he is cold and distant she feels she is not pleasing to him, and doubts her success as a potential woman. If, however, he oversteps the mark and an acceptably affectionate and flirtatious manner becomes the wrong sort of closeness, intruding sexually into her feminine privacy, then she feels soiled and degraded (see Chapter 7).

The way in which the girl thinks her parents and other relatives view a sibling will also affect her self-image. She may be disappointed that she is not the favoured brother, and feel femininity in itself to be a poor competitor against his valued masculinity. Or she may feel second best to a pretty and sexually competent sister.

If a woman has an inner fantasy that her femininity is bad, she may take certain life events as confirmation of her badness; for example, lack of affection from a parent, rejection by a boyfriend, damage by physical or sexual assault, pathology of feminine organs – from genital herpes to cancer – infertility, miscarriage, or the birth of a deformed or handicapped child. These events are discussed more fully throughout this book. When good feelings about her womanliness have developed, they need to be maintained by a caring relationship with her sexual partner (especially during pregnancy), and with her children.

What has happened, then, to the woman who is aggressive towards men and seems to take up arms to fight them? Some women attack men with words, cutting them down to size, showing no softness or pliancy, no tenderness or receptivity to ideas, no benevolence.

> A young woman asked for help because she wanted to enjoy sex, and become capable of a permanent relationship and of motherhood. Yet she dressed in leather jacket and trousers, rode a motor bike, and had attacked several men with knives. During the course of therapy this patient overcame her fear of men largely by identifying herself with her therapist–mother, whom she saw to be unafraid of them.

We believe that it is not so much a wish to be masculine, as Freud supposed, that promotes this sort of behaviour, as the fear of being submissive, of being receptive, and of being controlled by some man. Such fears may lead a woman unconsciously to deny that she has a vagina, hiding its existence by an outward show of masculinity.

The fear of owning a vagina/womb, which may be damaged by penetration, may not only give rise to masculine behaviour in a woman and to varying degrees of frigidity, but it can also be a factor in female homosexuality. The woman may enjoy the child-rearing part of her femininity and even the child-bearing part, but cannot face the vulnerability implied by intercourse. (One such patient dreamed of lying on a road with a man driving a steam-roller over her.) Confusion about femininity, for instance because of parental preference for a boy, or because of absence of the father, may be another pathway to homosexuality – the tomboy seeking out a female partner who is often the paradigm of what she herself would like to be.

Mature sexuality consists in each partner making the other feel good, successful, and potent. Each cherishes the other, and the woman progresses from allowing the penis to be successful to helping the child to grow and develop. The girl who has developed a strong feminine identity will enjoy her femininity and expect others to enjoy it, will feel reasonably sure of herself, and will be optimistic and confident that things will be fine if she becomes pregnant.

But is motherhood – or vicarious motherhood, as in fostering, teaching, or child care – the only way of fulfilment for a woman? Is the wish *not* to have children a failure of formation of feminine identity or is it a positive, alternative expression of it? Does a woman *need* a successful feminine identity, a *potentially* creative womb, in order to be creative in other spheres; to be fulfilled in the same way as a man is, by external creativity, such as writing a book, painting a picture, or running a business? Is it merely a matter of time before as many women as men will run the affairs of the nation? Or is there something inherent in the feminine identity that counteracts creativity in fields other than biological reproduction? Some recent work in the United States suggests that it is women's need for connectedness that prevents them reaching high office. Josselson (1987) concluded that a woman needs a *mentor* who is either a husband or an important person in her field of work, who supports her interest in her vocation, who believes in her and encourages her. Work will not really matter to her as a vital part of her identity, unless it matters to someone important to her. This links up with the idea of women valuing relatedness rather than career achievement for self-affirmation.

These are difficult questions to answer, because so many factors of judgement, definition, and fashion are involved. From our clinical experience as doctors and therapists, we believe that a woman cannot reach her full potential, nor achieve a balanced life, while conscious or unconscious issues concerning her identity as a woman remain unresolved. The medical and other caring professionals who try to help such a woman in distress may find it easier to understand her problems if they can conceptualize them in terms of her unique experience of being a woman. They would then be able to see how her behaviour is both an expression of it and a response to any threat to it.

Further reading

de Beauvoir, S. (1953) *The Second Sex*, London: Jonathan Cape; London: Penguin Books.

Eichenbaum, L. and Orbach, S. (1982) *Outside Inside*, London: Penguin Books.

Erikson, E. (1968) *Identity, Youth and Crisis,* New York: Norton & Co.

Chodorow, N. (1978) *The Reproduction of Mothering*, Berkeley, Cal: University of California Press.

Dinnerstein, D. (1976) *The Rocking of the Cradle and the Ruling of the World*, London: Women's Press Ltd.

Miller, J.B. (ed) (1973) *Psychoanalysis and Women*, London: Penguin Books.

Miller, J.B. (1976) *Towards a New Psychology of Women*, London: Penguin Books.

Mitchell, J. (1974) *Psychoanalysis and Feminism*, London: Penguin Books.

Chapter four

On becoming a mother

Psychodynamic issues of adolescence, mating and parenthood

Dinora Pines

> At the end of my long life I realise that what I was looking for I had at the beginning.
>
> Marcel Proust
> A la Recherche du Temps Perdu

> I would add that he was looking for the *fantasy* of what he had at the beginning, the generous, life-giving breast of the mother.

Choosing a partner encompasses the deepest experience of human existence, the search for physical intimacy and emotional closeness to another human being with whom we hope to find mutual love and understanding. We could say that we search for what we long for. Either we hope to regain what we imagine we had at the beginning of life, a blissful state of wellbeing in symbiotic union with a perfect mother, the nursing couple. Or we may hope to gain in a new couple that which was missing in the original one of mother and baby. Yet as adults we must also consciously maintain a sense of separateness from our partner that we have painfully acquired by giving up the symbiotic mother–baby relationship as we grow through the different physical and emotional phases of the life-cycle from infancy to adolescence.

All later relationships are based upon the early years of the child's life. At this time the parents and their relationship to each other create the atmosphere of the home in which the baby grows. The environment they provide, together with their attention to the baby's needs, lays the foundations for his view of life. A woman, usually the mother, is often the first important person in the child's life, although today young fathers play an active part from the beginning. If the baby's urgent needs for food and physical comfort are adequately satisfied by the mother, or by the father who substitutes for her, then that baby will feel bodily and emotionally satisfied by the mother and satisfactory to her and a mutual feeling of satisfying and satisfactory wellbeing and contentment will ensue for both partners of the nursing couple. The child in its internal world will have benevolent representations of the parents who care for it and feelings of love for itself and for others. This will lead to a basic trust in the generosity of life and a capacity for concern and love. If the baby's needs are not adequately met, then feelings of rage, frustration, and hate for the mother will lead to an impoverished and empty internal world and to a basic mistrust in the good experiences of life. Prolonged deprivation at this stage in which the child feels unsatisfied and unsatisfactory may lead to a low sense of self-esteem and a difficulty in giving and receiving love and concern later in life.

It is at this early stage that the two primitive opposing human emotions of love and hate are founded. Winnicott's (1960) 'good-enough' mother is able to accept the infant's split and projected feelings of hate and love, and integrate them both into his relationship to her as a constant figure in his life. This struggle between love and hate continues throughout human existence, since ambivalence, the fusion of feelings of love and hate directed towards oneself and the other, is inherent in all relationships. So we see that the mother and her attitudes are the basis for the first identifications of both men and women. As the child begins to differentiate between himself and his mother he will also differentiate the father from the mother and perceive the bodily sexual differences between his parents and himself. The little boy develops fatherliness later when he begins to admire father's masculinity and his own in identification with him, both proud possessors of the penis that mother does not have. The triangular or oedipal situation between father, mother, and child now replaces the earliest couple of parent and child. Freud called this situation the oedipal conflict, after the Greek legend.

In observing children's games we may see how early the wish to couple, and its accompanying wish to have and look after a child in identification with the parents, is foreshadowed in life, long before there is any physical possibility of fulfilment. We play mummies and daddies, mummy and baby. The little boy wants to give mother a baby, the little girl longs to bear father's child, and primitive passions can safely be expressed since the child's physical helplessness and immaturity are his best protection against these early primitive drives. So little Oedipus can safely wish to murder his father and marry his mother. But since children love and need their parents too, the oedipal conflict is at times repressed and at other times revived throughout his life, as is the wish to be part of a couple and to have a child.

It is for the first time in adolescence that the infantile oedipal wishes can be acted out in reality. The adolescent's physically mature body capable of giving and receiving full genital sexual pleasure, able to impregnate and be impregnated, is paralleled by strong sexual feelings and drives towards fulfilment in reality. He must now take responsibility for his own body and his own life and move from childhood to adulthood. A sexual partner will facilitate his move towards separation since in the new couple he hopes to replace the parental couple. The child can now give life to a new child and the childhood wishes can be fulfilled in reality. Yet a physically mature body, capable of adult sexuality, is no measure of parallel emotional maturity; and sexuality may then become a means of satisfying infantile emotional needs or of fulfilling unconscious early fantasies.

We frequently observe that adolescents use their newly matured body as a means of altering emotional states, whether they be those of pleasure or of pain. Adolescents in search of a mature identity have to perform certain intrapsychic tasks. Each adolescent girl has to establish her gender and sexual identity in the world outside her family since the intense sexual drive and longing that accompanies a mature body capable of reproduction also stimulates a revival of the oedipal conflict. Each adolescent boy has to live through the same development phase and deal with the pressures on him to prove his manhood. Thus, a boy who is doing badly at school may restore his self-esteem by numerous sexual encounters that prove to him that he is attractive in other ways. Or a child who is not assured of parental love may try to recapture early childhood feelings and satisfactions in genital sexuality. Premature sexual activity or promiscuity in adolescents has very little to do with mature relationships, since the body is used in a search for an object that is never found in real experience. Genital sexuality is frequently not enjoyed by the adolescent girl but is the price that is paid for the pleasure of foreplay, which satisfies her underlying longing to be looked after, cuddled, and fed in the same way as a baby is by his mother. The adolescent behaviour, experimentation, and promiscuity, that at first glance resembles the adult version of the childhood mummy and daddy game, sometimes at a deeper level masks the wish in both boys and girls to be the baby themselves. The coming of a real baby will inevitably alter this fantasy.

Adolescence, a turbulent stage in the life cycle, marks the renunciation of childhood ties to the parents, the assumption of responsibility for one's own body and its sexual drives, and the move from the family to the peer group. Genital sexuality and experimentation with different partners may be a necessary part of this developmental phase until a more mature identity, capable of loving a whole person both physically and emotionally, can be established. Hopefully, a lifetime partnership can be made.

In our society, romantic love is regarded as a fundamental factor in the choice of a partner to couple with. All love is based on infantile experiences and reactions. If our early parenting has been satisfying and we have internalized good and caring parents, then we may, in our beloved, hope to find again aspects of the mother who nurtured us and the father who provided for us. Resolution of guilt about the forbidden and unfulfillable oedipal wishes enables the young couple consciously to choose a partner of the opposite sex as in the parental couple. Unconsciously, a man may search for aspects of his father in his wife, and a woman may search for aspects of her mother in her man. A mature marriage enables the young couple to re-experience early bodily feelings of satisfaction in their sexuality and integrate them in a total relationship with each other. Pleasure in such a relationship, which deepens with the years of mutual growth, will enable them to pass from idealization to a good-enough reality.

If the earliest phase of parenting has been traumatic and unsatisfying, we find difficulty in loving ourselves and the internal representation of our parents. We hope to gain, in a new couple, that which has not been fulfilled in our childhood. Such a relationship may be immature since it is based on dependent infantile needs that have been unfulfilled. We then fall in love, not with someone who reminds us of those hurtful parents, but with someone who we hope will heal old wounds and give us hope of happiness. Unfulfilled infantile needs may also lead us to seek in another person an idealized view of ourselves as we long to be, and we are in danger of being overdependent on another for external sources of love and self-esteem since our internal world remains deprived and impoverished. Nevertheless, just as the baby with each feed takes in both the food and the loving care his mother gives him, so the lover, if he feels his love fulfilled, introjects the love his partner gives him. The strength of a partner may help him to replenish a deprived internal world and love himself as he feels loved by his beloved. A successful couple will replace the earlier idealization of each other by a stable relationship based on reality and mutual care and concern. Early sensuality and tenderness of maternal care will be recaptured in their sexuality and integrated with a deep emotional relationship to one human being, a relationship in which both partners can grow. A stable couple also learns to accept the integration of both hate and love in their relationship, and hopefully as love deepens it will outweigh hate.

The first pregnancy and the birth of the first child introduces a new dimension into the life of the couple, however stable it may be. Becoming a parent establishes a lifelong irreversible commitment to another human being – the child. The foetus, as yet unseen, becomes the forerunner of the third person; an infantile oedipal triangle is revived again. A further stage of identification with their own parents is forced upon the young couple, and pregnancy may be seen as a normal developmental crisis for them both.

The young woman's bodily experience of pregnancy introduces new physiological and emotional changes that profoundly affect her view of herself and her partner. Within her body she now physically bears a symbol of him that she has to incorporate into her representation of herself and her child. She knows that she alone will carry the baby and face the unknown solitary experience of birth, no matter how strongly her husband may empathize with her and give her loving support. She may feel sad at the impending loss of freedom, since the birth of her child will create the bond of the mother–child relationship from which she will never find relief.

Fortunately, pregnancy is an ongoing process, giving time for the future mother to adapt both physically and emotionally to becoming a mother herself. At the same time, she still has to remain the child she was in order to identify with her own child inside her body. Although unseen as yet, she may feel it to be an extension of herself, but as time goes on the experience of the baby beginning to kick and move within her body allows the young woman to regress and retrace the path of her early child-bearing fantasies and theories without shame or anxiety. As well as the revival of early childhood fantasies and theories regarding the inner world of the body, childhood sexual theories of how babies are made and how they are born are revived with the young woman's awareness of physical changes in pregnancy. She may feel confused and disturbed by these primitive fantasies becoming conscious. Uneasy conflicts belonging to past developmental stages reappear as they normally do at any transitional phases of the life cycle. Old ambivalent feelings towards parents and sibling are revived, and in particular the relationship between the future mother and her own mother comes into the foreground; for the pregnant woman has to learn to play the role of mother to her own unborn child while remaining the child of her own mother. Pregnancy, and in particular first pregnancy, can therefore be seen as a space in time for the young woman to achieve a new adaptive position, both within her inner world of childhood and the outer world of adult interpersonal relationships. It is the pressure of this internal stress that makes environmental support from her husband so vital to her at this stage.

His wife's pregnancy allows the young man to prepare for fatherhood himself. The further identification with his own father enables him to develop fatherliness towards his wife. He does not have to adapt to physiological change in pregnancy and can support her as she regresses emotionally during the nine months of pregnancy. His empathy and protective strength during this time contains and comforts the emotional child-part of his wife and sustains the adult woman in her. In this way pregnancy can be an enriching experience for them both and a preparation for parenting the real child once it is born. Fears, daydreams, and hopes for the future baby may strengthen their bond with each other.

Nevertheless, a man's attitude in pregnancy may also depend on his own need for mothering. The loss of sexual intimacy and his wife's inevitable emotional withdrawal as she moves towards term may revive previous feelings of deprivation in the relationship towards his own mother, and his sibling rivalry towards his unborn child as if it were a brother or sister. The repressed feminine identification with his own mother may also be revived, and we recognize that fathers can mother too. Today, many fathers actively wish to sustain their wives in labour and to share in the birth of their child. Some hospitals have adapted to this and, recognizing that the mother needs emotional care at this time, encourage the husband to assume this natural role as emotional caretaker to his wife.

The impact of the birth and of the baby's physical appearance brings reality into the parents' hopes and daydreams and their idealized picture of this baby must be modified. This is the moment when the baby is no longer a fantasy and certainly not a childhood toy. A real relationship with a real child must be established. The pleasure of anticipation and fulfilment of long-desired wishes, of pride in such an overwhelming adult achievement, must now be measured against frustrations, worries, and disappointment. Again, there is time, since parenthood is a lifelong process.

In the reality of the new situation the father has to share his wife with his child and his child with his wife. The new mother too has to share her baby with her husband and give up being his only child. The basic oedipal conflict, with its fantasized sexuality, is revived and repeated, but can be worked through in a more mature way in the presence of a real sexual partner and real child. Pregnancy and the coming of the first child for both parents can be called beginning again.

After the birth of his child, a father's feelings for it may grow rapidly. Our patients teach us to recognize the inherent bisexuality of every human being. There are often strong maternal feelings in fathers that they may express or deny. The father may share in the caring of his baby, and in this way express identification with his own mother and with his wife. Some men, who very strongly identify with their wives, find this new feeling such a threat to the balance between their masculinity and femininity that they have to re-establish their internal equilibrium as quickly as possible.

> A man who had attained material success in an aggressive competitive way, was deeply involved in his wife's pregnancy and very supportive to her. However, as soon as the baby was born he told his wife that he needed a holiday and went off in search of other women with whom he could reaffirm his virility and his masculinity. He re-established his internal image of himself as a

potent male like his father, to counterbalance the image of himself as his childhood caring mother, so that on his return he was very tender to his wife, and enjoyed sharing again with her the bodily care of the baby.

If we bear in mind the conflicts that are revived in both parents by the coming of a child, it is easy to understand their normal anxiety about the baby and their own relationship. The fragility of the baby and the additional burden of often divergent professional advice may well add to their difficulties. Disappointments and worries are as much part of the parent's relationship to their children as the more obvious joys and pleasures. It is essential for the baby's wellbeing and sense of security that its mother responds to signs of his distress as if he were a part of herself. Often it is possible to recognize mothers in difficulties with their babies from the very beginning. For instance, they may be afraid of unconscious aggressive feelings to the child and hold him as little as possible. Most mothers will cradle their baby gently and closely within their arms. Feeding is often a moment of intense pleasure for both mother and baby, whether it be from the mother's breast or a bottle. A mother who does not look at her baby's face while she is feeding it or respond to the baby's gaze may be having difficulties in attaching herself to that child. If a careful obstetric history includes a few questions on the outcome of previous pregnancies, such as stillbirth or late abortion, such observations may be very helpful. Unless a lost baby is allowed to have existed and been mourned, attachment to subsequent children may suffer.

Every new mother experiences normal anxiety and confusion arising from both physiological and psychological adaptation to the birth of the child. Every new mother feels insecure when beginning her task of understanding the cries of her newborn baby, since he can only express pleasure or pain. Each new mother is anxious to learn quickly how to empathize with her baby, to interpret his cries correctly, to satisfy his needs, and to learn to cope with her feelings of panic and frustration at her own inadequacy. Her baby has to teach her how to interpret his distress and give him the correct response. Each landmark in the baby's development, his feeding, toilet training, moves towards autoerotism, or physically crawling away from her may revive her own childhood conflicts. The way she has resolved them for herself may distort her view of her child, and she may indulge or forbid his wishes according to her own needs, rather than adjust to his.

The most devoted mother can experience times of loneliness, boredom, or even fierce anger towards her baby. She may feel resentful when he cries inconsolably no matter how hard she tries to comfort him. What can she do with her natural anger and frustration? To attack her baby is to harm him. Even to express hostile feelings is frowned upon by society. Many mothers feel an urge to smack a difficult baby at a time of stress, but to act upon this impulse and batter the baby generally implies an immature personality with poor frustration tolerance. Here again, the help of the other natural caretaker, the father, is invaluable. He can take over some of the functions of parental care and so relieve the tensions between mother and child.

Emotional support for the young mother – as if she herself were a baby – is vital throughout her pregnancy and the early stages of caring for her child. Yet, no matter how much she may be helped with the outward stress, if the inner problems are too great, sensitive maternal care and love may not develop however dutifully the mother looks after her child. Frequently, life and death are closely interwoven, and the coming of a child may in fantasy replace the dead person who was loved and lost.

> Jackie bore a normal and healthy baby, but she could not deal with motherhood, nor was she the best natural caretaker for her child. She had been adopted at an early age and had had a happy childhood until her adoptive mother died. She was aged 10 when she was left alone with an inadequate, severely depressed father. She insisted on his taking her to see her real mother who, to her astonishment, not only lived a few streets away, but was rearing Jackie's brother herself, while Jackie had been given away for adoption. All her hopes of a replacement mother were shattered because her real mother obviously wanted nothing to do with her. She was taken into care because her father was unable to keep her or the home going, but at 14 she ran back to her father and refused to be moved. She filled the house with 'adopted' stray animals and found a boyfriend. She not only wanted to be cuddled and loved by a boy, and so recapture early childhood pleasures, but also needed him to distance her from the threatening oedipal attachment to her lonely father.
>
> She seduced Bob who made her pregnant and to her surprise married her. She was happy, serene, and faithful since she felt she was now a woman and was no longer alone. She had a man to love and replace her dead mother and also to replace the original oedipal attachment towards her father. This was, of course, a normal development. When the baby began to kick and she could no longer deny the coming separation that birth would impose, she became depressed and stayed in bed. She knew that she would be alone again, just as she had felt alone and abandoned when death had separated her from her mother. No-one understood these feelings, least of all Jackie herself.

Her son was born when she was aged 17. She often wheeled him past her real mother's house hoping that she would come out to see her grandson, but the miracle never happened. Left alone with her baby, Jackie began to beat him whenever he cried or whenever she felt helpless and panic-stricken at demands she could neither understand nor satisfy. The baby represented a rival to her in many different ways. He represented the brother that her mother had kept while she herself had been rejected. Moreover, since her husband was a maternal figure for her, she resented his interest in the baby, and envied her own child the love he received. Any aggression she felt towards her husband was displaced onto her own child, whom she left whenever she could, abandoning the child as she felt she had been abandoned twice by a mother – once by adoption and once by death.

But most of all the baby represented aspects of herself that she disliked. Jackie had wet the bed until she was pregnant and gave it up at that stage since she felt that a mother should be clean and in being clean she also became frigid, because for her sexuality was associated with dirt and soiling. The baby was the concrete proof of her dirty sexuality and also denied her sexual pleasure. There was a helpless child outside her, crying, soiling, or wetting, behaving just like the child inside her whom she hated. She struggled hard to look after him, but from the beginning hated not only these features of herself in the baby, but also hated him for the loneliness and isolation at home, which she felt was due to the birth of the child. It repeated the incontinence and isolation of her adoptive mother's illness. At times these feelings were beyond control and she battered him. Yet part of her was a mother so that she became depressed and guilty about her compulsion to beat the baby.

Her husband tried to protect his child but he had to be at work all day and it was at his insistence that Jackie came for help. As a result of therapy she began to understand all that the child represented for her, and what she projected onto him. This made it easier for her to see the baby as a real child in its own right. Nevertheless, she could only deal with her ambivalence towards the baby by putting him into a day nursery while she went out to work and found companionship there. She could never achieve more than a modicum of care and concern and probably no true loving feelings. The day nursery was, in fact, the only solution for both mother and baby since there was no-one else to help or relieve her.

Motherhood and fatherhood are constantly adaptive tasks, changing with the baby's physical and emotional growth. Throughout, the mother is torn between fulfilling her own conscious and unconscious needs and those of her child and family. Among the tasks that a mother must perform for her child, beside the basic one of establishing feelings of trust and security, is that of separating gradually from him and encouraging him to separate from her. In this way he will develop his own identity. The quality of her love for him has to expand and change, so that she no longer loves him only as an extension of herself but also as a separate human being.

It is a vital part of a mother's task to encourage her baby, and gradually to teach him to tolerate frustration. He has to learn to substitute toys and other objects for her physical presence. The baby's capacity to crawl away from his mother, to remember her when she is out of sight, and to enjoy his body and the freedom of his own fantasy life, is an eventual step towards independence and a separate identity.

A harmonious family life necessitates compromise and balance between the needs of each member. The mother, too, needs replenishment of her own sources of personal satisfaction and self-esteem in order to maintain her own psychic health. Here again, the father has a crucial part to play in emphasizing her relationship with him and reminding her of the adult pleasures of being a wife. A woman eager to share life with her husband and capable of enjoying the sexual aspects of her marriage will firmly show her baby that she is determined to have some time to herself. If the father is indifferent to the mother, or does not encourage her to resume her sexual role as his wife, her unconscious needs for love may be transferred to her child. Too often we see in practice patients whose mothers have denied their children's right to a life of their own since they themselves cannot separate from them.

Pregnancy and parenthood produce an irrevocable change in the life of the couple and is a major landmark in the life cycle. Caring for the child is an integral part of creating the lifelong developmental process of true emotional parenthood, for children create parents. But it is accompanied by a revival of earlier conflicts of love and hate. The needs and wishes of the parents may conflict with those of their child, and parenthood becomes a supreme testing point of the capacity to compromise between their unconscious fantasies, dreams and hopes, and reality. Unlike physical growth, which is finite, psychic growth is a lifelong developmental process in which the capacity to be physically intimate and emotionally close to another human being, and yet to remain separate, is one of the goals of psychological maturation that few achieve completely.

No human being can satisfactorily fulfil the omnipotent demands of the infant, nor can any mother, however good, love her child without ambivalent feelings. No adult couple can totally fulfil the demands and wishes each makes of the other. We can only hope to be good enough for mutual care, concern, and growth.

Chapter five

Bonding and rejection

> Your children are not your children ...
> They come through you but not from you,
> And though they are with you yet they belong not to you
> You may give them your love but not your thoughts
> For they have their own thoughts.
>
> Khalil Gibran,
> *The Prophet*

Both intrapsychic and extrapsychic factors contribute to the satisfactory bonding between mother and child, and those that undermine this felicitous relationship lead to rejection through indifference, hostility, neglect, or abuse. The early years in a child's life profoundly influence his emotional make-up and personality, and any failure of early parenting provides the soil for emotional disturbance to flourish. The explorations and techniques of psychotherapy are constantly concerned with these failures of bonding.

The concept of bonding refers specifically to the mother's attachment to, and love for, her child, and does not include the child's attachment to the mother, which has been studied extensively by Bowlby (1969; 1973). Drawing from ethological studies of young primates and from long-term observations of children with their mothers or from clinical experience, he formulated his attachment theory. He considers that the primary drive in primates is not for food in the young or for sex in the adult, but for a social bond to protect against threatened danger. He believes that the infant, like other young mammals has a biological predisposition to become attached to an adult by proximity and contact.

Fatigue, anxiety, fear, pain, or distress stimulate the attachment behaviour in the child of crying, smiling, babbling, sucking, following, and clinging to the mother figure. These in turn elicit maternal responses of soothing and cuddling, thus creating a special bond between mother and child. If he is left alone or with strangers he will protest strongly until she returns and he can cling to her or be cuddled by her. In her presence he can dare to be adventurous and explore his environment.

A mother who provides this safe anchor will promote autonomy and independence in her child. If she does not provide this security he will be 'anxiously attached' and may grow up to be attention-seeking, impulsive, easily frustrated, tense, hostile, and antisocial, or passive and helpless. The need for attachment continues throughout life, taking the form of falling in love, continuing to love other persons, and grieving for them if they are lost. Threatened loss gives rise to separation anxiety, with fears of being abandoned.

Attachment theory relates to the child's part of the mother–child relationship; it is not primarily concerned with the mother's attachment to the child. Maternal attachment ranges from calm acceptance to a strong and primitive urge to fight for the child's growth and survival. Trouse (1981) lists five components: warmth or love towards the infant; a feeling of possession, devotion, and concern; a positive anticipation of close contact with him; acceptance of the obligations towards him that could otherwise be intolerable; and a sense of loss at the imagined or real absence of the infant.

Society expects 'mother-love' to be delivered in a package along with the infant, and assumes a mother will be delighted with her baby, will be devoted to him whatever the drawbacks, and will defend him from danger as a tigress would her young. Mothers are expected to be serene, gentle, pure, and endlessly giving; children are expected to be grateful, dutiful, and to respect and love their parents. In fact, parents and children have ambivalent feelings about each other. Many parents are unable to give affection to their children or are even cruel to them. A young child will remain attached to its parent even if it suffers rejection, punishment, or maltreatment. This remarkable fact is further dealt with in Chapter 15.

In this chapter the term 'mothering' is used to denote nurturing by the mother-*figure* who may, in fact, be the father or another woman – a grandmother, adoptive mother, foster mother, or nurse. Moreover, a baby can bond to a number of people – his mother, or father, or grandparents, or siblings – the presence of any of whom provide reassurance at a time of anxiety, when the mother is absent.

Intrapsychic factors in bonding

Several of the intrapsychic factors have already been discussed in the preceding chapters. The most important is whether the woman is at ease with her own femininity, feeling her womb will carry the child well and protect him, just as she expects that her arms will cradle the child well.

A woman's mothering capacity stems in large part from her

experience of her own mother. If she has experienced a pattern of good mothering, she will instinctively know how to handle her child – or make a reasonable attempt at it. But with no good childhood pattern to guide her, she may be confused and anxious, not knowing where to begin.

The facts of the conception will influence the way she thinks about the future baby. If she carries within her the seed of a loved partner and knows that the baby will be cherished in the strength of a loving parental relationship, she will exult in her pregnancy and feel easy about the future. In circumstances where the father has betrayed or failed the relationship by drinking, violence, or unfaithfulness, or where the child was conceived as a result of a loveless one-night stand or, in the ultimate extreme, by an act of rape, she is likely to resent it growing within her, feeling towards it the anger she feels towards the father. Again, when she conceives by her own infidelity outside the marriage, she may be overcome with guilt and reject the child.

> A young woman who had been abused by her father admitted during the course of therapy that she had often wondered whether he was her true father. She was dark, whereas the rest of the family were very fair, and her mother kept a photograph of a good-looking dark man. But her mother did not favour her, rejecting her, and calling her bad and wicked, while praising her other children. Her mother had also told her how she had tried to abort her, and this further devalued the patient and confirmed her view that she was worthless and should not have been born.

The presence or absence of the father's emotional and practical support for the mother is an important factor in her ability to be a good mother. If he welcomes the baby, shares the day-to-day chores, shows that he values the mother, and supports her when things go wrong, she will be enriched by his concern and, in turn, will feel she has something to give to the infant. The father's ability to welcome the baby will depend on his emotional maturity. Dinora Pines (Chapter 4) has described the way a baby re-evokes the oedipal triangle for both parents and also any sibling rivalry either parent may have. If instead of performing his 'parent' or 'adult' role, the father remains locked in his 'child' role, reacting to his wife rather as a mother, he may resent this new child that comes along, stealing his wife's attention and mothering away from him. He cannot then evoke *his* parental role in order to help support his wife. In the absence of the father, other carers including a therapist may provide the support a mother so desperately needs. It is important for this reason that any therapy should not terminate during pregnancy, but should continue until two or three months after a baby's birth.

Extrapsychic factors

The mother's social situation will, of course, affect her ability to be a mother. An immature, 17-year-old unmarried mother, rejected by her own mother for having an illegitimate baby, and living in financial hardship isolated from other caring adults will find it difficult to be endlessly giving to her baby and not to resent its demands, which allow her no time for her own enjoyment. She will feel impoverished and depleted by her babe's insatiable needs. And once the mould of good-enough mothering has been broken by her neglect of the child or by inappropriate punishments, it is all too easy for her to continue to behave in that way, with accompanying guilt and remorse that will erode her concept of herself as a good mother and further diminish her ability to be one.

Experience of a previous child will influence her management of a subsequent baby. If things had gone well the first time, she will be optimistic and confident; but if badly or tragically, the new baby will in some way bear the emotional burden.

Her experiences during the pregnancy and the birth will markedly influence the way a mother responds to her baby. Adequate antenatal preparation, with support and respect from doctor and midwife, will encourage her to be a good mother. But a traumatic delivery, with pain and fear of being abandoned by her carers, can leave a woman angry at the torture that pregnancy has forced upon her, feeling out of control of her own body and mind. Many women date their hostile feelings towards a child to such birth events.

> A young woman was worried that she could not love her 6-year-old daughter, who was a good child, and was afraid that this might harm her. There was no warmth or communication between them, and she did not see how it could ever change. She had planned for the baby and had wanted it, and the pregnancy had gone well; but she had been angry and disappointed that motherhood was not at all what she had expected.
>
> After a long and painful labour the baby had been delivered by forceps and put into a special-care unit. The mother had to express her breast milk so that the baby might be fed by tube, and she was so unhappy that she cried all the time she was in hospital. When the baby came home she could not get her to suck properly and, after struggling, gave up and bottle-fed her. The baby screamed continuously, hardly sleeping at all and vomiting often. The mother described the events to her social worker as if it had all happened yesterday:
>
> I felt like a zombie. I was so angry with her I used to shake her hard, and I told the GP and the health visitor to take her away or

> I'd kill her. John would come home and find supper not cooked, the Hoover out, the baby screaming, and me crying. He'd sit with her on his lap – he had more patience than me. At 6 months the child seemed a lot happier, but I wasn't. None of my friends could believe I couldn't cope. I'd fight with John over her and throw things all round the house, and hit him. I'd scream and swear and smash doors. He used to say I was mental.
>
> Her second daughter had an easy birth three years later, and although she was a 'defiant' child, the mother loved her and could be close to her.

The mother had had a difficult childhood background, with divorced parents, and no doubt this contributed to her disturbance and to her depression after the first baby was born. But it is likely that the difficult labour, the separation from her baby after birth, the resulting difficulties in breast-feeding and the lack of sleep resulting from the baby's screaming were major factors in her inability to 'bond' with that daughter.

A woman's mothering ability will also depend on her own physical and mental health. If her energy is depleted by poor health, she will find it difficult to meet the demands of caring for a baby. Where 'postnatal blues' progresses to a serious depression, or where a psychosis develops, a formidable barrier will be erected between mother and baby (See Chapter 14).

The baby himself influences the mother's attitude towards him. Ideally, when breast-feeding is going well, the mother will feel she is highly successful. Her body has nourished and brought forth this healthy child and now it continues to provide, without effort, for the child's needs. If breast-feeding is not going well, however, it is easy for the mother to feel a failure. Somehow, she is not competent; he refuses her milk and she feels rejected. This may well re-evoke other rejections that she has experienced in the past, crystallizing the present bad experience into a permanent rejection instead of a temporary hiccough in the mother–child relationship.

A mother may be disappointed if she – or the father – had wanted a girl and she finds she has produced a boy. (Verity Bargate's (1978) novel *No Mama, No* gives a chilling account of the disturbed behaviour of such a mother.) Or she may be disappointed because her baby looks ugly, or is sickly and passive; she then misses the response of his eye-contact, his chuckles, or his hand-grip, which would delight her and stimulate further responses from her. The injury to her mothering response is far greater if the baby is malformed (See Chapter 13).

The bonding doctrine

In the mid-twentieth century there was a liberal revolt away from the strict regime of baby management. In the 1970s attention became focused on the early hours of an infant's life, when the mother was supposed suddenly to develop mother love in a profoundly biological and emotional way, by seeing and holding her newborn child. If she was prevented from this early contact, it was considered that bonding might not occur. 'Bonding' was taken to mean a sort of instantaneous glueing of mother to infant, occurring in the early hours and days after birth.

Much research has been done on the duration and type of maternal contact and on the synchronicity of biological rhythms and mutual behaviour of mother and child in order to discover the effect on subsequent mothering behaviour and progress of the child. Pioneers of this work were Klaus and Kennell, (1976) who filmed mothers' first contacts with their babies and noted the universal maternal wish to be able to look into the baby's eyes 'to know you're alive'. Additional time with their babies in the first three days seemed to improve the mothers' ability to communicate with their infants during the first three months, but did not seem to have any persistent effect after that.

Medical technology, while improving maternal and infant survival, can distance a mother from her baby, intruding during the birth by continuous monitoring of the foetal heart, by drips to induce labour, and by Caesarian section; and after the birth of premature infants, by the glass box of the incubator and the technical expertise of the nurses.

> An overweight student with a poor self-image sought help for a long-standing depression. Her own attempts to diet were sabotaged by her mother whenever she went home. The mother tearfully related how this girl, her only child, had been born prematurely. She had been told by the nurses that she could take her home once the baby weighed 5 lbs. She had looked forward to that day, and arrived with the shawl and baby clothes all ready, to be told by the Sister, 'I'm afraid she is still a little under 5 lbs. You'll have to wait a day or two'. The mother was bitterly disappointed. Her reaction was to overfeed the infant, and as she grew to adulthood she continued to ply her with chocolates and other fattening foods; she had somehow failed to value her in any other way than by weight.

A difficult labour or being drugged and unconscious during the birth, or being separated from a newborn child who is frail and unresponsive, and may not even survive, are all experiences that can diminish any dawning mother love. Much thought has been given to such circumstances. Forward-looking hospitals have developed ways of promoting parent–child contact and fostering parental interest and care. Regimes designed to promote the safety of infant and mother at the expense of their psychological bonding have given way to a more liberal approach, influenced by the work of Odent and of Leboyer. Husbands are encouraged to support their wives during labour and to be present at the birth. The newborn infant may be placed on the mother's belly or at the breast immediately, rather than being whisked away by the midwife. Instead of the occasional visit to a premature baby unit, parents are encouraged to touch their infants, to ask questions about them, and to care for them completely for a 'nesting' day or two before taking them home. Some hospitals have even experimented with a regime adopted in Colombia for mothers to carry premature babies continuously between their breasts to provide warmth, movement, and easy breast-feeding.

The technique of artificial insemination can also intrude between parent and child.

> A man who was impotent and had had little or no sexual contact with his wife disclosed during therapy that his wife was undergoing artificial insemination from an unknown doner. Neither he nor his wife seemed to have considered that a child born into a home where there was no sexual intimacy might be deprived. Nor did they wonder whether the unknown donor or the 'authority-figure' doctor, who injected the sperm, might be unconsciously viewed by both partners as the instrument of the 'intercourse', however technical, and therefore the rival to the husband. Any resulting hostility on the part of the husband might easily be displaced onto the child.

Women in therapy while undergoing the tedious manoeuvres of artificial insemination by donor (AID) or artificial insemination by husband (AIH) often show much unconscious hostility towards their partner, as well as towards the medical profession. Despite the marvellous opportunities now offered to childless couples, technological developments such as the use of surrogate wombs and the freezing of fertilized ova have greatly complicated the issue of parent–child closeness.

The immediacy of the birth experience and the hormonal changes that the mother undergoes may make the early hours and days after the birth a particularly sensitive time for the development of bonding, but the research suggests that contact during the early days is not essential for it. Moreover, everyday experience shows that countless mothers have managed to love their children despite separation in the early postpartum days; and of course, couples who foster or adopt children – as well as fathers, who may be absent during the days surrounding the birth – can, in time, develop a very close relationship with them.

Bonding seems to be a slowly evolving and reciprocal process between parent and child, not wholly dependent on any specific period of contact.

Mothering

From the continuous containment of the baby in the womb, through the early years when a woman has to exert some control over the immature child, to the mother's gradual and increasing separation from him in order to allow him to develop autonomy, motherhood consists of a series of losses. Each stage can bring a pang of loss – birth, weaning, sharing a child with another carer or with the teacher, the first girlfriend or boyfriend, and finally, leaving the home.

Attempts have been made to classify mothers according to how they perceive and cope with their child. Ann Dalley (1976) has based her classification on three stages: enclosure in the womb; extension, when the child is physically dependent on her; and separation, when he becomes independent. But she considers that the mother's feelings associated with each stage lag behind chronologically. Thus, when the mother is nursing the baby, she feels that he is still part of her. When he is becoming physically independent she feels he is an extension of herself, and only when he is becoming truly autonomous does she feel at all separate. In a healthy mother–child relationship the mother passes through each stage successively as she increases in maturity, but some mothers stick at one of the stages or are only capable of achieving one stage. The 'enclosing' mother may smother her child and encourage him to cling, without respecting him as a separate person, while the mother who is stuck in 'extension' may force her child to perform in order to satisfy her own values and wishes; and the mother who can only be 'separate' may be unreliable or unavailable for his dependency needs and may deprive her child of the overt warmth and valuing that is necessary for his healthy development.

> A patient finally produced a living infant, after repeated miscarriages and stillbirths. Even when the child was a healthy 7-year-old, she seemed to be fighting tenaciously for its survival, still stuck in the phase of enclosure as a result of her earlier experiences.

Similarly, many mothers who have let their babies be adopted have not had a chance to pass out of the phase of enclosure, and still secretly feel the pangs of separation at each birthday, as they wonder how their child looks, what he is called, and whether he is being properly cared for (see Chapter 11).

Joan Raphael-Leff (1985) classifies mothers into 'facilitators', who see themselves primarily as mothers and who are on the whole warm and permissive; and 'regulators' who see themselves primarily as *persons* inclined to be controlling and somewhat hostile. The facilitator adapts to her baby, making it the centre of her life, 'the high point of feminine identity'. She breast-feeds at *his* demand, responding to his every need, delighting in her indispensability as a mother, and resenting any separation from him. The regulator, however, expects her baby to adapt to *her* routine. She feeds him at regular intervals; and may leave him crying, feeling that his demands on her erode her image of herself as a person existing in an adult world, often with job responsibilities. She feels trapped by pregnancy and lactation. The facilitator will bottle-feed, if she has to, by holding the baby close to her breast, while the extreme regulator will tend to keep her body separate from the baby while reading a book.

In both these classifications of mothers it is the unconscious self-image that influences a woman's performance as a mother, and this in turn depends on her childhood experiences, particularly with her own mother. Most women, of course, do not fit into rigid classification; each is part-facilitator, part-regulator, or fluctuates between the two or behaves differently with different pregnancies.

Rejection

In some families of several children, with apparently uniform social conditions, a mother may, for no apparent reason, feel unable to love one child. If there have been no adverse experiences surrounding the birth to account for this, it is often attributed to genetic differences between the children – that is, 'it must the child's fault'. Certainly some babies from the early weeks seem to resist being cuddled, preferring to keep in visual touch with the mother or to hold on to her skirt. Possibly they object to the constraint involved in being held close. It is easy in these circumstances for the mother to feel a failure and to stop trying to be close to the child. Nevertheless, this can only account for a minority of cases.

Women often seek help because they cannot touch, cuddle, or love a child properly. The reason for one chid in a family being singled out by the mother for rejection may be because she consciously or unconsciously perceives him as being a replica of someone she fears or hates, or as possessing that person's hated attributes. Of course, this also applies to fathers, but since the mother is so often the main child-carer, lack of her love is likely to be more damaging to the child. She may, for example, dislike her son because she sees him as being like her tyrannical father, or because his frequent illnesses allow him to obtain all the attention that her envied, ailing brother got from her parents. Or she may, for instance, see her daughter as her own demanding mother, her hated elder sister, her cruel aunt, or her critical mother-in-law. Even worse is her unconscious fantasy that the child represents a part of *herself* that she hates and wants to be rid of. If she, as a child, had experienced her mother as cold and unloving, she may identify her real child with her critical, insatiable, and hostile hidden baby-self and feel persecuted by it (Rafael-Leff, 1980). Or the child may be seen as a replacement for a previous lost child, and is blamed and punished for not coming up to the idealized standard or for being the 'wrong' sex.

A mother needs to soothe her infant when he is frightened. She has to absorb his terror and rage, somehow rendering them harmless, and reassuring the child that all is well. If she has black thoughts herself, perhaps perceiving the child as persecutory, she will put her own rage and terror into the child.

Parents living together in a hostile relationship, or who have parted and are living with new (and usually younger) partners, often see in their children the hated or feared qualities that they attribute to the other parent.

> A 15-year-old boy came home to such a mother, after going along to the pub with his older friends, smelling of beer and slightly drunk. She berated him for drinking under age, and he rebelliously pushed her aside to escape to his room. She shouted after him, 'You're drunk and violent, *just* like your father'.

> A 12-year-old girl and her friend were playing at being grown-up. They had tried out make-up and cigarettes belonging to the friend's aunt, and had bought a bottle of cider. The girl's mother returned unexpectedly and flew into a violent rage, beating her daughter savagely and cutting off all her long blond hair. She abused her, calling her a whore and a prostitute, and sent for the doctor, demanding that he carry out a vaginal examination, which he refused to do. The girl was humiliated and terrified, and deeply scarred by this experience. Some twenty years later, in psychotherapy for profound depression, she recalled this experience of abuse, and realized that her mother had at that instant seen her as the envied beautiful promiscuous younger sister of her own childhood.

Adoptive parents can make similar mistakes when they assume that the natural mother, because she was naive and unmarried, was bad in every way, and that her child must also be inherently bad. They may see any tentative sexual activity as 'the mother's promiscuity coming out in her', particularly if their own failure to have children was because of their own inhibitions and sexual failures.

This projection of bad attributes into the child tends to *make* the child bad by formulating his self-image in that mould. What you expect of a child he will generally produce, so that if you fear his violence you may be subtly encouraging him to be violent. Whereas if you trust in his goodness (being trustworthy yourself) he will usually grow into the nice person you expect. This projection of bad attributes into the child is a frequent factor both in child abuse, where the parent beats out of the child the bad characteristics he so much dislikes, and in 'Soul Murder', the equally damaging mental cruelty towards a child (see Chapters 4 and 15).

There is always some conflict between the needs of the parent and the needs of the child. It is easy to resent a crying child who is demanding to be fed or changed. A mother who was herself deprived in childhood often misinterprets behaviour that is appropriate for her child's age as wilful disobedience, and will clean his mouth or bottom roughly if he dribbles food or has a bowel movement, or beat him 'to teach him to do right'. Often a mother expected to fulfil her own parent's needs will expect her child to fulfil *her* needs by being perfect, happy, and responsive to her. If he is miserable and difficult, she will punish him for not being what she wants.

Help for these perplexed and unhappy parents lies in enabling them to recognize their own past deprivation and present needs. By helping them to unravel their own family and marital histories, they can discover where their hostility really belongs. Then they can come to see their children as separate human beings, with their *own* potential, distinct from themselves and their fantasies and fears.

Further reading

Dally, A. (1976) *Mothers: Their Power and Influence*, London: Weidenfeld & Nicolson.

Bowlby, J. (1979) *The Making and Breaking of Affectional Bonds*, London: Tavistock Publications.

Macfarlane, A. (1977) *The Psychology of Childbirth*, London/Shepton Mallett, Somerset: Fontana/Open Books.

Sluckin, W., Herbert, M., and Sluckin, A. (1983) *Maternal Bonding*, Oxford: Blackwell.

Schaffer, R. (1977) *Mothering*, London: Fontana.

Part Two

Distressed Womanhood

Chapter six

Hungry womanhood

Eating disorders

With eager feeding food doth choke the feeder

Shakespeare
Richard II

Over the past thirty years there has been a steady increase in eating disorders. Anorexia nervosa, the slimmers' disease, was rare in the 1940s, obesity little commented upon, and bulimia unknown. In the past twenty years, anorexia has occurred in epidemic proportions. As many as 50 per cent of women in the United States are thought to be overweight, and women with bulimia, who binge-eat then purge themselves by vomiting or by using laxatives, have been presenting themselves in large numbers over the past ten years. There are many more secret anorexic and bulimic patients who pass unnoticed. This means that a large number of girls and women in our society are constantly preoccupied with food, in one way or another.

Why is this so, at this particular time in history? Many reasons have been put forward to explain it. Certain facts are pointers. Anorexia and bulimia occur almost exclusively in women. They do not occur in countries whose scarce food supplies make actual starvation a real possibility. They do occur in western countries where eating is a social occasion rather than a life-maintaining activity. Anorexia seems to occur more commonly in middle-class homes where there is usually high intelligence and drive for achievement.

Since the Second World War there has been a rapid development of the power of the media in persuading a woman that to be successful in her career or to captivate her man, she must be slim and energetic, foregoing the luscious curves associated with successful womanhood in past centuries and in other cultures. At the same time she is portrayed at her most successful as a wife and mother, endlessly feeding and caring for her family, giving her own needs second place. It is at the family meal table that a woman is at her most valued and powerful, providing nourishing and delicious food for her husband and children. Despite this ultimate vocation as wife and mother depending totally on her sexuality, as an adolescent she has previously been, and in many cultures is still, expected to deny any sexual urges until marriage. On the other hand, the girl who is not ready to be sexual no longer has the protection of a chaperone to shield her from the intrusion of men, which means she is exposed to sexual expectations that she feels unable to fulfil.

There is enormous emphasis on food as having social significance and on body size as a social yardstick of success. The insistence of advertisements for dieting and the slender bodies of the fashion models adorning every newspaper, magazine, and poster leave no adolescent girl unaware of the importance her shape will have in her life, and of the way her body may let her down if she does not control it. It is therefore not surprising that, for so many women, food and shape come to be the vehicles for expression of intrapsychic and interpersonal distress.

One of the most subtle yet powerful ways for an adolescent to express her distress is by an eating disorder. It is difficult to stop a girl eating so that she becomes fat, and even more difficult to make an anorexic girl eat enough to become a normal size. The abnormal shape, be it too much or too little, silently mocks the family's self-esteem, particularly the mother's, announcing to all that the girl is not the shape a daughter should be, and the mother is thereby a failure.

The bulimic girl, on the other hand, keeps her binge-eating and subsequent purging secret as far as she is able, and appears on the surface to be a well-adjusted and socially adept woman, though inside she loathes herself.

These three main eating disorders, overeating, anorexia, and bulimia have much in common. In all three there is the constant preoccupation with food, and calories and weight, at the expense of concentration on schoolwork or of an interest in hobbies or even friends. There is a craving for foods that are self-forbidden because of their calories, such as biscuits, chocolate, chips, crisps, and ice cream. The overeater and the bulimic can binge on any of these, or even on a dry loaf of bread, stuffing it in without any real sense of hunger. They then feel uncomfortably bloated and excessively fat, and are full of guilt and self-hatred. The bulimic follows this, in the privacy of the bathroom, by purging herself with enormous relief of tension. She believes, mistakenly, that all the harm has been undone by vomiting or the use of laxatives, and that the excess calories are now all down the lavatory. An alternative method of ridding herself of unwanted calories is by violent exercise such as jogging or going for long bicycle rides. In none of these eating behaviours is the woman really attuned to the bodily cues of hunger and satiety.

The anorexic, while experiencing a craving for food, glories in controlling it, feeling she is demonstrating her superiority. As she triumphantly loses weight she has a sense of wellbeing that belies the true physical state; she is lacking in menstrual periods, oversensitive to cold, and probably has a low blood pressure and sluggish pulse.

The anorexic and the overeater, and to some extent the bulimic, have a distorted, almost delusional idea of what weight means to them. For each of them there is a phobic fear of the extra pounds that the ingestion of food will bring, with the resulting bloatedness and grossness; yet food cannot be totally avoided. One attractive young student said, 'I feel ugly. I can feel the fat sitting on my body. I feel I am a separate being to the fat. Only if I can eliminate the fat can I be myself'. The anorexic feels obese even when emaciated. She maintains that she is not ill at all, and asks to be left in peace, even when her loss of weight becomes life-threatening.

Girls who have become diabetic in childhood may develop eating disorders with potentially catastrophic consequences for their health. Strict control over their diets and excessive attention to food may have left them feeling deprived and excluded from much that other children take for granted, and craving the comfort of 'forbidden foods'. Indulgence leads to obesity and unstable diabetes with long-term complications. The anorexic constantly risks hypoglycaemic attacks. Either way, manipulation of both insulin and food intake is a powerful weapon of control over families and professionals alike. These girls are often very difficult to engage in psychotherapy, and if therapy is too disturbing, retreat into their diabetic problems, often with emergency hospital admission.

Susie Orbach (1978) has given us a fascinating account of the obese woman in her book *Fat is a Feminist Issue*. She suggests that, because society asserts 'the fat woman can't win', the overeater makes herself fat to *avoid* winning, that is, to avoid the responsibilities of being sexual, of competing or being competent in the world. She does not have to assert herself or express her feelings because the fat makes the statement for her. If she is fat 'she can take on everyone else's needs without them actually penetrating' her. She can swallow her rage and despair by eating them away, anaesthetizing her emotions by covering them – herself – with a layer of fat. The fat protects her both from the intrusion of others' attention and from revealing her true self to others. At the same time she feels so guilty when eating that food assumes a magical quality; and she becomes terrified of it, stuffing it down quickly so that it is no longer dangerous.

> A beautiful obese university student sought help over difficulties in personal relationships. She had always been the odd one out in the family, constantly picked on and denigrated by both parents

because she ate too much and was overweight. She never felt appreciated for what she was, for just being *her*. She had never excelled at anything, and was sullen, resentful, and rebellious at home. Once she got away from her family to university, she found that she was accepted for herself, particularly in a therapeutic group. She began to take part in life, becoming active in student activities, and discovering in herself a real talent for her subject. She did not at this stage lose weight, but made the whole of her body part of her true self, proudly holding herself well, instead of losing herself inside her fatness.

A typical anorexic story is that of an adolescent, apprehensive about the way her body has become totally out of her control through the changes of puberty. Then, as a result of a chance criticism about her 'puppy fat' from a relative or schoolmate, she decides to diet. Quickly the dieting acquires a momentum of its own; she rapidly loses weight and menstruation ceases. It will only recommence when she regains weight to around 7 to 7½ stones, depending on her height and build, usually well below the ideal weight for her size.

In childhood she was typically obedient and conforming, a pleasure for the adults to have around. In adolescence she still presents as a good little girl, with a facile manner of speaking, revealing no underlying emotions. She does not, in fact, recognize her emotions, nor her bodily feelings; seeming to be out of touch with her body, and only at ease with her intellect, which is usually of a high order. Many such girls find their way to university because the control that is necessary for putting aside self-indulgent pastimes in order to study for O and A levels can also be used to prevent any indulgent eating, in order to lose weight. In both types of self-discipline there is also the unconscious bonus of avoiding adult responsibility and sexuality.

A girl aged 14 was left at boarding school when her family went abroad. She had been a good bright child, and her father was proud of her, with great expectations of her academic and sporting success. Her younger sister had been a sickly infant, and was protected from such family pressures. During the holidays mother and both daughters began to diet, but she determined to be more successful than the others, continuing to lose weight after returning to school until she was causing concern. She longed for food and felt ravenous, but valued more the sense of power that she experienced from her self-control, and her weight and strength rapidly diminished. She was sent home to her family but since she refused to have a doctor in the house, consultations had to be conducted on the telephone by her anxious parents. Her increasingly skeletal appearance frightened them, and when her weight dropped below 5 stones they flew back with her to England. She heard a doctor say she was in danger of dying, and immediately began to eat, but spent many months in hospitals on drugs.

She then ran away to the family home in England, where she lived in a dressing gown, never leaving the house, and screaming if any outsider entered it. She began to binge, eating everything edible, including raw flour, lard, and cooking oil. She was paralysed by panic attacks and episodes of overbreathing, and was terrified of dying. Her family felt desperate at her control over them but were too frightened to confront her behaviour or her tantrums.

Eventually, at the age of 18, spotty and obese, she agreed to individual psychotherapy, and with difficulty began to talk. Much later she also joined an art-analytic-therapy group, which exposed her to others. At her first group session she did not speak, but drew an ice-cream sundae, making a powerful statement from her unconscious (I-scream). She later attended a therapeutic day hospital while her family obtained support from family therapy sessions, which had previously been 'too difficult' for them to attend. The bingeing ceased and she tentatively embarked on her missed-out adolescence, making some social contacts. She was still unable to live away from the family home, but managed to go to college and take some O Level examinations, which filled her with panic although they were well within her capacity. After six years, and a planned ending of therapy, she accompanied the family abroad, and wrote to say that she had a job and was enjoying life.

The inner experience of the anorexic girl is very different from the unconcerned cheerful outer mask. It has been well described by Hilda Bruch (1978; 1985) as an overriding feeling of ineffectiveness and helplessness, so that she attempts to be in control of her body to ward off her panic at being so powerless. Because she feels so inadequate and inferior, she feels she must be despised by everyone, and so has to strive to be 100-per-cent perfect to hide her true self. Since she does not really recognize her emotions, she feels empty and aimless. The necessary goal of dieting and the delusion that she is fat become rooted convictions for her which she cannot abandon. Eating or refusal becomes a pseudosolution of life's problems.

Another patient was the beautiful youngest daughter of a highly achieving family. Mealtimes were always a time of intellectual cut and thrust, in which she felt unable to compete. She developed anorexia as a way of rejecting the 'family food', longing to eat, but secretly gloating at her demonstration of power over the family. At university she developed a relationship with an 'unsuitable' man,

> and exchanged her anorexia for a turbulent and secretive love affair which still allowed her to flout family control and expectations.

On the surface, the parents of an anorexic provide everything for their daughter – material things, education, culture – but so often they do not really sense her needs, instead they tell her what her needs are.

> A student, recovering from depression, was silent during therapy sessions. She had been anorexic but was no longer so. The therapist was forced to conduct the sessions by making suggestions as to what the patient was feeling, leaving her to answer 'yes' or 'no', or 'perhaps'. At the end of the academic year, when some sort of trust had been built up, the therapist asked why she had 'almost had to stand on her head' to get some response out of her. The patient replied that her mother had always distorted whatever she had said about how she felt. If she had said 'I feel depressed', her mother would say 'No, you're not depressed, you're just moody'. In the end she said nothing, and feared that the therapist also would negate her true feelings.

Some patients feel that their mothers own their bodies. After all, many issues of parental control are fought on the battlegrounds of infant feeding and the family meal. A mother may force her young child to eat the food that she has provided, experiencing any refusal of it as a rejection of herself. It is not surprising that the adolescent's developing womanly body is identified with the mother's body, when it has throughout its life been fed milk, food, and opinions on how to behave by that mother. Parents continue to maintain their dominance by subtly preventing the girl from separating from the family, undermining her confidence and criticizing her friends.

It is probable, however, that the origins of anorexia do not arise during puberty but from the earliest days of childhood. In order for the infant to become aware of herself as separate from her mother she needs a mother who has special qualities, who is able to understand the infant's bodily needs and to respond to them appropriately. It is no use a mother *feeding* her infant when she is crying because she is cold: that will only confuse her about cold and hunger. A good-enough mother will provide the learning experience necessary by constantly helping her child to monitor her bodily needs. She must also be sensitive to her emotional needs, soothing her terror and allowing it to be expressed. Parents who cannot cope with the expression of any emotion often produce children who can only obtain attention by complaining of physical symptoms, who in later life tend to develop psychosomatic illnesses, their bodies continuing to be their only medium for the expression of their feelings. But parents of anorexic daughters tend to notice neither bodily nor emotional needs.

It is easy to envisage an extreme 'regulator' mother (see Chapter 5) failing to notice her daughter's needs, often because she is too upset by them. The child then feels guilty at upsetting her and learns to suppress her emotions, including her rage, and becomes good and compliant. In Winnicott's phrase, she develops a false self. He goes on to talk about 'primary maternal preoccupation', a function of the good-enough mother that enables her to:

> know about her infant's earliest expectations and needs, and makes her personally satisfied, in so far as the infant is at ease. It is because of this identification with her infant that she knows how to hold her infant, so that the infant starts by existing and not by reacting. Here is the origin of the true self.
>
> (Winnicott, 1960)

It is easy to equate this type of mother with the 'facilitator' mother, for she would be unlikely to create feeding problems for her children in babyhood or in later life.

Bulimic patients tend to be older on average than anorexics and are more likely to be sexually active. Between a quarter and a half of all anorexics are bulimic, so there is a good deal of overlap. They are helplessly caught in the cycle of bingeing and vomiting as in a trap. In general, they will not vomit if someone is present, needing to do it secretly. If they know they cannot vomit, they will manage to stop themselves from bingeing. For instance, going to stay with a boyfriend's parents will prevent it during that weekend.

Anorexics and bulimics may marry and have children, though anorexic women are likely to experience problems with their fertility and may need skilled help with drug treatment to promote ovulation. Usually anorexics who are actively starving themselves and have a very low body weight do not wish to become pregnant, even though they may be sexually active, and they often have a very controlling and mutually collusive relationship with their partners. They usually choose men who are caring and protective of them and avoid confrontation over the central issues of food, weight, and body size. The anorexic's preoccupation with food may lead her to cook constantly, and to 'feed up' those around her, as a cover for her own avoidance of food intake and a demonstration of her self-control.

Women with eating disorders risk developing a drinking problem. They may crave alcohol, bingeing on it as they would on chocolates and other goodies, and relying on it for relief of tension and distress, or developing a physical dependency upon it. When impulse control is poor, a woman may either indulge secretly or persuade others to take responsibility for protecting her from the impulse.

An emaciated professional woman in her mid-thirties sought help for her long-standing anorexia and bulimia. She began to drink wine as an alternative to stuffing herself, since the alcohol also provided relief from the mounting tension that made her binge. Her husband colluded with her lack of self-control by taking responsibility for the key to the larder and fridge so that she could not indulge herself in the home without his co-operation. He supported her attendance at an out-patient psychotherapy group, but their mutual fear of any conflict precluded any real possibility of change.

Bulimic women may appear perfectly normal, marrying and producing children, and presenting a glamorous outward appearance with maintenance of average body weight and shape. Typically, they appear to eat normal meals, but later secretly stuff themselves.

An attractive mother of two felt deeply ashamed of her secret bingeing, which she had successfully concealed from all around her, including her husband. She thought it would be impossible to share her secret, because it was so 'disgusting', and found great relief in revealing it in therapy without provoking the contempt from the therapist that she had feared. In subsequent group therapy she confided details of sexual abuse at the hands of her stepfather, which filled her with self-loathing and disgust, but was much more reluctant to reveal her bulimic habit, of which she felt even more ashamed.

The families of daughters with anorexia or bulimia have much in common. There may be unresolved conflicts within the family, with emphasis on an outward show of acceptability – a sort of 'keeping up with the Joneses'. The bingeing or food refusal then becomes a potent communication of the daughter's distress, at the same time exposing, by the obstinacy with which it is maintained, some of the denied anger and self-assertion. Both parents and daughter get stuck in a habit of treating the daughter as prepubertal, needing continued protection, unable to live her life as an adult by looking after herself, and tolerating some gloom and depression. Sometimes the girl has 'chosen' her anorexic role in order to hold the family together in their concern for her, fearing that tensions within the marital relationship, or maternal depression, may lead to family breakdown or catastrophe if she frees them from their parental obligations by growing up and becoming independent.

Any therapy must be aimed at enabling the girl to experience and express her needs. By listening attentively and valuing what she says she may begin to value herself, and realize she has a right to obtain satisfaction in life. Educating her about the effects of starvation, and of vomiting or the use of laxatives, and helping her to alter her false perception of eating, and weight, and body image are important facets of treatment.

Any sudden weight gain will make her terrified of losing control completely, so a slow steady weekly weight gain must be the aim towards a target weight that is a little lower than the ideal weight for her size. The patient may find it more acceptable if food is 'prescribed' by the doctor in liquid form to be taken as medicine.

Life-threatening effects of starvation, or suicidal depression, may necessitate hospital treatment for a time, and perhaps medication. Anorexic patients often seem obstinate, manipulative, and deceitful to nurses and doctors on the ward, who do not understand the intensity of their false beliefs and how imperative they feel it is for them to be in control of their eating. Moral judgements about unco-operative behaviour and deceit are unhelpful, though clearly clinicians need to be aware how their well-meaning endeavours may be flagrantly overturned, for instance by a patient pouring food into the pot plant or down the lavatory, or concealing it behind the radiator, rather than eating the carefully planned diet. The most important aspect will be understanding the meaning of such displays of distress if lasting help is to be achieved.

Various behavioural regimes have been developed for coping with the actual eating habits. The eating can be controlled by insisting that the patient only eats three planned meals a day: or the vomiting can be prevented by not allowing the patient to be on her own for two hours after meals. Once the rigid eating patterns have been broken down, the patient can be encouraged to eat foods she has hitherto avoided; and to eat in different situations – at a picnic, at a supper party, or in a restaurant.

The family may be treated as a whole by helping the members to communicate their feelings to each other, and to resolve conflicts. The parents are encouraged to unite in their attempts to help their daughter to eat normally. She is encouraged to take part in activities outside the home or, if appropriate, to leave home.

It has been noted that the families of girls with eating disorders and the families in which childhood sexual abuse occurs both fail to satisfy the children's needs, but at the same time overprotect them by denying them any degree of independence or self-determination. There seems to be some association between these two disorders (Calam and Slade, 1987; Sloan and Leichner, 1986).

Since many of the anorexic's problems stem from the underlying lack of a proper concept of identity, a student patient can be treated in a group with other university students. This will contain other young men and women with identity problems who have promoted the intellect at the expense of suppressing their feelings. In contrast to the brittle assurance of the anorexic, they present themselves in varied ways, from the brilliant automaton who can cope with a computer but not with other people, to the depressed girl who sits and weeps. The anorexic discovers her identity, who she is, from the reflections she receives from the other members of the group. But it is difficult to hold an anorexic girl in therapy; the habit of evasion of emotions is set hard and she often flies from treatment. Self-help groups may help her where formal therapy has failed.

Whatever the treatment chosen, the therapist must avoid reproducing the characteristics of her mother by appearing to be controlling, demanding, or critical – or by 'knowing what she really feels', which will merely entrench her in her defensive behaviour. These patients can make greedy demands on the therapist's time, 'phoning her home, or asking to see her between sessions. The therapist must set clear limits and firm boundaries, which may be experienced as rejecting, but will provide security for the patient.

With so many young women at risk of developing eating disorders, we should begin to think about prevention – in secondary schools, in ballet or athletics classes – and particularly by the media. Just as conversion hysteria in women seemed to be common at the turn of the century, slimming diseases seem to be, at this point in the social and economic history of the west, the present fashion. They may in due course spontaneously change or disappear, giving way to a new syndrome by which young women can communicate their distress.

Further reading

Bruch, H. (1978) *The Golden Cage*, Shepton Mallet, Somerset: Open Books.
Orbach, S. (1978) *Fat is a Feminist Issue*, London: Paddington Press.
MacLeod, S. (1981) *The Art of Starvation*, London: Virago.
Orbach, S. (1986) *Hunger Strike*, London: Faber & Faber.

Useful addresses

Anorexic Aid,
The Priory Centre,
11 Priory Road,
High Wycombe,
Bucks.
Tel: (0494) 21431

The National Information Centre for Anorexic Family Aid,
44–48 Magdalen Place,
Norwich, NR3 1JE
Tel: (0603) 621414.

Chapter seven

Womanhood despoiled

Childhood sexual abuse

> The expense of spirit in a waste of shame
> Is Lust in action;
>
> Shakespeare
> *Sonnet 129*

Incidence

In 1961, Kempe shocked the world with his account of the way in which small children could be battered by their parents (Kempe and Kempe, 1978). It is only in the past twelve years or so that we have become aware of the way in which parents and other members of the family abuse children sexually. We have been amazed at the increasing number of women giving a history of sexual abuse. This is partly because the subject has been highlighted in the press and on television. It is also because we, the professional carers, have at last begun to ask the right questions. While our minds were closed to the possibility of this type of trauma, no-one could tell us of the awful things that had happened to them, and we could not hear them if they tried.

There is a whole spectrum of child abuse, from extreme physical violence on the one hand to serious mental cruelty on the other. Child sexual abuse is one of the ways in which adults use children for their own purposes, and it overlaps with both physical and psychological abuse. Physical and psychological abuse are discussed in Chapter 15.

It has been estimated that between 10 per cent and 30 per cent of adult women have a history of some sort of childhood sexual abuse, and that in 75 per cent of those cases the perpetrator is known to the child as one of the family or a relative (45 per cent), or as an acquaintance such as a mother's boyfriend, (30 per cent); in only 25 per cent is it a stranger. Three-quarters of all cases of incest are between fathers and daughters. Stepfathers are much more likely to victimize a daughter sexually (as are adoptive or foster fathers) than natural fathers, perhaps because the blood-bond taboo is absent. Only rarely does a mother abuse her daughter sexually; more often it is a brother, a grandfather, or an uncle. It is estimated that four times as many girls as boys are abused, though boys are generally more severely abused, and for longer. It occurs in all social classes.

Variation in the reported incidence of abuse may be due to varying definitions of what constitutes sexual abuse, and to the fact that we only know about the cases that are reported. We do not know of those cases in which the victims remain silent.

Adolescent girls may report incest in order, for instance, to damage a stepfather and later retract the accusation, so that it is difficult to know what the truth is. On the other hand, patients in psychotherapy may find it so difficult to talk about incest that they only do so after trust has been built up with the therapist over weeks, months or years. They recoil from breaking the family secrecy, feeling intensely disloyal to both father and mother, and fearing to break their father's prohibitions, with threats of punishment if they tell anyone. They dread stirring up unbearable pain and evoking disapproval or rejection from the therapist. It is easier to report assault from a stranger. Whatever the true incidence, since the majority of victims are female, childhood sexual abuse is a significant and continuing cause of distress and suffering in women.

The effects of childhood sexual abuse

The effects of child sexual abuse depend on a variety of factors, particularly the age and developmental maturity of the child when it begins, the type and duration of the abuse, the closeness of the relationship with the perpetrator, whether physical abuse is associated and whether it has been disclosed to outsiders, and with what consequences.

The younger the child when the abuse begins, the more damaging it seems to be. For a child, genital manipulation and intercourse are quite different experiences from the observation of an adult exhibitionist. Yet, continuous voyeurism from a father, so that a child or adolescent feels that nowhere in the house is she safe from his prying eyes, may be more damaging than a single affectionate genital contact. Assault from a stranger or an acquaintance outside the family seems to be less damaging than assault from within it; since family members are not involved, they can comfort the victim and protect against further assault. A wide age gap between the perpetrator and the victim seems to be more damaging than a small one.

The affective nature of the relationship can also mitigate damage. A father who flatters with his attention and is affectionate, gaining willing consent from the child, seems to cause less harm than a father who threatens rejection or physical punishment, who uses force, or who alternates violence with sexual behaviour. What makes the event traumatic is where the child suffers pain and fear, feeling betrayed by someone she ought to have been able to trust. A comparatively mild sexual assault from a stranger may be made more damaging if the child is again 'assaulted' by police questioning, or a police surgeon's physical examination. Finally, if pregnancy results, the trauma is greatly increased.

Although victims may remember a definite occurrence as happening just before puberty, it often emerges that the assaults began much earlier in childhood. The most usual time for a parent's assault to begin seems to be either between 3 and 6 years of age or after puberty. The child accepts what is happening as part of life, since she knows no other pattern. She may not realize that all fathers do not behave to daughters in this way until she discovers, usually at secondary school when sexual matters are being discussed, that other fathers do not do it to their daughters. She then becomes deeply upset and resentful. She may suppress the knowledge of what has happened until an event in adult life, such as childbirth or a television programme on incest, triggers the memory. She develops symptoms at the point at which her defence against her distress breaks down and the knowledge comes into consciousness.

What happens then to these girls who have suffered sexual abuse? First, there are the personality and identity problems arising from the abnormal family constellation, and these are evident whether or not past sexual assault is talked about. The family will have been one in which all interpersonal relationships are disturbed and distorted, and which does not meet the needs of its members for nurture, care, and affection.

In such families the mother is usually cold and distant. She is likely have been herself the victim of childhood sexual or physical abuse. The father, while dominant and authoritarian in the home, may appear outside as lacking in confidence, or as being a hardworking pillar of society, though with few friends. He may himself have been abused physically, sexually, or emotionally as a child. His use of alcohol may have contributed to the incest.

The marital pair do not respond to each other's needs for affection or sex. The wife has abdicated, allowing her daughter to take over her role. The husband, instead of seeking the sex he needed outside, has found it within the home. The family becomes isolated from the community, trapped with their secrets and their denial, feeling that any separateness from each other would lead to the break-up of the family.

If the incest occurred at a very early age, the act may be perceived by the child as excretory. Her confusion is increased when the next day she searches for confirmation from her father that what she remembered actually occurred. But he acts as if it never happened. So she waits, frozen, for it to happen again. She cannot trust her own perceptions and judgement. One patient remembered how, when she was paralysed as a 6-year-old, her grandfather would come regularly at night when she was asleep and take her into his own bed, placing her face downwards. She could not move, and she could not scream because he placed one hand over her mouth. Yet in the daytime he continued to behave as the respected and upright older man.

The girl spends much of her childhood wondering whether she should tell someone – her mother, her grandmother, a sister, or a teacher? But they might not believe her, or if they did, they might blame her for it. Her molester has probably warned her that he will kill her, or her mother, or himself, if she tells. In any case, a young child does not know the words to use. What happens to her is not part of the everyday life at home or school; it is something separate and secret, yet it pervades every waking moment, and disturbs her sleep with nightmares.

If she does try to tell her mother, she is often accused of making up stories, is thought to be mad, wicked, or a pervert, or is ignored. She may not try to tell anyone about it, but suppresses her anger and despair. She is condemned to remain silent and cannot explain why she suddenly turns away from a relative with whom she has hitherto been playful, or why she has suddenly become silent, withdrawn, and tearful. The grown-ups never seem to wonder why, or try to understand.

If she does manage to tell her mother or a teacher, and they actually listen and believe her, she starts a chain of events that may provoke a worse situation than the incestuous one. At least she can pretend to act at home and at school as if life was normal. But disclosure may result in her father going to prison, the family blaming her for his loss, for revealing the incest to the neighbours, for the loss of income, and sometimes for the resulting loss of their home. When he comes out of prison, he will not be allowed to stay in the home while she is there, and her mother may choose to have him at home rather than the children, forcing them to go into care. The daughter is well and truly punished for her crime of allowing and disclosing the incest. Away from home she may willingly or unwillingly become involved with men, and find herself in further trouble. Some girls choose homosexuality in order to avoid men. Whether she tells or not, she cannot win. Her life is scarred for ever.

She is bitter with her mother for permitting the molestation. Why does she not acknowledge what happened?

> One patient said she thought her mother might have known of her older brother's abuse of her because when she was aged 7, her mother had said, 'Twin kittens should not mate'. Yet when as a

grown-up she told her parents of the assault and her brother denied it, her parents believed him. 'It's the men who are always believed, and the women get the blame.

If the child is told she has led her father on, she believes it. In addition, she feels massively guilty, knowing the incestuous relationship is in some way wrong. She is guilty for usurping her mother's place, and for gaining more paternal attention than less-favoured siblings. She may be jealous of a younger sister who becomes favoured in turn. She is in a special powerful position; preferred to her mother, she has a secret power over her father, and is alienated from her siblings. The only touching is sexual, a poor substitute for real love or affection.

These losses, the anger, and the helplessness about her predicament make her unable to enjoy any part of her life. She has a very low self-esteem, and becomes depressed. One girl summed it up, 'My father grasped the delicate flower and crushed its petals.'

Since we do not know the true incidence of incest, it is impossible to know how many victims lead normal average lives, with no ill effects. But what of the children that we *have* come to know about? The young child may reveal her disturbance at the time with bed-wetting, sleep problems, nightmares, somatic symptoms such as tummy pains, behaviour problems, learning difficulties, fear of adults, or precocious sexual curiosity and activity.

In adolescence, incest at the very least makes for great difficulties in relating to peers. The girl feels uniquely different from the other girls. She cannot join in when they are talking about dating, first kisses, or what happens in lovemaking. She is terrified of somehow revealing what is happening at home if she opens her mouth, or undresses in front of the others. Her body feels dirty and ugly. No-one could ever love her. She may be so terrified of drawing attention to herself that she becomes very good and compliant at school, though she dreads standing up and speaking in front of the class.

A young woman related how she shared a bedroom with her two older sisters and lay in bed at night listening as her drunken father came to the oldest each night; then as that sister became pregnant, came to the next sister who was now pubertal. Finally, he came to her. She could not look anyone in the eye for fear they would, by looking at her, know what happened each night, and would not like her any more. After some psychotherapy she said, 'I visited my mother and I was able to look at her without feeling she could see into me, and see what had happened. She wasn't well, and for the first time I felt sorry for her. I can look at people in the street, now.' Her whole social life began to improve as people no longer felt she was either 'stand-offish' or intensely shy.

The adolescent's deep unhappiness may result in her taking an overdose, though she may not reveal the true cause to the doctors. Her depression also leads to various forms of acting out – truanting, running away from home, drug or alcohol abuse, stealing, and other delinquent acts.

Many adolescent girls behave badly at home or are disruptive at school in order to be put into care and be taken away from home. They often express their despair and anger by further anti-authoritarian and delinquent behaviour, even ending up in a long-term residential home or Borstal. Until quite recently, the caring professions have not understood that one of the commonest reasons for the seemingly inexplicable deviant behaviour of adolescent girls is sexual abuse.

Such girls may become promiscuous, undervaluing themselves, really longing for the basic caring love they never obtained in early life from their mothers. They may run away from home to the big cities, often just as they have begun to have a sexual relationship with a boyfriend, and the father is becoming jealous and punitive. They accept shelter from pimps or prostitutes because they need security and some sort of relationship, and slip into prostitution to keep themselves. Recent studies in England and in the United States have shown that a high proportion of prostitutes had their first sexual experience with their own fathers, and that almost half had been raped.

A large proportion of drug abusers have been rape or incest victims. The combination of incest and rape in the histories of prostitutes is not chance; there seems to be a definite increased likelihood of the female incest victim being raped. It is probable that the helplessness, lack of confidence, and sexually placatory behaviour make the girl an easy victim for the rapist. It is as though she expects to be abused and has never had permission to stand up for herself and to say no. Some of the most damaged victims of incest, therefore, may be lost in the statistics of alcohol or drug abuse, prostitution, or successful suicide.

When they reach adulthood these women cannot form satisfactory personal relationships with men, women, or their children. Rather than finding sex as part of a loving relationship they try to find love through sex, by a series of affairs, accompanied by break-ups and abortions. They break off relationships to punish the men, indirectly punishing their fathers. Very often they cannot enjoy sexual activity at all. They have varying degrees of sexual unresponsiveness, from spasm of pelvic and thigh muscles (vaginismus) when sexually approached, to the absence of any enjoyment from orgasm. Their sexual response is inhibited because consciously or unconsciously, they see their partners as their fathers, with the associated guilt and feeling of degradation.

Individual patients report specific sexual problems. One woman could not lie on her side with her husband facing her back because she had a flashback of her father's penetration from behind, once she had struggled free of him on top of her. Another could not bear her husband's lovemaking in the morning, because that was when her father had come into her bed. Another vomited after sex. One woman's young son jumped on her while playing with her, and reminded her of her brother who had regularly assaulted her. Yet these women cannot avoid sex altogether, as they so badly want the physical affection. Their sexual problems stem not only from their relationships with their fathers, but from the fact that their mothers have not provided them with a pattern of a sexually attractive, good, and successful adult woman for them to identify with.

They cannot trust men, seeing them as taking sex where they want it, but having no real concern for a woman. 'They wolf whistle, only wanting one thing, and grab you for it.' Fear of attack from men can lead mothers to become agoraphobic as their youngest child goes to school; in some way they feel that their child protects them from men's assault when they go out of the house.

They either choose husbands who are 'understanding' and impotent and accept their frigidity; or choose men who beat them up and let them down.

> A woman who had been forced to have oral sex with her father as a child seemed compulsively to take overdoses despite the stomach washouts. She was later able to understand that only after a washout did she feel clean. Another patient who, as a child, had been assaulted by a big dark-haired relative, could not give up an unsatisfactory relationship with a youthful rather feminine-looking man. During the course of therapy she became really attracted to a swarthy masculine dark-haired man, but was, at the same time, frightened, and let him down so often that he broke off the relationship. Another patient had an understanding husband who tolerated her need for seven month's celibacy. She felt for the first time that she was a virgin, saying that she had never been one. Once she felt 'untouched' she could choose to have sex with her husband.

Victims have difficulty with medical examinations and with using contraceptives. They cannot relax during vaginal examinations, feeling that the authoritarian figure of a male doctor reminds them of their father. Even with a woman doctor, the positioning for such an examination brings back bad memories. One woman said that when doctors and students watched her having a baby, she felt like a slab of meat. Another had rows with her husband because she could not handle her contraceptive cap: it felt slimy, as her brother had done when he abused her.

Even if these women manage to achieve what appears on the surface to be a stable marriage, there may be much pain and unhappiness experienced by both partners.

> One woman wept as she told how her husband expected her to deal with her daughter's wet bed. She got angry and behaved exactly as her own mother had behaved towards her, slapping the child and threatening to send her away to a home if she did it again. She was angry with her husband – then she realized it was really anger at her mother.

They cannot look at their children's bodies, particularly as they approach puberty. Their sons' developing masculinity frightens them. Their daughters' sexuality makes them fear they might molest them, or that their husband or a stranger might do so. They cannot feel neutral about them.

They have difficulty with women friends. They imagine that people think that they asked for the abuse, or enjoyed it; and although some may with reluctance and shame state that they did enjoy what little sexual stimulation they received, the sense of horror, terror, pain, and degradation overwhelmingly cancelled out any pleasure.

> One married woman managed to break through her reticence and tell a friend about her abuse. The friend's response was to say she did not want to see her again, nor want her children to play with her daughter. This confirmed that patient's sense of worthlessness and her mistrust of women.

Most victims long to confront their parents with what happened to them, and long for acknowledgement from both father and mother, but they fear it would upset the mother so much that it might kill her. If they do confront their parents, it is a difficult time for all. The parents have usually blocked off the memories and do not want to be reminded of them and made to feel guilty and responsible. They may deny it, or the father may agree and shrug it off. The mother may be distraught at the disclosure, or she may reveal that she knew all along. Or she may side with the father, blaming, criticizing, and belittling her daughter.

> A daughter was called a whore for having an illegitimate baby; because it was black her mother said it was like a monkey and she knitted a matinee coat for the child with a hole in it 'for the tail'. She refused to acknowledge that the father had abused her daughter, and that she had colluded with this. The daughter felt so

repelled by her white father that she could only be drawn to black boyfriends.

One patient did manage to confront her father and to her surprise he cried, and said he was seeing a psychiatrist for depression. His own father had done it to him and to his brother and sister. (This was the kindly grandfather she had let her daughter play with.) He begged her forgiveness. Although she could not forgive him, she felt as if a burden was lifted from her, and she could allow herself to have some sympathy for him, as well as the hatred.

A young women found it relatively easy to tell of her father's physical, emotional, and sexual abuse, but very difficult to admit to her hatred of her mother for her collusion with the incest, and for her accusations that she had 'asked for it' from her father.

Everyone would like to be proud of both parents. It is often easier to blame oneself for being bad than to be critical of parents. This badness is centred in the woman's sense of her own femininity, her womb/vagina, which has been despoiled and degraded. This may affect not only her sense of her sexuality, but her feelings about her capacity to mother, to 'hold' a baby in her womb or in her arms. One mother felt her son had Down's syndrome because she had been 'damaged inside' by her father's abuse. A woman may resolve never to have children, a resolve that is reinforced by her fear that any child might be seriously abused by her husband.

The pattern of physical or sexual abuse may be repeated in the new family. The father, coming from an incestuous home, does not see why he should not have sex with his daughters; and the mother, by her inability to give real affection to husband or daughter, promotes the incest. Her inability to assert herself and her low self-esteem make her acquiesce in any abuse of her children by her partner. She may actively collude with his sexual abuse of them by going out to work in the evening, or sending her daughter to rub her father's back in the bath. Some women find themselves actually abusing their own children, torn between the anguish for themselves as victims and the self-loathing for themselves as molesters.

In summary, the after-effects of childhood sexual abuse for a woman are shame, guilt, denied anger, and deep feelings of badness and ugliness, helplessness and fear. She is unable to trust either men or women, has profound difficulties in personal relationships, and is unable to assert herself because she seels that, since her boundaries have already been breached, she must satisfy any man's sexual needs. She feels there is no hope for her. One patient wrote:

Can knives caress
Or torn flesh rejoice?
Can cracked bones dance
Or stuffed mouths sing?
Can the bound embrace
Or the imprisoned fly?
Can broken hearts trust
Or the betrayed forget?

Clinical management

Leaving his spoil perplex'd in greater pain
She bears the load of hurt he left behind
And he the burthen of a guilty mind

Shakespeare – The Rape of Lucrece

Sexual abuse should be considered as a cause when a child shows any otherwise unexplained symptoms, especially of sexual precociousness; or when an adolescent girl repeatedly runs from home, asks to be taken into care, is involved in delinquency or promiscuity, becomes a prostitute, or makes a suicidal attempt for no obvious reason. Woman victims also present themselves to doctors with the usual wide variety of psychiatric symptoms: depression, phobic anxiety, alcoholism, drug abuse, eating disorders, psychosexual problems, and difficulties in relationships, particularly with men and with their children.

> A teenager was referred to a psychiatrist because she had panic attacks at night, when she felt she could not breathe and would die. Because her father was known to have had an incestuous relationship with her, she was referred for psychotherapy. She could not meet anyone's eyes as she felt 'they were boring into her'. She said she felt rejected by her friends, 'but what else could she expect, being so ugly and so horrible?' She had tried buying new clothes but she still felt dirty inside. When the therapist had linked her fear of choking to her father's tobacco-tasting breath when he came into her bed at night, her panic attacks ceased. When her individual therapy and brief group therapy ended, her depression lifted. She was taking typing exams, had moved away from her family, and was able to enjoy a relationship with a boyfriend.

Many victims of childhood sexual abuse, as of rape, have recurring nightmares of the assault, reliving it night after night, and are afraid of going to sleep. One girl dreamed of her grandfather following her down a dark corridor from which there was no escape, pursuing her faster and faster until she reached the end and woke up terrified. Many dream of knives: this should make one wonder about the possibility of sexual abuse.

> A young woman was irrationally jealous of her boyfriend whom she loved very much. A dream of a knife alerted the therapist to the possibility of abuse and led her to explore this further. It emerged that the low self-esteem that allowed the patient to feel that her boyfriend would easily put her aside for some other woman had been produced by her father's advances, which had gone beyond the bounds of what was acceptable between father and daughter without her realizing it. She had felt guilty for not loving her father enough. During therapy she saw that he was the one who had been at fault. As she became able to stand up to him, her self-confidence increased and her jealousy subsided, as did her depression and her headaches.
>
> Another woman had dreams of rotting meat, swarming with worms, that revealed her image of her inner self, hidden behind what *she* felt to be a mask of a charming and talented woman. After talking during therapy about the relatively minor assaults from acquaintances in her childhood, which together with coldness from her mother, had greatly disturbed her, the bad dreams stopped. Instead, one night she dreamed that she opened the refrigerator and inside was a plate of pink glowing *healthy* meat. She then went to the oven and inside was a joint roasting and sizzling away, with a delicious and appetizing smell coming from it. It was clear that her image of herself was now quite different.

A particular phenomenon seen in abused women is a hallucination of a form, something like a man, or their father, standing at the foot of the bed at night. They wake up in the night and see this form and are very frightened. It takes some time for them to realize it is not really there. These patients are in no way psychotic.

One rare outcome of childhood sexual abuse is said to be that of multiple personality in which a woman slips into behaving at different times as different people. We have not seen such patients, but we have seen, particularly on the wards, patients who have behaved in a bizarre way that technically could at different times be called hysterical, psychotic, or borderline. There seems to be an element of play-acting and attention-seeking in their verbal and physical disruption of the ward, in their violent swings of mood and generally tiresome behaviour that tend to alienate the nurses and doctors looking after them. We believe that the possibility of childhood sexual abuse should always be considered in these cases. If such a history should be elicited, these patients usually need long-term psychotherapy. One such patient later admitted that her parents could not accept that she had been abused, and attributed her distress to 'mental illness', so she had to act 'mad'.

Less bizarre, but nevertheless, odd behaviour may alert professionals to the possible underlying cause.

> A patient described her depression in the third person. When asked how she was, she replied, 'She's not so depressed at the moment'. It emerged that her defence against her father's nightly assault was to imagine herself floating out of the window, then it was 'she' who was left in bed. After some weeks of therapy she was able to say 'I'; she was daring to be herself. Like many other patients, when the incest was talked about in sessions, she squirmed and shook in her chair, almost as though the assault was occurring in the present. She wanted to please the therapist by talking about it, yet clearly felt repulsion and fear, and looked like a girl being forced to do something terrible. The therapist felt as though she was indeed 'the rapist'.

However victims of sexual abuse present themselves, they usually have at least one of the four typical symptoms. The first is obsessive rumination about the events, turning them over and over in their minds. The second is an extremely low self-image, with feelings of badness and worthlessness, making them feel outcast from the rest of the world. The third is difficulty with personal relationships, especially with men, and the fourth is sexual unresponsiveness, because of the flashbacks and the guilt at any sexual enjoyment. One or more of these merit psychotherapy, directed at dealing with the abuse, whatever the other traumas that have led to other symptoms.

Once a woman has disclosed that she was sexually abused as a child, she needs to know at once that she is going to receive help and support. The urge to deny it all again is great, and if help is not forthcoming she may evade therapy. Many of our patients opt out of individual or group therapy; or do not turn up for the initial assessment appointment. For this reason, an assessment appointment should be sent out as soon as possible after referral, even if the date of the appointment has to be delayed (Hall 1987b).

We believe that assessment should, ideally, be made by a woman therapist despite the fact that the disclosure has often first been made to a male doctor, social worker, or counsellor. The patient needs the safety of a woman therapist rather than what she feels to be the implicit threat of a man. Adequate time should be allowed for the initial interview – as much as two hours. Only with time will she be able to reveal the facts of the abuse, which should be elicited at least once. If she cannot bring herself to say exactly what happened, the therapist can help her out by asking specific questions about possible acts and possible parts of the body, allowing her to nod or shake her head in reply. If she thinks that the therapist is avoiding the facts (which she herself is only too ready to collude with), she may assume that the therapist also cannot face them because they are too awful to contemplate; and retreat once more into denial. No healing will then occur. A woman therapist, while asking for explicit details in the most matter-of-fact and straightforward way, acts very much as a good mother. She must be calm and reassuring, but at the same time must communicate her understanding of the patient's pain and humiliation. One patient said to a woman therapist, 'I've tried to tell a number of doctors or psychiatrists, but you're the first person who's really understood, who has made me feel all right about it'. Another said to her therapist, 'You accept it all, you just being there is something. You've stood back to let me move around in my feelings.... I'm not oppressed or punished.... Whatever I've done or said, you've still been there. I now feel a lot calmer and safer and relaxed.'

It is worth finding out at the initial interview if the patient has recurrent dreams about the abuse. If so, it is helpful to teach her 'dream rehearsal' (Marks, 1978). In the clinic she is asked to relive her dream in fantasy until she gets to the frightening part and is then asked to fantasize an ending of her own choice. For instance, she might choose to push her molester over, or punch him, or suddenly find herself safe in the sitting room with her husband or her mother. She should practise this dream rehearsal twice a day and after a few days she may find that she can *dream* the good ending instead of having the nightmare ending, or that she can wake up before she reaches the really frightening part. This gives her more confidence in herself and enables her to go to sleep without being afraid.

If the patient is experiencing sexual problems with a husband or partner, it is helpful to see them together. However much men are intellectually aware of the cause of their partner's inability to respond sexually, they almost invariably feel hurt and rejected. 'Surely she must see that (unlike her male abuser) *I* am kind and loving towards her, and that my sexual urgency arises out of that love and affection?' It is useful for a woman therapist to explain his wife's sexual difficulty to him since she herself finds it hard to do so. The men experience relief at their dilemma 'being understood by somebody'.

> One older woman victim wrote some months after the end of therapy that while the therapist was talking about communication in sex and sensate focus exercises 'I was sitting there trying to be adult, and smiling and making the right noises, but inside I felt sick and wanted to scream at you, biting my tongue to stop myself.'

> Eventually, she was sometimes able to enjoy sex without guilt, and even occasionally, to initiate it.

It is possible for a patient to fail to disclose a history of abuse even during prolonged therapy. Even if she does manage to disclose it, and makes some improvement, she can be left with an impoverished life, still unable to be assertive, or self-confident, or to trust anyone enough to make a good relationship. Individual therapy can help many patients, but group therapy can often achieve in a few months as much or more than individual therapy can achieve. Perhaps the ideal treatment programme for most victims is individual therapy followed by group therapy. Most patients, having admitted that they are victims, can go straight into a group, but there are some badly damaged women who cannot trust enough to manage a group, and who definitely need individual therapy.

Should the therapist be male or female? There are advantages and disadvantages in both. It is easier for a woman patient to talk to a woman, and she can learn much by identification with the therapist acting as a 'good mother'. On the other hand, a male therapist can come to be perceived by the patient as a trustworthy man who will not abuse her but will value her as a person. In our group we consider it helpful for the woman therapist to have a male co-therapist with her in order to focus the anger the group members feel towards men, and to enable them to work through it (Hall 1987b).

Some psychotherapists think it is unwise for a patient to have more than one source of therapy or counselling. We think that these women have so much to contend with in their lives and so much unhappiness, that they need all the support they can get. Some of our patients see outside counsellors or have marital therapy, and we simply encourage them to bring important outside matters into the group. We regularly liaise with other agencies where necessary.

Group therapy

One of the aims of any form of therapy is for the victim to be able to place the responsibility for the abuse on the perpetrator. A child cannot be held responsible. Any encouragement of the parent by the child, or any sexual pleasure experienced by the child must be acknowledged if the resulting guilt is to be laid aside, but must be seen as a natural reaction of any child to what is a wholly abnormal and confusing situation for her. Victims have extreme difficulty in blaming the perpetrator rather than themselves, but in our group they found themselves blaming the molester when *another* member talked about *her* experiences, and could then relate this to their own abuse. Having freed themselves from the responsibility and from much of the guilt, they still had to break the habit of always being the victim in life, and to learn to stand up for themselves.

Members find group-therapy sessions very painful. As other members relate their experiences this stirs up their own painful memories, and their symptoms can become worse for a time. But they also experience great relief, finding that they are not alone, that other apparently normal people have been through the same fear and degradation. They begin to feel part of the human race instead of considering themselves as outcasts.

Over the course of a few months, the group members become more self-confident and talk more freely. They are more assertive and many, on their own initiative, confront their molester or tell their mother. They become less afraid of men, and begin to dress in a more feminine way, for instance discarding their defence against the male threat, be it their tight jeans, their voluminous skirt, or merely their drab clothes, for a more attractive outfit. Because their sense of their true selves is emerging, they begin to make changes in their lives, take exams, find new jobs. They begin to enjoy life and even to enjoy sex. The main improvement, however, usually takes place *after* they have left the group.

Once a victim has confronted her molester it seems to prove a turning point in her recovery. She achieves a sense of mastery over her life instead of feeling always at the mercy of persecuting people or events. She has demonstrated that she has boundaries and will maintain them.

Many of Freud's women patients told him of their past experience of incest; and he at first considered that sexual seductions in childhood were an important cause of neurosis in adults. He later, however, denied this knowledge, in a letter written in 1897 to Wilhelm Fleiss. In retracting evidence that, in 1896, he had accepted was true, he was protecting parents in general by maintaining the universal secrecy and denial that had been the pattern for centuries, and still continued until about fifteen years ago. Unable to believe the truth of the histories of incest in his women patients, he hypothesized that all young girls have incestuous fantasies towards their fathers, as do boys towards their mothers, and that the reports of incest from his women patients were merely fantasies. This false premise has prevented psychoanalysts from hearing what their patients have told them about their childhood sexual abuse, and as Alice Miller (1983) has pointed out, has led the analysts to perpetuate the denial of their patient's parents. It has held back psychotherapeutic help for victims by about seventy-five years.

Far from instances of childhood sexual abuse being based on fantasy, or being exaggerated, they are likely to be underestimated by the caring professions. If the children lie at all, it is likely to be denial rather than fabrication. In adults, it may take six months or more of a trusting therapeutic relationship before sexual abuse can be talked about.

> A patient had had a year's weekly psychotherapy with a skilled female therapist, and had ended therapy, having improved a good deal, without mentioning the abuse. She then developed acute phobic anxiety and came into therapy again, this time with a male therapist. After four months, following the interpretation of a dream about tadpoles in a vase of dirty water, she was at last able to reveal the awful secret, although at that stage she was still unsure whether it was true.

Many patients are unsure at first whether their memories are false, and are relieved if they obtain corroboration from a relative. This uncertainty stems from the fact that the memory has been repressed for so many years before emerging into consciousness during therapy.

From our own experience we believe that, far from patients making up stories of childhood sexual abuse, we never find out about many of our patients who have experienced it, particularly adolescents who have overdosed or run away from home. How often in the past have we failed to help our patients, because we did not consider the possibility of actual incest and so did not ask the right questions? We fear that we may have let down many who were looking to us to make it possible for them to tell us; and we may thus have fulfilled their transference expectations of our being uncaring mothers.

We now believe that it is bad parenting, with some combination of cruelty or psychological or sexual abuse, that distorts normal intrapsychic development. Since this is a process that repeats itself from generation to generation, it is essential to try to prevent it, not only by helping the distressed victims who do present themselves so that they will not abuse or collude with abuse in the next generation, but by seeking to help the male perpetrators who are in the same inter-generational trap.

Many girls and women who are seriously disturbed and often suicidally depressed present themselves to the psychiatric services, but are unable to disclose the original assault. No-one has guessed the cause of their distress and they cannot reveal it. Treatment will be to no avail unless the dark depths are probed and the painful facts are shared with the therapist, enabling these patients to come to terms with their unhappy past.

Further reading

Renvoise, J. (1982) *Incest: a Family Pattern*, London: Routledge & Kegan Paul.

Forward, S. and Buck, C. (1981) *Betrayal of Innocence*, London: Penguin Books.
Ciba Foundation (1984) *Child Sexual Abuse within the Family*, London: Tavistock Publications.
Butler, S. (1978) *Conspiracy of Silence*, San Francisco: New Glide Publications.
Moggach, D. (1984) *Porky*, London: Penguin Books.
Miller, A. (1984) *Thou Shalt Not Be Aware*, London and Sydney: Pluto Press.
Angelou, M. (1984) *I Know Why the Caged Bird Sings*, London: Virago.

Chapter eight

Lesbian womanhood

Female homosexuality has attracted little attention, excitement, or invective in the past. It has been generally supposed that this was because women were regarded as too lowly and contemptible for their sexual preference or practice to be of any importance. Certainly, female homosexual relationships, lacking the potential for issue, presented no threat to inheritance and were unlikely to shake the foundations of society. Until recently no publicity was given to lesbianism, and women who loved other women were unremarked and unremarkable. There was a general attitude of pity towards women who did not marry, since social position and financial advantage were associated with the married state, and it was assumed that all women would wish to have a husband and children if the opportunity was available.

Those few exceptional women throughout the ages who broke the limits traditionally imposed on their sex did not usually combine their activities with marriage and motherhood. Even with abundant domestic support, the limitations of child-rearing would have severely restricted those women who travelled and became explorers, artist and writers, scientists and reformers, who became educated and influential against overwhelming odds. Their sexual orientation was not a focus of attention or concern.

Lesbianism is a form of sexual preference and orientation. It is a practice that is displayed by a substantial minority of women in our culture. It is not a perversion, nor an illness, and it is unhelpful to regard it as such. In common with many other minority practices, powerful feelings of prejudice, condemnation, hostility, and fear may be aroused in others by lesbianism, due to ignorance and the threat of difference. Discrimination and oppression is mainly personal and social. Lesbianism has never been subject to punitive laws since, unlike male homosexuality, it has not been perceived as a threat to the social order nor as an abuse of personal freedom or power likely to contaminate others.

Homosexuality is thus not a psychiatric disorder, and is not of itself a cause of distress. Social attitudes, prejudices, and certain religious views may contribute to personal difficulties experienced by women who have a sexual preference for other women, but in most other respects relationship conflicts are similar to those experienced by primarily heterosexual women. We find it helpful to view sexual orientation and preference and the capacity for making relationships as a continuum, with a degree of overlap and flexibility of expression which may change with circumstances, opportunity, and time during the course of the life cycle. Given every woman's intimate experience of another woman, her mother, it seems to us unsurprising that women may find satisfaction in close relationships with other women. This does not necessarily involve genital sexuality, nor an avoidance of relationships with men. Women may choose a lesbian relationship, not only because they find themselves sexually excited by women's bodies, but because they have a need to be cuddled, and enjoy being close to another woman's body.

Some women choose to live together for mutual support and care. One such woman became depressed when her companion abandoned her for a mutual woman friend. 'I don't think I am truly lesbian,' she said, 'I didn't go much for sex, but she needed me and I thought we would always be together.'

Lesbian women may be exclusively homosexual in their attachments and orientation, or bisexual to a greater or lesser extent. During childhood and puberty it is usual for girls to admire other girls and to have crushes on older schoolfellows, teachers, or other idealized figures. This is a normal part of growing up and is associated with the loosening of the tie to their all-important mother, allowing identification with other models of womanhood. Sexual stirrings may lead to self-exploration, and masturbation fantasies may involve female figures. Sometimes this stage of development includes a fascination with other girls' bodies, which may lead to mutual exploration and discovery.

Many paths lead to preference for one's own sex as the literature on the aetiology of homosexuality demonstrates (Bell and Weinberg, 1978). Any simplistic causal view is unlikely to be applicable to the majority of lesbian women. Some not uncommon experiences are factors in the development of lesbian orientation in *some* women: childhood seduction by a woman or a man; experience of or exposure to heterosexual activity that is aggressive or frightening; experience of a critical, rejecting, and hostile mother; an exclusive preference for women as objects of affection from an early age, often in the absence of a male figure; an overpowering or brutal father; and experience of an exploiting or limiting heterosexual relationship.

A woman in her late thirties had just married for the third time when she sought help. She was embarrassed by her habit of gazing at women's genital areas, 'mentally undressing them', and was becoming preoccupied by the pubertal development of her only daughter. She could not look people in the eye and was concerned with her inability to sustain relationships. In group therapy she explored her patterns of communication and developed some awareness of her own needs. She left her husband, who was in any case intruding sexually on her daughter. She was able to look at her attachment to another woman in the group, who represented her sister, and long-repressed memories emerged of sharing a bed with her older sister. During adolescence they gained excitement and satisfaction in mutual masturbation, which united them and compensated for a lack of affection in the family, but when she was aged 17, her sister married and emigrated, leaving her alone with her uncaring mother.

After the group ended she asked to continue in therapy and used individual sessions with the female therapist to deal with the uncomfortable feelings that had been denied for so long. This rapidly relieved her symptoms and her long-standing depression. Her relationship with her daughter improved dramatically when she was able to acknowledge her lesbianism, finally deciding to 'come out' and seek the company of other lesbian women.

Whereas her sister had matured into heterosexual orientation and made a successful marriage, our patient's denial of her homosexual desires had caused serious distress over many years with symptoms that seemed bizarre until she understood the real meaning for *her*.

Few lesbian women conform to the stereotype of butch masculine individuals, in contrast to many homosexual men who emphasize their feminine characteristics for deliberate display. But some lesbians have a masculine build and gait, seem by nature unsuited to feminine dress, and are more at home with male pursuits. They attract and are more attracted by delicate and feminine partners and adopt complementary roles accordingly within the relationship. Some deliberately dress in a sexually unattractive way, shunning artifice, so that they will not attract unwelcome attention from men. However, the majority conform largely to the dictates of peer group, class, and fashion and are unlikely to advertise their orientation by their appearance or behaviour, although they may display signs recognizable to other homosexuals.

Jo was in her early twenties when she was referred for help. She looked butch and wore an anorak, jeans, and trainers at all times. She had been distressed by her feelings for an older woman colleague who had made love to her. A young man on the staff had recognized her lesbianism and had encouraged her to 'come out'.

She had a history of violent outbursts throughout her school days, and had several times attacked other girls. She was deeply protective of her invalid mother, and felt that her father always disapproved of her. She had moved away from home because she was depressed and grief-stricken following the sudden death of her closest friend with whom she enjoyed a very special, though non-sexual, relationship. She sought help because she did not know how she could face her family with her decision to 'come out', and she used brief individual therapy to help her to express her grief, and to look at the way in which she related to others.

Several years later she accompanied her partner Louise to therapy, but made it plain that she did not wish for further therapy herself. The couple had met at a women's group that Louise had attended after leaving her husband. A pretty and feminine girl, she had married her long-standing boyfriend but was forced by parental pressures to have a termination of an unplanned pregnancy prior to their marriage. She never forgave her husband for this and became increasingly irritated by his incompetence and his lack of manliness, feeling it was 'like living with a backward 3-year-old'. At the women's group she found support and began to talk openly about her feelings for the first time. She was grateful for Jo's protective attitude towards her and soon they were inseparable. However, Louise longed for a baby to replace the one she had lost and became profoundly depressed. She spent a considerable time in individual therapy, grieving the loss of her first aborted pregnancy, and exploring the conflict between her wish for a child and her attachment to Jo. She was unsure whether she could bear to have sexual intercourse with a man in the hope of becoming pregnant, or whether to ask for AID. Eventually the couple moved to another area, so we do not know how their story continued.

As human beings we are social animals and inherently bisexual, each of us possessing the capacity to be attracted to our own and to the opposite sex, but not necessarily desiring sexual contact as a part of any relationship. Most people have a range of relationships, from casual acquaintanceships, through increasing friendship and intimacy with family and closer friends, to a few special relationships of great intimacy. For many people the ideal relationship entails the sharing of thoughts, feelings, confidences, and activities with one special person. The closeness is enhanced by a loving and fully sexual expression of this intimacy. Such an 'ideal marriage' with another is likely to be an exclusive partnership, characterized by loyalty, consideration, generosity, mutual trust, and self-restraint, since it will meet most of the needs that the partners have of a mature relationship with a special other.

Such fulfilling relationships are not commonly achieved and some needs usually remain unmet. The ideal relationship exists only in fantasy and all adult relationships include a degree of ambivalence, although devoted stable partnerships are likely to meet many of the requirements of both individuals involved. Sometimes these will be met by having several close relationships of real importance, of which only one may include sexual intimacy. Typically, a woman may be secure in a happy marriage and family life, but seeks stimulation and confirmation of her worth as an individual in a job or activities outside the home or by creative and absorbing hobbies that can be shared with others. Her feelings about herself and her world may be shared with a special friend and confidante who is privy to aspects of herself that she does not feel able to share with other important people in her life. Sometimes her mother or sister will fulfil this function for her, and it may offer a very important safety valve.

A marital relationship is often enriched by companionship and activity with others which does not threaten the stability and central importance of the union. This is usually with a companion of the same sex, thus avoiding the partner's jealousy. A man will typically engage in sport or join a club of some sort, obtaining companionship by these activities. Occasionally, one partner seeks sexual satisfaction outside the marriage with another of the *same* sex, which disturbs the equilibrium in a special way. A woman may feel able to fight a mistress, but cannot compete with her husband's desire and need for a homosexual lover. Such situations cause great distress to all those concerned, and any solution involves a degree of compromise and loss. Often a couple cannot bring themselves to part, but tolerance is rarely sufficient for continued marital harmony unless both partners have a degree of autonomy and satisfaction from their lives and from other relationships such that the marriage is enhanced by them. Nigel Nicholson movingly describes the marriage of his parents, Harold Nicholson and Vita Sackville-West in his book *Portrait of a Marriage*. Their unusual partnership survived early storms and continuing homosexual infidelities by both partners, which apparently enriched the powerful bond between them.

Women are better able than men to demonstrate affectionate feelings for their own sex in our culture. Women may kiss and embrace others. Touching and close physical contact does not invoke the taboos applied to men, which seem only to be waived on the football field. Unless a woman finds her marriage intolerable or falls passionately in love with an available woman, she may satisfy her needs for female companionship and intimacy by a loving and special relationship that never becomes fully sexualized. A woman who realizes that her primary sexual orientation is lesbian may nevertheless choose to marry and have children, as may a primarily homosexual man, preferring the social acceptability of marriage and family to the problems inherent in declaring homosexual preference. Many women, however, never question their sexual orientation, and embark on marriage and motherhood as a matter of course. Subsequent recognition of powerful loving feelings for another woman may cause intense confusion and distress, leading to breakdown. Such a situation has much in common with that of a married woman who falls in love with another man, but the unfamiliarity of the experience, the self-doubt and confusion created by the acknowledgement of the previously unrecognized lesbian feelings, and the degree of social disapproval that it attracts, may create overwhelming conflict.

> A woman in her mid-thirties was admitted to hospital in an acutely distressed state. During childhood she had been brutally treated and emotionally deprived, and had sought refuge in marriage to a dull man who made few emotional demands on her. On a study course she met a warm and maternal woman, a few years her senior. As the friendship deepened, the older woman confided that she was unhappy in her marriage, burdened by the care of her elderly in-laws, but devoted to her adolescent children. The two women were astounded to find themselves falling in love, and their relationship progressed to provide physical warmth and satisfaction from sexual intimacy. They made plans to set up home together and found a flat, but when it came to the crunch the older woman felt unable to abandon her family responsibilities. Our patient was full of anger and disappointment, and her distress required hospital admission.
>
> Her friend visited her regularly while she was in hospital, clearly upset by her reaction but unable to make the decision to leave her family. The women attended joint therapy sessions that enabled them to explore the difficult dilemmas that each faced, and our patient subsequently went into long-term therapy. She found various excuses for discontinuing when she experienced the therapist as another hostile rejecting mother, unable to give her the love for which she longed. Her friend remained with her family and their affair eventually withered.

A woman may find it impossible to acknowledge her lesbian feelings openly, fearing that doctors will view her as perverted and abnormal. If she feels ashamed, she may prefer to accept hospital admission, drug treatment, and even ECT, rather than admit the underlying cause of her seemingly inexplicable and resistant depression and distress.

> A nurse had suffered from prolonged and disabling depression requiring a number of hospital admissions and courses of ECT, but the roots of her depression had never been clarified. She constantly threatened suicide, and when she was referred for a consultation, her handbag was stuffed with hoarded pills. Each of her breakdowns had been associated with difficulties in her working life, when she had developed powerful affectionate feelings for senior nurses that she felt were unacceptable. The first breakdown had followed an upsetting incident when she and a friend had become rivals for the affection of a senior colleague. She had been preferred and the other girl had made a serious suicide attempt.
>
> She had never used the word lesbian or declared her orientation and her feelings about herself to anyone. She had never engaged in any expressions of physical intimacy with the objects of her love, but felt that she was abnormal. She was thinking of marrying a man who had loved her for many years, since it would make her parents happy. Unable to resolve the conflict of feelings that this aroused for her, she became depressed and suicidal. She gave the therapist sufficient clues to realize the true nature of her problems but her sexual orientation was by no means certain and she worked on her difficulties in long-term individual therapy. It eventually emerged that she had been seduced by her father as an adolescent during her mother's absence through illness. The conflict that this had aroused in her led to an avoidance of men, and difficulty in acknowledging her right to be sexual. Her crippling depression disappeared, but her ambivalent feelings about her sexuality continued.

Declaring herself a lesbian may be traumatic for a woman, largely because of other people's attitudes. The understanding and support of other lesbians is usually generously offered to a girl who 'comes out'. Lesbian relationships in general are characteristically loyal and affectionate, lacking much of the competitiveness that women often demonstrate towards one another in their heterosexual conquests. But the distress and intolerance of relatives may be a major problem for a lesbian girl.

> An attractive mother in her forties, recently remarried after her first husband's sudden death, was referred for help with depression that had resisted treatment over several years. She discovered by chance that her adored only daughter was in love with a married woman some years her senior. She was so distressed by the 'loss' of her daughter and of her hopes for the future – grandchildren and

a new family – that she made a serious suicide attempt. Her daughter was undeterred and set up home with her woman friend, who left her husband and children. The mother could not reconcile herself to her daughter's choice, experiencing it as a personal attack and a public sign that she had failed as a mother. It seemed an insult to her late husband's memory, and she considered the other woman to be an intruder into her relationship with her daughter. She used brief therapy to express her rage and disappointment that her daughter should fail her in this way.

Sometimes a woman will recognize her lesbian tendencies from an early age, and yet be unable to cope with the implications that this has for her life. She may form passionate attachments for other women, who may or may not reciprocate them but she may not be able to handle rejection by others, nor any open acknowledgement of her needs and orientation. This may lead her to an unrewarding and unsatisfactory situation in which she denies herself the very opportunities for the loving relationship for which she longs.

A woman and her brother grew up in a fatherless family and had no contact during childhood with any adult males. An outstanding pupil, she delighted in discovering how things worked, and had little interest in the teenage preoccupations of her school friends. She always felt herself to be apart from the others, and had several crushes on girls whom she particularly admired. In late adolescence, she began to declare her affections more openly, but only where she felt it safe to do so. In her twenties she fell in love with a colleague who was engaged to be married, and plucked up the courage to declare her feelings. The colleague's fiancé sought her out and threatened her in an abusive way, which led to her making a serious attempt on her life. Her mother's response on visiting her in hospital was, 'Where did I go wrong?' The daughter never forgave her for this, and was deeply resentful of her mother's failure to accept her sexuality, which mirrored her own inability to accept herself for what she was. Her successful professional life was punctuated by episodes of deep depression, which were always related to the development of a passionate attachment for a heterosexual woman who found her attentions distasteful and rejected her in favour of a male partner. She rendered ineffectual a number of attempts at psychotherapy, by pitting her considerable intellect against the therapist's attack on the underlying problem. Eventually, in middle age she joined a therapy group that enabled her to explore her pattern of relationships with others, her idealization of women who attracted her, and her inability to acknowledge her lesbian orientation openly.

For each of these women their lesbianism was not in itself a cause of distress, but the attitudes of others towards it, in reality or in imagination, caused profound embarrassment, unhappiness, and even despair. We never see women who are seeking to change the direction of their sexual orientation, but we often see women who are uncertain about themselves and their sexual preferences. They are usually confused about their relationships with others, and are experiencing difficulty in making and sustaining intimacy. This in no way differs from the issues that bring heterosexual women to therapy, but the social and personal implications of a women's preference for her own sex are inevitably similar to those facing a homosexual man, and influence her choices regarding child-bearing and child-rearing. Social pressures and public opinion make it difficult for a woman to gain the care and custody of her children if she leaves her marriage to live with a lesbian partner. If she enters into a relationship with another man, a mother is much more likely to gain custody of her children.

The majority of co-habiting women have a harmonious relationship with their sexual partner. There is good role differentiation, with a sharing of parenting tasks and housework, but it is usual for the mother to do more of the actual child care. A study of schoolchildren reared in lesbian households compared with matched controls brought up in heterosexual single-parent households showed no significant differences in psychosexual development, emotions, behaviour, or mannerisms. (Golombok *el al*, 1983) The authors concluded that rearing in a lesbian household did not lead to atypical psychosexual development or constitute a risk factor likely to create vulnerability to psychiatric illness.

Donor insemination is available in some centres to unmarried women who wish to conceive, and private services may not enquire about the reasons for a woman seeking AID. Other centres may be deeply opposed to offering a service to lesbian women or women without a partner, and some lesbian women who long to become mothers will deliberately seduce a man in the hope of becoming pregnant. Others may displace their mothering instincts into caring for their partner, working in a situation that offers an outlet for 'mothering', such as nursing or residential care, or may sublimate their energy into other activities. Many homosexual partners lavish care and attention on their pet animals, often successfully breeding pedigree dogs and cats, in whom they take parental pride.

Lesbian orientation should not be regarded as abnormal, or in itself a cause of distress. Rewarding and stable lesbian relationships would be the choice of many women. Unsatisfactory relationships are a significant cause of distress whether they are homosexual or heterosexual. For some women, inherent bisexuality may be recognized with changing circumstances and opportunities.

> One woman had worked and lived with her partner for twenty years and was shattered by her death in a road accident; she later married her bachelor neighbour and found new happiness.

The power of falling in love may radically change long-standing patterns.

> A hard-drinking chain-smoking woman, who swore like a trooper, rousing fear and ridicule in her acquaintances, lived with a pretty blonde and wore men's clothing at home. At a time of personal difficulty after starting a new job, she confided in an older male colleague, widowed several years earlier after a devoted childless marriage. They fell in love and became inseparable, to the astonishment of old friends. She was transformed, no longer outmanning the men, and they married. She gave up her job when their first child was born, revelling in motherhood and family life.

Lesbian women in distress seek understanding of the meaning of their distress, which will be as varied and as uniquely personal as that of any other individual. It should never be assumed that the distress is an inevitable consequence of lesbianism.

Further reading

Dickson, A. (1985) *The Mirror Within*, London: Quartet.
Hodgkinson, L. (1986) *Sex is not Compulsory*, London: Sphere.
Walker, A. (1983) *The Colour Purple*, London: The Women's Press.
Nicholson, N. (1973) *Portrait of a Marriage*, London: Futura.

Useful addresses

The Albany Trust,
Secretary Mr D. Neville,
24 Chester Square,
London SW1 9HS.
Tel: 01 730 5871.
(Counselling and Information service)

Gemma,
Secretary Ms E. Beckett,
BM Box 5700,
London WC1N 3XX.
(Organization for Lesbians).

London Lesbian Line,
Tel: 01 251 6511.
Offers information, counselling and referral service.

Chapter nine

Childless womanhood

The womb
Rattles its pod, the moon
Discharges itself from the tree with nowhere to go.

Sylvia Plath (1932–63)
'Childless Woman'
from *Collected Poems*, Faber, 1981.

A woman's capacity to create, bear, and nurture a child is the very essence of her womanhood, her unique and special capacity – prized, feared, envied, protected, and celebrated. Birth is the only defence against the inevitability of death, an intimation of our immortality, of our new hope for the future. When a woman has a child, she confirms for herself and for others that she is a complete woman, fertile and capable of the biological task of creating and perpetuating life. She rivals her own mother, by becoming mother of a child in her turn, and completes the reproductive cycle that began with her own conception in her mother's womb.

The psychological importance of the uterus and the results of its malfunction, leading to failure of conception, abortion or miscarriage, stillbirth, imperfect babies, and neonatal death, are significant because the uterus is an organ associated with fundamental aspects of wellbeing, of 'being well' as a woman. It is usual for women to experience some doubts and uncertainties about the prospect of conception and parenthood, as indeed do men. Sometimes this ambivalence may be sufficient to prevent conception, or lead to the sabotage of medical efforts to promote conception if help has been sought for infertility. Sometimes a woman will repeatedly become pregnant and yet seek to have the pregnancies terminated, reassuring herself that she can become a mother and yet choosing not to do so, as if unready for the whole experience of motherhood. Another may dread the thought of pregnancy and childbirth, and feel unable to mother her own child, and yet choose to reproduce to satisfy the needs and expectations of her partner, her parents, or society in general. Others may choose not to have children because they lack a supportive partner, or because it would threaten their health, their relationships, or other valued aspects of their lives, such as careers or special interests. Such decisions about whether to have a child are never lightly undertaken, nor are they decisions that can be put aside once and for all without further thought.

Biologically, a man may father children throughout his adult life. For a woman, fertility is likely to be limited to a space of some thirty years, with diminishing prospects during the latter ten or fifteen years. Such knowledge, whether conscious or unconscious, exerts an influence on the choices women make. There is fear of leaving motherhood too late because of the increased chance of bearing an abnormal child or, if something should go wrong, that there might not be time enough remaining for a second chance.

There are women who have enjoyed full and rewarding lives, without time or desire for children, who are suddenly confronted with the biological reality that their potential for childbearing is running out. They go to great lengths to try to have a child before it is too late and may become inexplicably depressed as they mourn the loss of what might have been, and face the reality of their future without heirs. This is one of the reasons why the fortieth birthday – the big four-O – looms large as a landmark in the lives of women, marking not just the passing of the years, but the ending of their reproductive phase.

For a woman who longs to become pregnant and is sexually active, life may come to revolve around the monthly flow, with alternating hope if her period should be late, or despair when it appears, dashing her hopes that she might have conceived. For women who are exceptionally fertile, and who find themselves pregnant in spite of every effort to prevent conception, the monthly flow relieves anxiety and reassures her that she will not be carrying an unwanted child.

Childlessness

Failure to conceive may cause deep unhappiness. It may threaten relationships and lead to profound depression and a sense of worthlessness. (The relationship between psychological factors and infertility is dealt with in more depth in Chapter 10.) A woman may feel excluded from longstanding relationships when her friends become preoccupied with their babies, or feel she is a freak and failure in her family when sisters and sisters-in-law produce children for the proud grandparents. The sight of pregnant women, or young mothers with babies, may give rise to envy and bleak despair. If she works with a group of young women who may well become pregnant, she feels increasingly isolated and left out.

Seeking medical advice on the matter can be difficult for some couples, who fear being asked intimate questions about their sexual relationship or being subject to embarrassing physical examinations and investigations. Lovemaking may become subservient to the desire for conception, with temperature charts and efforts to determine the most fertile periods of the cycle dominating the relationship. Husbands may feel degraded by this and find themselves unable or unwilling to perform to rote. One said, 'I feel that now she only sees me as a stud. She's interested in my giving her a baby, but not in loving me.' Conversely, the wife who fails to conceive when she knows that her husband has a great desire for children fears that he will leave her for another woman with a fertile womb. Although a man's contribution to infertility is important, the popular myth and stigma of the woman's responsibility remains central to the way in which women view themselves and in which society as a whole views childless marriage.

A deeply depressed woman was admitted to hospital after a serious suicide attempt. Since her childhood she had suffered from painful and disabling arthritis that was only kept in check with powerful drugs. When she did not become pregnant, she and her husband went to the infertility clinic and were subjected to extensive investigations, to no avail. When she stopped her medicines in case they might be responsible for her failure to conceive, her arthritis worsened. She began to think that her childlessness was a punishment for her sickness and deformity, and that she was 'unfit' to be a mother. This was reinforced when she and her husband were rejected as potential adoptive parents, and she attempted suicide.

In individual weekly psychotherapy sessions, she began to grieve her lost hopes, and to share her feelings about her body. She had always felt unattractive as a woman and she felt trapped in her sick role by her inability to become a mother. She wanted a perfect healthy baby, a representation of herself as she had been before illness struck, to love and to nurture safely into adulthood. She wanted to create a child with her husband, feeling that his care for her sick self was parental, rather than the passion of a mate. She had never talked about the extreme suffering she endured as a child, and her feelings about her family's attitude to her illness and their incomprehension of her pain. She poured out anger and tears that had been dammed up for many years and was surprised to find herself experiencing sexual excitement that she had not known before. She considered returning to the clinic for more investigations, but decided that she had felt 'a patient' all her life, and that now she was beginning to feel like a woman. When she

> concluded therapy, her depression had gone completely and she was finding much satisfaction in voluntary work in several spheres. She said that psychotherapy had opened up a new era of her life.

> A woman in her early forties had never married although she had always longed for a family of her own. After a sudden bout of severe abdominal pain, a hysterectomy was advised for fibroids of her uterus. She was deeply shocked. Even though it seemed unlikely that she would ever have a child, the possession of her uterus was important to her. It represented a hope, albeit an unrealistic one, and to lose her womb would be the end of her dreams, the end of her *potential* for motherhood. She used a single psychotherapy consultation to explore these feelings, and decided to retain her full womanly potential, and to refuse surgery, thus avoiding the sense of loss and depression a hysterectomy would have caused. She continued to hope for a special relationship and marriage, and felt her solitariness each time she was invited to a wedding. Holding on to her uterus seemed to be some protection against the emptiness within her, but as the ensuing years took her beyond any possibility of child-bearing, troublesome menopausal bleeding led her, in her early fifties, to seek hysterectomy. It was important for her that *she* had chosen the time to part with the womb that had such significance for her.

For these women, as for so many others, childlessness was a condition that they were unable to change, but their feelings about what they perceived as incompleteness or failure were resolved to some extent by having the opportunity to explore, share, and reflect upon them within the safety of the therapeutic encounter. In the second case, her capacity to seek a consultation about her *feelings* – rather than about the gynaecological symptoms – gave her a degree of control over her subsequent treatment that most patients surrender to their doctors with sometimes devastating emotional consequences (see Chapter 20).

We have been struck by the number of depressed young women referred for therapy, with considerable problems in their close personal relationships, who have been investigated and treated for infertility but who had given themselves no chance of conceiving, since they were not having intercourse with their partners.

> A couple consulted a gynaecologist privately for investigation of their childlessness. They were reticent about their sex life, but it turned out that since the husband drank himself stuporose on home-made beer each night they had not had intercourse for many years. The wife seemed to need to go through this gynaecological ritual before she could leave the marriage, nine months later.

Possibly, the ritualistic attendance at infertility clinics meets a need for self-punishment, or for acknowledgement of worthlessness. Nevertheless, the evident ambivalence of such women towards becoming a mother is very different from the deep despair of those women whose maternal instinct is involuntarily thwarted.

A young nurse was referred for psychotherapy because she was infertile, depressed, and disabled by severe back pain. She was good at her work, enjoying being needed, but developed spinal problems and was unable to cope with the physical demands of nursing. At around this time she married a young man whom she scarcely knew, before he was posted abroad. She determined to have a child to look after as soon as her husband returned, but did not conceive and attended an infertility clinic, where eventually fertility drugs were prescribed. The likelihood of conception was indeed remote, since her husband was posted to another town and she had chosen not to accompany him. They infrequently shared a bed, and although her husband came home most weekends, intercourse was rare.

Her difficulty in getting together with her woman therapist reflected her difficulty in getting together with her husband. Her obsession with her menstrual cycle and the prospect of conception was a defence against acknowledging her inner feelings of emptiness and loss, and the poverty of the marital communications. The clinic had colluded with her pretence, since they *assumed* that sexual intercourse must be taking place.

In therapy she glimpsed the deep pain of her childhood with a mother who did not love her and did not want her, but threatened to cut off all contact if she communicated with the divorced father. She felt torn between them both, and had escaped from her own inner sickness by caring for it in others. When injury had forced her to become a patient, her pain – both physical and mental – was intolerable, and her rage found expression in depression and suicide attempts. The 'distant' marriage offered her a new role and the hoped-for baby would have given her someone else to look after. She developed incapacitating headaches which, together with her back pain, prevented regular attendance for therapy, so that she rendered the therapist's efforts useless, as she had the clinic specialist's. Like her mother, she did not really want a child, but she could neither admit that, nor face the disasters of her own experience. She dropped out of therapy when her sabotage was challenged.

Childlessness is a relative condition. Sometimes both partners of an involuntarily childless union will conceive with new partners.

Sometimes a woman remains childless for social reasons, lacking a partner or the opportunity for motherhood. A woman may fear that her partner will leave her if she has a child, and therefore shuns motherhood even if she longs for it, or chooses abortion if she finds herself with a pregnancy unwanted by the father. Sometimes a woman who has already had children finds unexpected difficulties in having a further child. Sterilization may have been chosen as an alternative to other methods of contraception by a woman who feels that her family is complete, but a change of circumstances – such as a new marriage or the death or loss of existing children – may lead to a renewed desire for children, which may become an overwhelming obsession, even more powerful than the original urge for motherhood, and rendered more urgent by the sense of time running out. Sometimes the sterilization may be reversible, successfully leading to conception, but failure may cause severe depression, with marked guilt and self-blame, and a conviction that this is a punishment that she has brought upon herself for having left a marriage, or having somehow been responsible for losing a child. Women who have been unsuccessful in achieving a desired pregnancy, whether through failure to conceive or by repeated early miscarriage, sometimes request sterilization or hysterectomy as a form of self-punishment.

Lost hopes are not easily mourned. Grief and rage are more easily expressed when a loss is tangible, less easily when the loss is intangible. Women are often wounded and humiliated by chance thoughtless remarks, which are not meant maliciously. The state of childlessness and the complex emotions associated with it should be broached with delicacy and sensitivity.

Further reading

Dowrick, S. and Grundberg, S. (1980) *Why Children?* London: The Woman's Press Ltd.

Useful addresses

CHILD,
Farthings,
Gaunts Road,
Pawlett,
Nr. Bridgewater,
Somerset.
Tel: 0278 683595.
(Self-help for couples with infertility problems.)

NAC (National Association for the Childless),
318 Summer Lane,
Birmingham.
Tel: 021 359 4887.

Chapter ten

Barren womanhood

Psychological aspects of infertility

George L. Christie and Mike Pawson

The observations of anthropologists, sociologists, and psychoanalysts can deepen our understanding of what prepares a human being to become a parent or to remain childless. Human birth rates are influenced by sociological forces, mediated through both human physiology and cultural practice. Thus, when an agrarian tribe moves into a nomadic phase, where children can impede travel, the birth rate falls as a result of various bodily adaptations. Girls do not menstruate until late, fertility is similarly delayed, and mothers breast-feed their children for much longer, with correspondingly reduced fecundity. When the tribe settles down again in one place, these processes reverse, and the birth rate rises again.

Over the greater period of human history man's numbers overall have remained fairly constant. Whenever plagues, famines, or wars have reduced the figure, the fecundity has increased and the birth rate has risen. Whenever the figure has increased beyond a certain level, or when food supplies have become inadequate for the existing level, a number of culturally ingrained practices, including abstention from intercourse, abortion, and infanticide, have brought it down again.

So the balance between the human need to have a child and the human need not to have one is something that varies from time to time, influenced by many forces. It is important to remember that the harbouring of ambivalent feelings about having children is not necessarily abnormal. It is, in fact, an inescapable part of the human condition. There is even evidence that anxiety, mixed feelings, even emotional turmoil, are normal in pregnancy, and can represent forces promoting internal readjustments within women, particularly during first pregnancies, preparing them for their important new role – a preparation that includes further internal separation from their own mothers, and increasing readiness to bond with a new human being.

In this chapter we are concerned with the barren womb, some of the causes of infertility, and the consequences for the individuals involved.

There is a huge body of knowledge about the physiology of reproduction and about the nature of pathological bodily processes involved in infertility. There is much that remains unexplained, however, about the psychological and social forces that might contribute to the barren womb (or the unproductive testicle). We are familiar with the anguish of the involuntarily childless, but we are on less familiar ground when we try to explore the possibility of emotional origins for their plight.

Many sound physicians believe that psychological influences are unimportant in fertility, and can produce scientific evidence supporting their view. On the other hand, general practitioners and gynaecologists can offer numerous clinical vignettes strongly suggesting the operation of such human factors. Many analysts and psychotherapists can also produce case material indicating that conception may follow the acquisition of new insights and the resolution of inner conflicts.

The series of case histories that follows demonstrates such a connection between infertility and the emotional life of women (and men), e.g. their unresolved griefs and motivational conflicts. These histories reveal the power of the human dilemma that lies behind the empty womb.

Case 1

> A 30-year-old businesswoman with primary infertility consulted one of the writers early in his career. She had been trying to conceive for several years without success, despite much gynaecological investigation and treatment. She was seen only once in psychiatric consultation, and no evidence of psychological disturbance emerged. Towards the end of the session some discussion arose about the possibility that her competitive business life style was in conflict with her aspirations towards motherhood. The writer never saw her again, but shortly afterwards she telephoned to say that, after thinking about the discussion, she had wound up her business, had taken a helping job in the local kindergarten, and had conceived the same month. She made sure also that he heard indirectly about the arrival of subsequent babies. Such a story is not uncommon in general and gynaecological practice.

Case 2

> A Roman Catholic nurse complained of secondary infertility. Her only previous pregnancy had resulted in a stillbirth some two years previously. She had not been given the opportunity to see the baby or to hold it, and no photographs had been taken. She had declined

to make her own funeral arrangements and the hospital had disposed of the baby.

She became increasingly tearful during the initial interview, as this aspect of her history was explored. She had no idea of the hospital routine for disposal of stillborn babies, but, when asked, agreed she would dearly love to know where the baby was buried. She was asked to return in a week's time. In the meantime, a phone call to the chaplain of the particular hospital established where the baby was buried, and the plot number of the grave. The woman was given this information at her next consultation and was encouraged to visit the grave.

The importance and relevance of coming to terms with her dead baby was explained to the woman and discussed with her. A few routine and simple investigations were undertaken, but she was told no treatment would be started unless something radically wrong was found. She was also informed that, in the opinion of the writer, the most important aspect of the treatment would be the visit to the dead baby's grave.

Returning a few weeks later she confessed that she had not been able to find courage to make the visit. Her feelings about this were discussed, and the writer suggested that her husband might go with her and support her. The following weekend, being their wedding anniversary, seemed an appropriate time for the visit.

When she returned for her follow-up appointment, six weeks later, it was clear, as soon as she entered the room, that the situation had changed. She had a confident and relaxed air and reported that they had visited the grave several times. She conceived four months later, no other treatment having been necessary.

Case 3

A woman of 24 was referred with secondary infertility, and secondary amenorrhoea of some duration. She had been fully investigated elsewhere and was referred purely for treatment with fertility drugs. This treatment was given, and she conceived on the third course, being subsequently transferred back to the hospital that originally referred her.

When she reached 28 weeks gestation, the writer was asked to see her again as she appeared to be rather large, and ultrasound scanning revealed that she was expecting triplets. There was considerable staff rejoicing and self-congratulation at this diagnosis. The remaining antenatal care was continued in the department where she had been treated, proceeding to a successful and relatively straightforward vaginal delivery of three healthy babies. All went well on the postnatal ward and when feeding was established and the babies were of adequate weight, she was discharged home. It was then that her real nightmare began.

Her mother-in-law was brought in to help in the home but three new babies were all too much. Within a few weeks of her discharge the writer had a phone call from the local district general hospital to say she had been admitted with an overdose. She survived this, but, when she subsequently returned to discuss what had happened and her future, the true story of her past life began to unfold. She said that she had not really wanted children yet, but had agreed to treatment for the sake of her husband who was anxious to have a child. She described how she had fallen pregnant at 16 and had a child by the only man she had ever really loved. Her parents forbade her to continue the relationship. She was not allowed to keep the child, which, because of some complications during delivery, was regarded as being unsuitable for adoption and placed in a home. She had been mourning the loss of this child ever since and had never had a normal spontaneous period in all that time. Because of her unresolved grief, she clearly had not been ready for another pregnancy, which had been artificially forced upon her by the use of fertility drugs.

Case 4

An Indian girl in her early twenties was referred for a second opinion concerning her primary infertility. She had secondary amenorrhoea and was therefore not ovulating. All investigations returned normal findings. She had been treated with appropriate fertility drugs, but had not conceived.

She had been born in India, the unwanted fourth child in a well-to-do family. Soon after birth she was given by her parents to a grandmother to look after and, when she became too much for the latter, she was sent off to boarding school aged about 5 or 6. There she stayed, seeing little of her parents, who appeared uninterested in her, even during school holidays.

At the age of 17, an uncle showed her the only warmth and affection she had ever received from any of the family, but he also got her pregnant. The family arranged for the pregnancy to be terminated, but she was in disgrace. No longer a virgin, she was unable to marry within her own social stratum, and a marriage was arranged with a lower-caste Indian in the United Kingdom. As the facts emerged, her failure to ovulate seemed less and less surprising.

Case 5

The patient was a Catholic woman in her late thirties presenting ostensibly with primary infertility. The initial impression was of a very ordinary person; average brown hair streaked with early grey, average height, and average femininity. She may not have been easily remembered had it not been for the story that eventually unfolded.

She gave a history of a marriage in her twenties. There had been no pregnancies and the couple had separated after six years. She had met her present partner six years previously and they had been trying to conceive for approximately three years. Interestingly, the referring doctor's letter had made no mention of the earlier marriage, presumably because the patient had not revealed it. There was nothing remarkable in her gynaecological history, and all fertility investigations returned normal findings.

She was seen in the follow-up clinic six weeks after her final investigation, and was labelled 'unexplained infertility'. At this stage, even obscure possibilities warranted exploration. The writer felt there was one area of enquiry. It was clear that Catholicism mattered very much to her, and in the Church's view, of course, there was no sanctioned marriage. In view of this implicit conflict, she was referred by the writer to a psychotherapist attached to the fertility clinic for his opinion. At her first interview with him, no new features to her story emerged. However, the therapist gave her a phone number at which she could contact him if she felt the need for a second visit. Ten days later she rang him, very distressed, asking for an urgent appointment. A different story then began to emerge.

At the age of 20, unmarried, and still living with her parents, she had conceived. Despite her strict moral Catholic upbringing, she had decided to have the pregnancy terminated and did not confide in her parents. An illegal backstreet abortion was performed when she was three and a half months pregnant. She described vividly her visit to the abortionist, who ruptured the membranes with an instrument and sent her home. That night, with her parents asleep in the next room her pains started. She squatted on the floor, delivered the foetus and placenta, and wrapped them in tissue. When she had recovered in the early hours of the morning, she broke up the foetus and placenta, flushing them down the toilet before her parents awoke. Two years later, she returned home from work to find her father dying on the floor of the same toilet, the last rites being administered.

Since that time, she had been tormented by guilt. Had her baby felt anything? Did her baby have a soul, and if so, where was it? Had God killed her father as punishment? The therapist was the only person with whom she had ever discussed these events in the seventeen years since they happened. She had tried to obtain help from the Church on two occasions, but each time had seemed to be thwarted by twists of fate that had prevented her from getting an interview with the priest.

The next time she visited the fertility clinic she repeated the whole story to the writer, a nurse, and a medical student. It was a moving experience for all to see her sitting there, weeping as if purging herself of seventeen years of guilt and misery. At the end of her story she said she could not possibly now contemplate a pregnancy, and wished to take the oral contraceptive pill. It was agreed that she should continue to see the therapist but that arrangements would also be made for her to visit a wise and sympathetic Catholic priest. She continued psychotherapy once or twice weekly, while in parallel with this, she discussed her story with the priest. He proved to be a caring spiritual counsellor, who helped her to explore her doubts and answered her religious questions.

Three months later she returned to the fertility clinic, complaining of pains in the chest and attributing these to the contraceptive pill. She said she now wished to discontinue the pill. Within six months she conceived, without any other treatment and was delivered of a healthy normal son.

Case 6

This patient was referred with secondary infertility, having always had an irregular menstrual cycle, her periods appearing at intervals of up to three months. She had been investigated earlier in the USA with no abnormal findings. She had conceived spontaneously two years before her referral. A disastrous medical error had occurred during labour, as a result of which the child was stillborn. The baby was cremated and the parents scattered the ashes at the church where they were married.

In her early twenties she had obtained her birth certificate and discovered the fact of her adoption. She had always been suspicious of this possibility because there were no photographs of her in the family album before the age of 6 months, in contrast to all the photographs of her elder brother, a true child of her adoptive parents. The adoptive mother had seemed unable to answer any of the patient's questions relating to her birth and this had increased her suspicion of an adoptive origin.

The patient had considerable insight into why she might not be

> conceiving. She agreed to wait and to come to terms, as much as she could, with her past history, before taking any active steps in relation to medical treatment. However, as time went by, and her periods became less and less frequent, she eventually requested treatment with fertility drugs. These were prescribed. She now ovulated but still failed to conceive. She continued to attend regularly, and at these visits, her past history and background were always discussed. She was encouraged to try and trace some of her true family. She knew that, although her true parents were dead, there were some half-brothers and half-sisters who should still be alive. She was finally successful in tracing a half-sister. A meeting was arranged, which resulted in a happy, fulfilling, and successful day.
>
> The patient is now pregnant. Perusal of her temperature charts show clearly that it was on the day of the reunion with her half-sister that she ovulated and conceived.

We believe that consideration of such histories bears witness to the need for members of helping professions to explore infertility with a holistic approach, and with a sensitivity to the moving issues involved. Methods of treatment are only really appropriate, we suggest, if they serve to help infertile individuals (and couples) to grow and to achieve optimal emotional adjustment in life.

It is an unfortunate fact that treatment measures are sometimes instituted without recognition of relevant emotional issues. Of particular concern to many is the way our growing edge of knowledge concerning psychosocial aspects of human fertility and infertility is being left behind by the growth of an ingenious technology in methods of fertilizing eggs that otherwise would never have been fertilized. This can be a valuable procedure if used wisely, but there may be a price to pay, if not. If the desire to conceive becomes an obsession, as in some individuals defending themselves against an unresolved unconscious problem the result may be 'a hard-won child, wrested from Providence'. There are disturbing reports of the appalling case histories of some children forced into life in this way.

This is not to argue that the infertile are more psychologically disturbed than the fertile members of the community. Controlled research studies suggest that this is not so. In fact, consideration of such cases suggests that infertile women may be more sensitive, at a deep bodily level, to the fact that they are not ready to bear a child under the current circumstances, i.e. that it is not time for a child to come. In this, the infertile woman may be potentially a more caring parent than the woman who can conceive at any time.

Adjustment to lasting infertility

At the end of a long period of gynaecological investigation and treatment a couple and their physician may have to face a conclusion that the position seems hopeless, or that no diagnosis can be made. The couple must be helped to adjust to this, and work through their grief and other feelings if they are to be able to use alternative avenues to parenthood.

For some, the final diagnosis brings an element of relief, a response to their wish for a definite answer one way or the other. However, a final verdict of infertility is always traumatic for the couple, no matter how much inner conflict has been generated by the prospect of parenthood. The trauma may well be experienced by the couple when they are already exhausted from prolonged physical and emotional strain and marital tension consequent upon a comprehensive and protracted period of medical investigation and treatment.

So the verdict of infertility always evokes a crisis for the couple, however much they may deny any emotional reaction to it initially. Under favourable conditions, and helped by an understanding professional, the initial shock gives way to a protracted period of human suffering, with an eventual resolution of feelings and recovery. Nijs and Rouffa (1975) report a sequence of four stages, reminiscent of the changes following bereavement: a feeling of confusion for one week; puzzlement, rebellion, and doubting for two to three weeks; sexual dysfunction for two to three months; and a period of depression, which may last for six months.

The initial sense of shock is accompanied by feelings of confusion and numbness, often associated with isolation and loneliness. The couple may feel anger, associated with a sense of losing control over body and destiny. The individual may experience a threat to his or her identity, including sexual identity. Grief is felt not only over the loss of fertility, but also over the implicit loss of a natural and idealized child. In addition, many couples subscribe to the myth that an inability to conceive is somehow linked with an inability to be a parent.

It is a failure to work through and resolve such emotional reactions to the diagnosis of infertility that can interfere with subsequent success in taking up one of the alternative avenues to parenthood. Wiehe (1976a,b) has demonstrated how this resolution is rendered more difficult by the initial inclination of infertile persons to deny or repress their feelings, usually with a tendency to show a neutral or even positive outward attitude to the verdict. One indicator of such denial is the emergence of a frenetic wish to rush into adoption, artificial insemination, or *in-vitro* fertilization, or to go off to an undeveloped country to buy an alien baby.

Mourning and death are desperately difficult to cope with when one is faced with creating or nurturing life, and the reverse is also true. Just as a couple who have suffered a stillbirth need to mourn their loss before starting another pregnancy, so should a couple mourn the loss of their fertility and their idealized fantasy child before embarking on any alternative approach to parenthood. The physician's role at this stage is to help them through the period of grief.

This means that the doctor himself also has to face up to his own feelings about the failure of the treatment. It is not good enough to dismiss the patient to the nearest *in-vitro* fertilization clinic or adoption agency. The primary goal of medicine is healing, with compassion. An integral part of traditional medical training, however, has been its objectivity, and this can help the doctor to acquire a self-protective skin that will prevent him from suffering with the couple; and they can collude with him in this.

If the physician can stay with the couple, suffer with them, and help them work through their feelings, he may be rewarded by seeing the achievement of an optimal adaptation to reality, a renewal of hope, the emergence of sound initiatives, and a freeing of their natural parenting capacities. Such an approach requires time and the help of others, such as relatives, friends, professional counsellors, and self-help organizations.

When ready, the infertile couple have a number of options open to them. These now include not only adoption or fostering, but also the new procedures that separate out fertilization from marital intercourse, i.e. artificial insemination by donor (AID), and *in-vitro* fertilization (IVF), possibly combined with donor eggs and/or semen, or surrogacy. Changing social attitudes to contraception, abortion, and single-parent families have drastically reduced the supply of babies for adoption, thereby increasing the demand for the other options.

Several studies have demonstrated a significant relationship between the ability of couples to accept and resolve the feelings about their infertility, and their subsequent success as adoptive parents. Wiehe (1976a,b) quotes two such studies. Other workers have shown that the ability of adoptive mothers to discuss their feelings about their infertility correlates significantly with their later ability to communicate successfully the fact of adoption to their children. It has also been found in a follow-up study of adopted boys that the adoptive mothers' inability to accept their own infertility correlated with the later emergence of hypochondriacal concerns in the boys.

Menning (1975) has described how parental inability to resolve feelings about infertility may negatively affect the relationship between adopting couples and children throughout their lives. She points out that this is especially predictable at certain milestones in the lives of the adopted children, such as the explanation to them of their adoption, the onset of their puberty, the striving of adopted adolescents to reach intimacy with the opposite sex, and their eventual marriage and subsequent bearing of children. Any or all of these events are likely 'to hook the old unresolved feelings of infertility' in the adopting parents. Menning adds that resolution of infertility feelings is in the interests of the entire family: 'It would be best if all the family resources could be invoked towards constructive management of the problems at hand, not towards fighting old phantom fears and grieving losses' (Menning, 1975). She goes on to say that the process of resolution may take a long time:

> It should never be asked of the couple that they complete it on some sort of schedule. The best we may ever ask of couples is that they try to acknowledge and experience their feelings; that they try to re-work their concepts of sexuality, self-image and self-esteem. The dynamic state of a couple, actively trying to cope, is infinitely healthier than that of the couple who have denied or repressed all of their reactions, or who feel these feelings can be quickly or easily dispatched.
>
> (Menning, 1975)

Similar considerations apply to the choosing of other avenues to parenthood, as discussed in a thoughtful paper by Nijs and Rouffa (1975), with special reference to artificial insemination. They argue that the eventual resolution of feelings (anger, guilt, and loss) about infertility must be accompanied by a new self-definition without the procreative dimension. A new sexual identity has to be built up in each partner. Sexuality and procreation have to be separated. The two partners have to affirm each other in the new situation. Even when only one partner is biologically infertile, they have to recognize and accept each other as an infertile couple. And they must achieve success in the painful process of separating from the idealized image of their own natural child. All this has to be done in a sort of psychosocial vacuum, as relatives and friends tend to avoid discussing these issues.

The couple must have achieved a genuine shared wish for a child, a wish that does not just represent a negation of their biological infertility. It is only when a good sexual relationship is re-established, on this new level, that the true generative urge can reappear. A child has a right to parents, and the good parent is, primarily, a good partner. Each partner has to place the child in the perspective of his or her relation to the other one. The re-establishment of a sexual relationship is also important in terms of the child later finding its own sexual identity. Artificial insemination is thus contra-indicated, according to Nijs and Rouffa (1975), if the male partner is impotent.

Who is available to help the infertile couple to resolve their feelings about the diagnosis of infertility and make a final choice about the most appropriate option open to them? Menning (1975) suggests that it is unreasonable to ask people who have suffered a major crisis and who may have been traumatized by medical technology to diagnose and treat their own feelings and then present themselves 'cheerfully resolved' at the desk of the adoption social worker.

We doctors do not always handle these problems well, and sometimes do not even acknowledge the existence of a problem. We may be too quick to tranquillize the distress or attempt to elevate the mood by treating the grief with an antidepressant drug. The outcome for such couples can be more constructive if we can not only discuss with them their own feelings about the infertility and the treatment options left for them, but also share with them our own feelings of frustration and helplessness. The grief and guilt associated with infertility may be lightened by the doctor openly bearing some of the responsibility, and pointing out that not enough is yet known for doctors to be able to explain or treat their particular problem. It may also be helpful to point out that not everyone will conceive, and that there may be good reasons why nature is not allowing them to reproduce. But such an approach must be delicately handled.

All couples who are looking for alternative pathways need continuing support, as well as preparation. Social services often provide aftercare for adoption and fostering, but not for artificial insemination or *in-vitro* fertilization, unless specifically requested. Self-help groups can be very supportive during treatment programmes and the period of adjustment to a verdict of infertility, and they are now available in most parts of the western world.

Modern technological procedures, such as AID and IVF, are frequently unsuccessful. The task of helping a couple to adjust to lasting infertility can be the most difficult part of management, and the one for which the physician is least prepared. Professional counselling should be available for such couples at all major infertility clinics, with access to community self-help groups, where these exist.

Chapter eleven

Motherhood thwarted

Miscarriage, stillbirth, and adoption

Believe me, I loved you all.
Believe me, I knew you, though faintly, and I loved,
I loved you
All.

Gwendolyn Brooks
the mother.

Early abortions and miscarriages

Abortion and spontaneous miscarriage may both be experienced as profoundly distressing events, even though physically they may cause little upheaval if the pregnancy ends at an early stage. For young fit people, pregnancy may be the first occasion when medical attention is sought; the first experience, apart from childhood ailments, of being a patient and perhaps a first contact with hospital.

A spontaneous abortion or miscarriage occurring early and without complications may not require hospital admission or emergency treatment. Nevertheless, it is likely to come as a great shock, and may cause revulsion if the conceptus is recognizable as a formed foetus, perhaps passed into a bucket or the lavatory pan. The need to dispose of this as waste may become a haunting memory.

A miscarriage may be the first unexpected event in the married life of a young couple who have been anticipating a normal pregnancy and a joyous birth. If the pregnancy has been planned and wanted, the disappointment may be intense; if the pregnancy has been unplanned, though not necessarily unwanted, miscarriage may be associated with some relief, but may bring remorse in its wake. Husbands often feel guilty and unable to offer support and help, indicating their bewilderment and sense of exclusion from an event that, while involving the woman in an intimately personal and physical way, is quite literally outside the husband's experience. He may seek for rational explanations for this untoward occurrence, express anger that it should have happened, be embarrassed at any mention of the event, or be irritated at his wife's grieving. A husband may be alarmed and confused at the change in his partner if she becomes seriously depressed, especially when the doctor reassures him that miscarriages are commonplace.

Relationships often become closer when partners have shared and supported one another through a crisis. However, if a couple are unable to share their emotional reactions, the woman may become resentful about his perceived lack of interest in her and the man may feel excluded from the relationship. They may grow further apart, and experience problems with sexual intimacy, which in turn increases the distance between them. It is not uncommon for partners to seek comfort outside the marriage at such a time, perhaps indulging in a brief and secretive sexual affair for reasons that they do not fully understand – both reassuring themselves of their attractiveness and punishing their partner.

A further pregnancy may be both desired and feared. Despite her rational understanding of the situation, a woman usually feels that her 'bad womb' is to blame for the loss, never the 'bad seed'.

Termination of pregnancy

Termination of pregnancy may be sought or advised for many reasons, including serious risk to the mother's health or because the unborn child is developing abnormally. It may be a lesser evil than continuing with the pregnancy, but the decision is never a simple one. The loss of the child-that-might-have-been may be re-experienced repeatedly and needs to be grieved. Choosing termination means taking responsibility for killing a part of oneself, and the anguish can be such that grieving is avoided. The significance of the event is often minimized in order to avoid the guilt and shame associated with it. Acknowledgement of the powerful emotions that accompany such an episode will help facilitate the normal mourning process, so that depression is less likely to follow.

> A cheerful energetic woman sought help in her late forties because of recurrent episodes of bleak depression that suddenly enveloped her 'like a black cloud, without warning'. She had married young and was shocked when her husband later made it clear that he wanted no children, but she continued to mother him and express her maternal feelings in her work and in caring for the children of friends. She now regretted that she had conscientiously practised contraception and denied herself the children that she so desired. Eventually she found a lover, but felt unable to leave her husband.

By chance she conceived on the only occasion that she ever had unprotected intercourse, and described her joy and pride at her realization that she was pregnant. This was swiftly followed by the feeling that she had *stolen* a baby from a man who had not *chosen* to have a child with her, and that she had no right to have the child. She sought a termination and the wise gynaecologist asked her to be very certain that she wanted to give up this special chance. She described her excitement at seeing 'her baby' on a scan, and the anguish of making her decision. She proceeded with the termination, knowing that there would never be another opportunity for her to experience motherhood. The most important thing for her was to know that the doctor understood how much she longed to have the baby, and how great a grief it was to give up this one and only chance. She could not talk of her secret to anyone else. Therapy offered an opportunity not only to grieve the abortion, but to deal with all her other losses and to explore her difficulty in taking anything for herself and asserting her needs as an individual.

Termination may be imposed upon a woman, not only by medical advice, but by other important figures in her life. Often parents insist on their daughter having a termination, particularly if she has become pregnant very young, and may have no understanding of what this means to the girl. We see women who have been unable to withstand pressures put on them by families, partners, and doctors, but who deeply resent the enforced loss of their pregnancy, and who have suffered from the consequences for years. Even though a woman may acknowledge that abortion had been the best solution, and that she had been unready for the responsibilities of motherhood, she cannot forgive their insensitivity to her feelings and wishes. She may hate the parents who destroyed their own potential grandchild, and perceive the event as a murderous assault on her developing womanhood, an envious attack on her womb.

A late termination of pregnancy requires a woman to go through the process of labour and birth of her child, a physically arduous experience that results not in the joyous arrival of a longed-for infant, but in the miserable and untimely confirmation of her failure. If the pains are not experienced, or the birth is lost in the mists of anaesthesia, the trauma may be worsened by the sense of unreality.

A woman had been expecting twins, but in the sixth month of her pregnancy one had died. The scan showed that the remaining twin was suffering from severe malformation of the brain, which was not compatible with life. She was advised, therefore, to have the labour prematurely induced – in effect to terminate the pregnancy –

in the hope of reducing complications with delivery. She had finally agreed to this but could not come to terms with it. She had not seen or held her babies, since one was macerated and the other grossly abnormal, and it had been thought too distressing to expose her to this sight. Perhaps she had killed the second twin, perhaps after all it would have been born alive in spite of the terrible abnormality. She felt stigmatized by having produced abnormal babies, and alienated from the women who attended antenatal clinic with her, envious of their healthy babies. She could not talk about her loss, nor could she identify with other mothers since none had had the identical experience. She longed for a baby, but dared not risk another pregnancy in case she, who had produced two monsters in her womb, should have another failure. Her husband was at his wits' end, and sexual contact had ceased. The 'monsters' had assumed such gigantic proportions that the couple's despair had become a wall of silence between them, paralysing the husband's efforts to comfort her. He also needed comfort, to be reassured that she still cared for him, and did not blame him for his 'lethal gift' to her womb. Joint counselling sessions with the couple enabled the unspoken feelings to be put into words and facilitated their grieving.

There is no one way, no right way of dealing with these individual disasters. However unpleasant the reality, the fantasy is usually far worse. It is better for a couple to see their malformed baby, with sensitive support from professional carers, than to avoid the experience. If a woman has had to carry this imperfection intimately within her, surely her hands can be allowed to touch it and her eyes to see it and weep. Talking about the experience – the feelings of disappointment, revulsion, rage, and grief – is essential for healing. Recovery cannot occur if it is dealt with by denial or is trivialized. Professionals may find it all too easy to collude with a couple's avoidance of their feelings, unconsciously avoiding their own painful feelings in the process.

Sometimes a late termination of pregnancy is sought for complex social and emotional reasons, when there are no compelling medical indications for it (such as a damaged foetus or a threat to the mother's life). Whatever the reason, later terminations involve the woman giving birth to a fully formed and recognizably human baby, who has been experienced as a separate 'other' within her, kicking and moving and demonstrating life. Although she will have fantasies about the child it might have become, it will be difficult for her to mourn this child, who has not had an independent existence and who cannot be acknowledged to the outside world.

A young woman was admitted with a recurrence of severe depression that had, on previous occasions, been treated with drugs and electroconvulsive therapy, but she had never revealed anything about herself that shed light on its origin. A woman doctor working on the ward felt sure that her depression was not innate or 'endogenous', but that it must have been related to some life events. She noted from the records that some years earlier the woman had had a termination of pregnancy, and referred her for psychotherapy.

The woman had fallen in love with a man who was not free to marry her, although they planned that he would come to live with her. She was delighted to find herself pregnant, and kept her exciting secret while she waited for him to join her. He was aghast at the news, and told her that she must get rid of the child or he would be ruined. She was not asked what she wanted and at the private clinic, submissively accepted examination and injections, numb with fear, and dreading her lover's anger as she had dreaded her father's. She was left alone during labour, and realized too late that she longed to keep her baby but that she could not stop the inexorable process of expulsion from her womb. She longed to die and screamed for help in her pain, but no-one came. Later, she could not express her anger to her partner and turned all her destructive feelings against herself in guilt and despair.

She slowly learned to share these experiences with her therapist, and as the depression lifted sufficiently for her to allow long-buried feelings to emerge, she relived her tragic and violent life. She began to recognize the pattern of her submission to brutality and exploitation, her fear of sexuality in herself and others, and her perception of herself as worthless and undeserving of love; which contributed to her tolerance of her lover's empty promises and her inability to separate from him. The loss of her baby had triggered catastrophic depression, but the whole of her life had been one long disaster. The pitiless termination had repeated the violence she had experienced as a child victim of incest and evoked the same feelings of helplessness and repressed rage. In therapy, the exploration of present pain had unlocked the past and offered the prospect of freedom from its tyranny.

When a pregnancy is sacrificed to protect the mother's health a woman may experience a particular form of survivor guilt. Renal failure, heart disease, cancer, and pre-eclampsia are some of the conditions that may lead to a woman being advised to give up a pregnancy. Termination reflects the conflict of interests between mother and child in the survival stakes, the mother's life being regarded as more precious. The guilt and sadness at the sacrifice may be relieved in some measure by a sense of duty to her partner and any other children. But there is an irony in giving up the hope of immortality in the shape of a new child for extra time in a body that is wearing out. This problem may be especially acute for a young woman who develops cancer. The tumour may be experienced as taking her resources, feeding off her in much the same way as does the foetus, and the contrast between the destructive growth and the creative growth can lead to a sense of acute confusion and threat, with severe anxiety, depression, and a sense of hopelessness, which in itself militates against her survival. The recognition of her need to ventilate primitive rage may be life-saving in this situation. The conspiracy of silence about such an uncomfortable situation makes it difficult for the sacrifice of her baby to be given due acknowledgement.

Stillbirth and neonatal death

Pregnancy should be a normal and healthy event in a woman's life, and the outcome of a satisfactory pregnancy is a live and healthy baby. The hopes and expectations, not only of the parents but of their family and friends, are part of the preparation for each baby and are ritualized in the creation of a nursery, the purchase of equipment, clothes, and toys, and in the choice of a name. Most births take place in maternity units in hospitals, and women go there expecting to leave with a baby in their arms. Midwives are drawn to their profession primarily because it is a branch of nursing that uses skill in the service of health and normality, not of sickness and pathology. The arrival of a baby is cause for celebration. Congratulations are showered on the proud parents and gratitude expressed to the staff for each miracle of new life.

In such a context, stillbirth and neonatal death represent tragedy. A woman feels that she has failed if her baby fails to survive. She alone has empty arms and breasts burdened with useless milk. She is surrounded in the maternity unit by mothers nursing the babies that they have successfully produced. She has prepared for a new life and a beginning, and instead she has to cope with a death and an ending. It may be the first death that has ever touched her.

Stillbirths and neonatal deaths need to be fully grieved if they are to be buried and relegated to their proper place in the life of a family. If there has been ambivalence about the pregnancy, grieving may be even more difficult. A conspiracy of silence, intended to protect against distress, may serve to make the dead baby unmentionable. In order to protect her from further stress, equipment and baby clothes may be put away by helpful relatives before the mother returns from the hospital, and she may be prevented from registering the death or attending the funeral service. The child may not have been named, nor if stillborn, given a marked grave.

> A young wife's first child was unexpectedly stillborn. She did not see or hold the baby, and the body was whisked away immediately after birth. Her husband arranged the burial, but the grave was unmarked and she never visited it. She could not cope with the distress she felt, and did not even know the sex of the child until some twelve years later, after three further pregnancies had given her two children. She had blocked off her grief, but was a martyr to physical pain and weakness, which depressed her deeply after her marriage failed. Psychotherapy was offered twenty years after that first loss, which had remained undealt with because of her avoidance. She found exploration of her feelings intolerable, and could not bear to re-experience the pain, so she opted out of therapy and continued to seek medical help for her somatic symptoms.

It is important for parents to have the opportunity to see and hold their dead baby and to take their leave of it. Even severe deformities can be partially or completely concealed by swathing the baby or dressing it in a gown. Privacy for this leave-taking is essential, so that the parents can openly express their grief and share it with one another. Many maternity units now have cameras to photograph dead babies, so that parents can have a record and memento of their lost child. This is particularly important for a parent who has not felt able to see a dead child and say goodbye, but who may later regret the fact, and be obsessed with fantasies about its appearance. These may be relieved by seeing a photograph. If permission is given for a post-mortem examination, the results of the report should be discussed with the parents, and their wishes concerning burial or cremation and any arrangements for a form of service should be respected.

A particular problem is the late miscarriage, since a woman who loses her baby before twenty-eight weeks of pregnancy has not legally given birth, and therefore no death certificate can be issued. Such a foetus has traditionally been disposed of in hospitals as pathology waste. But increasing awareness of the significance of the loss of a baby, and the importance of facilitating grieving if subsequent morbidity is to be prevented, has led to improved and sympathetic management of these sad events, not only by hospital staff but also by burial authorities. The burial of a stillborn child of less than twenty-eight weeks gestation is at the discretion of the individual cemetery; a doctor's note instead of the usual registrar's certificate provides authority for it. Some enlightened authorities now permit a stone to be placed to mark the tiny grave.

Stillbirths present a difficult problem of mourning (Lewis, 1976) since although the infant is fully formed, it has never had an independent existence, and the woman experiences grief for loss of a part of herself rather than for a cherished separate other. Because it is so difficult to mourn a loss-that-never-was, a woman may continue to fantasize that the child is alive and growing up, unable to relinquish him, emotionally neglecting other real children that she may already have, or who may be born subsequently.

> A woman presented as an emergency in a most dramatic fashion, with razor slashes to her abdomen and breasts. It was clear that she had inflicted these injuries upon herself, but she was appalled at this suggestion and had no recall whatever of the circumstances of the 'attack'. The psychiatrist who saw her recognized that she was severely depressed and a serious suicide risk, and referred her urgently for a psychotherapist's opinion. It emerged that several years earlier, when the family were living abroad, she had lost a baby at birth. Because she had not participated in the death and burial, it had remained unreal to her, and she had never mourned the loss of this baby whom she referred to by name.
>
> A year previously her much loved mother had died suddenly, while she was in hospital following the birth of a daughter. She referred to this child simply as 'the babe', an indication of her inability to let this new child become important to her, since her feelings were still engaged with her dead baby. Her mother's death had resonated on the earlier unmourned loss.
>
> The terrible episode of self-injury had served to express her pain and bring it to attention in a way that she could not *consciously* do, particularly since she was regarded by others as 'so capable and reliable'. Brief focal therapy resulted in a dramatic improvement and complete recovery, enabling her to grieve both losses.

If a baby lives for a short time after birth before dying, it may be easier for the mother to mourn it. The urge to support the life of her child is strong – a biological attribute that has been essential for the survival of immature human young. However, this can create intolerable conflict if a mother's natural desire to hold her child close to her body, to maintain comforting skin contact, and to put the child to the breast must be sacrificed to the very different priorities of high-technology care.

> A 40-year-old woman was referred for psychotherapy because her severe depression had not responded to intensive treatment. Her first-born son had died three days after birth, and she had been excluded from his christening, death, and burial. She described how she had longed to hold him to her, certain that the powerful life force within her would ensure his survival, and that he was

dying from the separation. When she had been taken to see him in the baby unit, he became pink and relaxed as she held him to her, and she was confident that she could have given him the care that he *really* needed better than the hospital staff. Her rage and grief at his death found no expression. But after her next child was born she became catastrophically depressed. Because she had delivered a normal healthy child, her depression was seen as an ordinary postnatal depression; no-one linked it with the death of her first child.

Parents are frightened if their child is at risk, and may accept restrictions on their access to him, handing over his care to highly trained nursing staff in a specialist unit. It is particularly helpful for such staff, who are themselves subject to considerable stress in their difficult and responsible work, to encourage parents to talk about their feelings and their fears. This helps them not only to gain the confidence to handle their delicate child, who may perhaps also suffer from severe congenital abnormalities, but also to begin to come to terms with a death that may be inevitable. All of the conflicting feelings in such a situation may be magnified for the mother, but both parents will have love and concern for their baby. The more parents are able to share both their involvement with their child and their anxiety about him, the more each will benefit from this mutual support, and their relationship will be strengthened.

Sudden and unpredicted death shortly *after* birth is, like any unexpected death, characterized by shock and disbelief. It is a major blow not only to the new parents, family, and friends, but also to staff. It is even more difficult for professionals to deal with than stillbirth and anticipated perinatal death, since it may appear to reflect a failure in their competence.

A woman who loses her baby has also to cope with the bodily aspects of her loss; with changes in her figure, with enlarged breasts that may painfully remind her of the baby she expected to suckle, and with the return of menstruation and its implicit invitation to become pregnant again and replace the baby she has lost. Other mothers may cut off contact with her, feeling embarrassed to display the evidence of their own success or to demonstrate their love and pride in their own baby in the face of another's loss. Friends and relatives may avoid the painful subject, treating the episode as if it had never happened. Colleagues and acquaintances who knew that she was pregnant but have not heard the outcome of events may greet her warmly when she returns to view, and enquire after the baby. They are embarrassed when she tells them that she has lost it, but if she weeps at the telling, the embarrassment and distress is magnified for both parties, and may perpetuate avoidance, not only of the subject, but also of the unhappy woman. Previously enjoyable social contacts, such as the congregation of pram-pushing mothers at school gates collecting older siblings, may become intolerable. Childhood rivalries may recur when a brother or sister appears with a baby, to family acclaim and grandparental pride.

Older siblings may be puzzled and distressed by the event. They may be too young to understand what has happened or to verbalize their feelings, but may be disappointed that the promised new baby has not materialized. In some way they may feel responsible for the loss, secretly glad that they need not share their mother with a demanding new competitor. They will be affected by their mother's depression and try to take care of her, or demand reassurance and attention. She may find comfort in cuddling another child, or she may be irritated by his demands, resenting the distraction from her preoccupation with her lost baby. If the sex is the same, the child reminds her of what might have been; if different, there may be enhanced feelings of loss because the son can never be the daughter who was lost, or vice versa. The dead baby is, in the mother's imagination, free of faults. Any defects and failure will be the mother's.

It is now recognized that the advice given to a woman who has lost a baby, 'Two normal periods and try again' – fails to take into account her need to grieve her loss and satisfactorily complete the mourning process before becoming pregnant again (Bourne and Lewis, 1984). The circumstances of the loss and its meaning are obviously highly individual, and the quality of communication and relationship with her husband and family, as well as her previous life experience, are major factors influencing her recovery from the loss of the baby.

Pregnancy, the flowering and nurturing of a new life, is not compatible with mourning the loss of a life. A woman cannot grieve a lost baby while preparing for the birth of a new one. She must have sufficient time to recover her equilibrium and relegate the experience to the past where it belongs, before embarking on another pregnancy, however much she longs to fill the gap. Such delay may be seen as a major obstacle by the older woman who knows that her fertility is diminishing as she waits. A lost baby may also create an unwelcome age gap between older children of a family and one born later. The grieving process for most women seems to be adequately completed in a period of one to two years after the loss, although individual variation is considerable. Sensitively aware professionals, who encourage involvement in the dying and in the ritual aftermath of death, and who acknowledge the value of the natural expression of grief, may expedite the process dramatically. Most importantly, by giving permission to rage and mourn they may protect the woman and her family from years of depression and disturbance.

Unrecognized for what it truly is, mourning over the loss of a baby may last for many years and be difficult to treat. Long-standing depression, which apparently comes out of the blue in an otherwise healthy woman, may never be linked to the loss of a baby. The woman herself may deny its significance as a defence against exploring old pain.

> A woman in her mid-fifties was referred with a twenty-five-year history of depression after her doctor had heard one of the authors speak about apparently intractable depression in women. When medication had failed, treatment for dietary allergies and for pre-menstrual tension had been followed by hormone-replacement therapy at the menopause without success.
>
> Shortly after her marriage she had had a miscarriage. After a difficult second pregnancy, the child was nursed in special care and she was not allowed to see it or hold it. On the third day the baby died and her husband arranged the funeral. All reminders of the baby had been cleared away by the time she went home. She put a brave face on things, and denied the importance of what had happened to her. In due course she bore a healthy son, but following his birth she became suddenly and inexplicably depressed. Although fluctuating, this depression never left her, spoiling her life, and she never allowed herself to get close to her two children, each of whom experienced difficulties as they grew up.
>
> Initially she denied that her depression could be due to the loss of her baby. 'How can you expect me to grieve?' she demanded. 'I didn't give birth to a life, I gave birth to a death. I've got nothing to grieve over.' But eventually in therapy she gave up the antidepressant pills that she said 'shrouded me in cotton wool' and kept her feelings at bay. She remembered once, when her son was small, telling her doctor that she could not take her mind off the baby that she had lost. 'Pull yourself together woman', he said, 'and don't give it another thought.'
>
> In therapy she was able to weep and to express her rage as she remembered the pain and desolation of her experience. As soon as her mourning was expressed in therapy, she found herself not only free of the tyrannical depression, but able to work and express herself creatively as never before, literally starting a new life.

Adoptions

Occasionally, a woman may decide to continue with an unplanned pregnancy, knowing that she cannot keep her baby and bring it up herself. Unwilling to destroy life, she chooses to give her baby for adoption, thus ensuring the survival of a precious part of herself and hoping that her child will have a better life than she could give it. Although she may know that the decision was sensible, she may also grieve at the parting and long to know how her child is faring. If she has kept it a secret, she will not be able to talk about it to friends or relatives, and denial of her feelings will be almost inevitable, protecting her from the pain. Even if she subsequently marries and has a family, she may be preoccupied with fantasies about the fate of the child she gave away, noting anniversaries and feeling special concern when important stages in the child's life would be reached. She may hope to be reunited with the child one day and may idealize him if subsequent children disappoint her. She may have told her husband about such an episode in her past, but because it has not been important to him, it is unlikely to be mentioned again. We have seen women who have sought one consultation only, often at a significant time when the child given away would be embarking on a new phase in his life, or in the case of a daughter, would have reached the age when the mother had become pregnant with her. If she has hitherto had no opportunity to talk about them with anyone in her everyday life, it may be helpful for a woman to share thoughts and emotions about the child given for adoption many years earlier.

The process of mourning and separation after an adoption is similar to that of the mother who has a stillborn child, or one who dies in the neo-natal period. The greater the mother's involvement with her new baby after birth, the more painful it will be to give up the child. Yet if there is no contact after birth, fantasy will have to replace reality, the experience of the child as separate from herself will be avoided, and the loss will become even more difficult to grieve. Seeing single mothers who have kept their children may arouse envy and open old wounds.

> A schoolgirl became pregnant at the age of 14. Her family kept her pregnancy secret and after the baby was born she was not allowed to hold her, and only glimpsed her briefly before she was adopted. When she returned to her convent school, she felt adult and different from the other girls and rapidly dropped out of education, but managed to cope by denying the importance of her loss.
>
> Two years later her father died and her grief at his death resonated on the loss of her baby. She began to starve herself, developing anorexia nervosa and becoming again a prepubertal child for mother to care for. Her sexuality had rocked the family boat; her anorexic avoidance of it served to keep them together after the father's death. Her physical health was precarious for years and she had many hospital admissions. She strenuously avoided discussion of her feelings, and used alcohol to numb them.

> When her daughter would have been 14 years old, a cousin had an illegitimate baby, and proudly kept the child. The patient was filled with jealousy, and began to dream about her own baby. In an initial psychotherapy consultation she talked at last about the significance of her experiences, and the powerful emotions of love and grief evoked by thoughts of her daughter. But her own mother sabotaged the planned therapy.

Lack of support may prevent a woman expressing her grief, and she may see no future for herself – a reflection of the lost future that her child, now lost to her, represents. In the last case, denial protected the patient and her family for many years from acknowledging the meaning of her loss. Her distress was expressed by starving herself so that she was literally at risk of dying for want of nourishment – which blinded her doctors to the grief that really needed treatment. Her apparently supportive and nurturing mother was greedy for her daughter's company and continued to bind her in a symbiotic relationship from which she could not break free. She could not subject her mother to the pain of abandonment that she herself felt for her own daughter.

> Another patient felt unsupported and unloved when at 18 she had become pregnant by her fiancé, who promptly left her for another girl. Her disapproving parents turned her out, and eventually she agreed that adoption seemed the best solution. Six years later she was referred for psychotherapy, deeply depressed and overweight. She ate constantly and consumed large numbers of chocolate bars, trying unsuccessfully to assuage her feeling of emptiness. She felt there was a great hole inside her, left by her baby, gnawing at her constantly. She felt unable to risk sex with her current boyfriend who might impregnate and abandon her as the baby's father had done. She wept constantly, but in therapy the tears turned to rage at her parents and fiancé. Her depression lifted as she shared these emotions, and she began to allow herself to acknowledge her sexuality.

A girl who has herself been adopted may frequently wish to become pregnant because it allows her to identify with her own natural mother. The only thing she knows for certain about the mother who had given her away at birth is that she had conceived her, carried her inside her womb, and given birth to her. She may long to have a child of her own, so that she can have someone of her own flesh and blood to care for. The fact that she will be passing on some of her own inheritance from her natural parents to the baby makes her baby into 'real family'.

> A 16-year-old girl admitted to an irrational fear that she would, like her adoptive mother, be unable to have children. She deliberately

engaged in unprotected intercourse in order to reassure herself that she could become pregnant and to hurt her cold adoptive parents by proving that she could do something they could not in conceiving a child of her own. The father of the child was a casual acquaintance who would know nothing of the baby and have no claim on it. Her parents had forced her to have a termination with the help of a psychiatric recommendation. She later sought therapy 'to find out who I am', since she had no real sense of identity.

Women whose babies are lost to them, for whatever reason and at whatever stage between conception and successful birth, experience deep distress. When the child who has grown within her emerges to occupy her arms, a woman has a precious extension of herself to love and nourish. To lose this, whatever the circumstances, is a major blow to her self-esteem and diminishes her confidence in herself both as a woman and as a mother. A sensitive appreciation of the significance of these events by professionals involved in them can help a woman to cope with the inevitable distress, rather than delaying her recovery by failure to recognize her misery.

Further reading

Borg, S. and Lasker, J. (1982) *When Pregnancy Fails*, London: Routledge.
Leroy, M. (1988) *Miscarriage*, London: MacDonald Optima.

Useful addresses

The Miscarriage Association,
18 Stoneybrook Close,
West Bretton,
Wakefield, WF4 4TP.
Tel: 092 485 515.

SANDS (Stillbirth and Neonatal Death Society),
Argyle House
29–31 Euston Road,
London, WW1 2SD.
Tel: 01 833 2851.

SATFA (Support after Termination for Abnormality),
c/o 22 Upper Woburn Place,
London, WC1H OEP.
Tel: 01 388 1382.

TAMBA (Twins and Multiple Births Association),
292 Valley Road,
Lillington,
Leamington Spa, CV32 7UE.
(Offers support where one twin dies and is miscarried.)

Association for Spina Bifida and Hydrocephalus,
c/o 22 Upper Woburn Place,
London WC1 0EP.
Tel: 01 388 1382.
(Offers support for couples offered termination after amniocentesis.)

Chapter twelve

Motherhood bereft

Loss of a child

> Give sorrow words: the grief that does not speak
> Whispers the o'er-fraught heart, and bids it break.

Shakespeare
Macbeth.

A sick man asked Sengai to write something for the continued prosperity of his family, to be treasured from generation to generation. The Master wrote:
– Father dies, son dies, grandson dies.
The sick rich man was indignant.
– Is that what you write for the happiness of my family? A tasteless joke!
– No joke intended, said Sengai – if your son would die before you, that would be very sad. If your grandson would die before you and your son, you would be broken-hearted. If your family dies in the order I have written down, isn't that prosperity and happiness?

Sengai

Failures of conception, development, and birth constitute a major area of distress for women. Nevertheless, all these traumas pale into insignificance compared with the untimely death of a much loved child. The ravages of malnutrition, poverty, and infection have been, for practical purposes, eliminated as serious threats to survival in our civilized western society. Thus the death of a child is a savage and unexpected blow that runs counter to all reasonable parental expectations. Accidents and childhood malignancies are the most common causes of death in otherwise normal children and, if the mourning process is impaired, are followed by significant morbidity in other family members. Mothers may never recover from such a catastrophe and the surviving children of a family may suffer seriously after the death of a sibling. Not only will they have sustained an important loss at an age when it may be difficult or impossible for them to verbalize their feelings about the experience and its significance for them, but resulting parental preoccupation and depression may create further problems.

> A young woman had severe headaches for which no physical cause could be found. In therapy she related how her older brother had died of leukaemia when she was an adolescent, and her headaches had followed this. When the therapist suggested she felt responsible for her brother dying, she said she felt 'blocked', which she experienced as a block in her head. Her brother had often told her she was stupid, a block of wood. The therapist linked the headache with his cancer. She said no, it was just coincidence, her headache was due to the electric lights at work and now, in the consulting room. She remembered the bright lights in the ward the night he had died and then realized that she had at that moment 'taken his cancer into her', as symbolized by the headache. During the course of therapy she was able to grieve for him. Once she had achieved that she could relinquish her guilt at surviving him, and her headaches disappeared.

Parents may sometimes withdraw from contact with a surviving child or children, and can become overprotective and unduly controlling of them, or take no interest and pleasure in their activities and progress. Parental depression may be experienced by their other children as emotional abandonment.

The sudden infant death syndrome (SIDS), commonly known as 'cot death', may be especially difficult for a family. An apparently healthy normal baby is suddenly found dead, and the suspicion that the death may have been unnatural and the whole rigmarole of police questioning, post-mortem, and inquest adds to the natural grief and guilt of the devastated parents. Other small children may be too young to understand why the baby has disappeared, and horrified friends may withdraw.

> One mother, recounting her experience, recalled the worst part, 'They took my baby away from me, they would not let me hold her. She was mine but I felt like a criminal. I wanted to love her and I was crying. I never held her again. She was in the coffin when we saw her again.' Her older child was showing signs of disturbance when her continuing depression led eventually to her referral for therapy.

Children may feel that they are blamed by their parents – either directly or indirectly – for the sibling's death, that the 'good' or 'favourite' child has been lost, and that their parents regard them as a poor substitute. If there has been marked sibling rivalry and fierce competition within the family for parental attention and affection, the survivors may struggle with a heavy burden of guilt for years. The powerful negative feelings involving fantasies of destruction – 'I could kill you', and 'I wish you were dead' – which are a feature of sibling relationships, albeit transiently, may give rise to a persistent sense of guilt and responsibility for having caused the death. Siblings present at a fatal accident may be devastated by the experience and haunted by memories of it throughout their lives, reliving over and again their failure to prevent disaster.

> A young mother of two was referred with marked depression that her general practitioner found inexplicable. She had presented to the surgery with overwhelming attacks of panic, during which she feared she would die, and it was plain that she had an underlying depressive illness that was souring her supportive marital relationship and limiting her activities. Her two small children had become clinging and anxious, and she was overprotective to the extent of not allowing them to attend a play group, nor to be out of her sight at any time.
>
> She had completed our department's usual confidential questionnaire before attending for an assessment consultation. It was noted that she had lost a brother in childhood. On enquiry about his death, she became distressed and full of panic. During early life, she and her older brother had been sent to a children's home while their mother was in a sanatorium. They had been inseparable. 'We meant the world to one another', she said. When she was 9 years old, she saw her brother drown while playing by the river. His body was recovered by the police; she had to give a statement then and had to answer questions at the inquest. She was not allowed to go to the funeral, and her parents never spoke to her again about her brother's death. She believed they blamed her, and she certainly blamed herself for having been unable to save him. She carried his photograph in her handbag, but had never been able to express her feelings about his death, nor tell her parents how she felt that they had let her down.
>
> Motherhood had reawakened memories of her own early childhood, and she was determined to give her own children the security and affection that she herself had lacked. But her feelings about them resonated on the loss of her 'very special' brother, and she unconsciously feared that she would be unable to take care of them sufficiently to protect them from harm. As they grew out of babyhood, she knew that they could not always be within her sight, and so the panic attacks developed.

The clear evidence of unresolved grief, with idealization, preoccupation with his memory, and persistent nightmares about her brother's death prompted the diagnosis, and brief focal psychotherapy was offered for one hour weekly. She experienced rapid relief of her nightmares, the panic attacks ceased, and her mood improved steadily. She dealt with the unfinished business of her emotions from the past, and became free to relate to her children as themselves rather than as replicas of herself and her brother. Despite the separations and privations of her childhood and the long-standing grief, she recovered fully within four months, and she and her family have not presented for further help. Failure to recognize the root of her problems would have perpetuated the family pathology.

A mother's morbid grief may last a lifetime, with incalculable consequences for one or more of her surviving children, and disorder in subsequent generations.

The only daughter of a cultured family sought psychotherapeutic help when she was aged 40. Her family's attention had focused on the youngest brother, who suffered from an inherited abnormality, incompatible with survival to adulthood. Their mother was passionately involved with this child and the daughter became the 'good girl', subsequently training as a children's nurse in order to look after her little brother. She nursed him as he became more disabled, and cared for him until he died. Her mother's failure to grieve him healthily was never challenged by the family, and her idealization of the dead child was reinforced by family and friends, who still marked every anniversary of his death after more than twenty years by sending letters and flowers. Her powerful and controlling mother demanded appreciation of her own grief, but never acknowledged what the ordeal had meant for her daughter, who had been forced to care intimately for him, but was unable to prevent him from dying. She had felt that she had 'no right to grieve' as she was only his sister, but her sorrow had been compounded by her guilt – 'Why couldn't I have died – instead?' and her fear that somehow she had not done all that could have been done for him. She had never been able to acknowledge her jealousy of him for being so special – and for usurping *her* place as mother's baby. His weakness and his need inspired pity, but often his infected chest and his desperate weakness revolted her. She had longed for recognition of her own fear and exhaustion as she devotedly nursed and comforted her brother.

Our patient was frequently disabled by lack of energy and uncontrollable weeping and panic, and she retreated to bed with sleeping pills for lengthy periods, unable to cope with everyday life and exhausted by her two children and domestic routine. She idealized her intelligent and capable son, and identified strongly with her sensitive anxious daughter. Her own mother continued to overwhelm her and reinforced her feelings of helplessness whenever they had contact of any sort, as did her daughter's headmistress and other female authority figures.

She had a lengthy history of psychiatric hospital admissions and treatment when she joined an outpatient psychotherapy group, and had inevitable problems in getting to the group on time, and bringing her pain and sickness into the group instead of retreating to bed. However, she slowly gained confidence as she confronted her experiences in the group setting, and allowed her own strengths as well as her weakness to be acknowledged by herself and others. After confronting authority within the group, she managed to be assertive enough to stand firm against her mother's life-sapping demands, and gradually achieved a new health and balance in her life. The ritual mourning of the brother's death was relegated to the past, and decently buried.

This progress continued after therapy had ended, and she made several important choices against the wishes of her mother and other powerful figures in her life, which gave her continuing satisfaction. Several years later her mother developed cancer, and she was able to nurse her through a distressing terminal illness. Her children also blossomed. Her daughter, once relieved of her crippling self-doubt, showed late promise of academic brilliance; her son tossed away the family expectations of his intellect, and gained satisfaction from a craft apprenticeship. They no longer felt the need to be excessively dutiful but enjoyed a relaxed family relationship freed from the necessity to protect their mother from her depression and 'sickness'.

Women who have lost a precious child may feel that life will never again be worth living, and that they will never be able to trust again. If death occurs suddenly and without warning, as in an accident, the shock and denial of the episode may contribute to the perpetuation of grief. The occasional accident of drowning, climbing, air disaster, or fire may leave no body to be buried, no evidence of death to be mourned. If there is no body, there is no evidence of lifelessness, and the sense of unreality cannot be challenged by experience. A mother may irrationally expect her child to return, and may keep his memory alive by attention to minor routines such as washing his (unworn) clothes and keeping his bed aired, in preparation 'for when he needs them'.

The horror and outrage resulting from the death of a child is sometimes accompanied by the wish to avoid seeing the child's dead body, as a way of avoiding the unthinkable. This may result in collusion between professionals and family, ostensibly to prevent further distress to a grief-stricken relative – perhaps because they wish to protect her from the sight of distressing injuries. Professionals are usually greatly relieved when relatives accept tragedy without giving way to anger or tears, thus protecting them from embarrassment and pain. 'She was absolutely wonderful – took it very well – didn't make a fuss.' But if these natural emotions find no outlet, mourning cannot be completed and morbid grief may result.

> A woman and her husband were proud of their four children, enjoying family outings and activities. She was troubled by heavy periods after the birth of the youngest child, and decided to have the recommended hysterectomy shortly after the child started school. While she was in hospital, this child was fatally injured in a road accident. She was stunned by the news, and could not believe it. The hospital staff were stunned too, aware that the recent surgery had left her without the possibility of having another child. They found it difficult to face her after such a tragedy, and it was not easy to get them to agree that she could be allowed home to be with her family. The undertaker advised that she should not see her child's body, because of the injuries, and so she was denied the opportunity to say goodbye. She was excluded from the inquest, and although she went to the funeral service – the first she had ever been to – it seemed totally unreal and she could not connect it with her lost child. The previously happy family was devastated. The dead child's toys and clothes were preserved as they had been left. The circumstances of the accident were not talked about since the subject seemed too painful and too dangerous. She blamed herself for having been in hospital; the other children and her husband thought she blamed them for not having taken better care of the child.
>
> After some months she returned to her part-time job, but she was irritable at home and restricted the children's activities outside the house. She had several spells of depression for which her family doctor prescribed antidepressant drugs, which helped her over the worst of the symptoms. As the second anniversary of her child's death approached, she talked of suicide. She felt that she was in a black tunnel with no light at the end, and everything was pointless. She was profoundly depressed and unable to work, spending her days at home watching her dead child's favourite video film and cuddling his favourite toy, while she gazed at a greatly enlarged school photograph taken just before the tragedy. She resented the

interruption of her reverie when the other children came home from school, and family relationships were seriously strained.

She was reluctant to be referred for psychotherapeutic help, telling her doctor that she wanted to die and join her baby. However, she did come for therapy and painfully struggled with her reluctance to say goodbye to her child. She talked of her murderous rage towards the driver who had killed her child, and what she would do to him should she ever see him. With difficulty she returned to the crematorium with her husband, and was shocked to find there was no exact spot identifiable where the ashes had been buried. Following this visit, the couple talked with their other children about the catastrophic episode that was dominating their lives, and they were able to weep together and describe in detail exactly what had happened and how they had felt about it at the time. She was able to acknowledge that even if she had not lost her womb, another baby would not replace her precious child, and to remember the happy times with him. She discovered that to say goodbye was not the end but a new beginning, and that family life, though different and tinged with sadness, had to go on. No longer preoccupied with her lost child's memory to the exclusion of everything else, she found herself able to laugh and joke once again.

Accidental deaths strike suddenly and without warning, so that shock and disbelief is a major factor in each tragic episode. The death of a previously healthy child from illness is sometimes sudden, as in overwhelming virus infection, and may leave family members shocked and worried that they have failed to recognize the signs of illness and impending tragedy. If medical attendants have been involved, they may be angry that the doctors have been unable to prevent the death, and think that hospital admission or specialist opinion should have been sought – which may be quite unrealistic, but is a way of struggling to make sense of an episode that is incomprehensible and too awful to accept. The anger and sense of outrage is a part of the normal response to death – anger at the event itself; anger at God, at fate, at the dead beloved for abandoning them in this way. It may become focused (and displaced) unfairly onto professionals. It is important that such hostility is not taken personally by doctors and nurses, as this leads to defensiveness and a combative stance towards the relatives. An acknowledgement of the anger as a natural emotion in such a situation may be a very helpful way of 'giving permission' for feelings that will be even more destructive if they remain bottled up.

When there has been a fatal illness, lasting for months or years, there will have been a prolonged period of distress for the family before the eventual death of the child. They dread being overtaken by tragedy and feel powerless to control it. After the initial shock at learning the diagnosis, depression may be thrust away and every moment occupied with pursuing the finest available care for the child and even a magical cure. Hope is enormously important, and should be realistically encouraged together with the acceptance of the inevitable outcome. Having good times together – a family holiday or an outing, doing something special, looking forward to a treat – are important in sustaining morale during this difficult time, but are also the source of happy memories for the future. Death may be inevitable, but dying may be a long-drawn-out process that can provide times of real intimacy and joy, the more poignant and memorable because they are transient.

The first indication of serious illness in a normal healthy child may be bizarre, or stumbled on by accident. A patient discovered a big hard lump in her daughter's tummy when she felt it after a bath. Another found that her son grew out of his new shoes within a couple of weeks and his trousers would not fasten round his expanding waist. A third noticed that her agile daughter was clumsy, and took her for an eye test. This is the moment when anxiety really begins for parents, and delays in seeing doctors, getting specialist opinions, and being sent for tests may create overwhelming stress, which is not readily appreciated by the professionals who are used to working in the system. The doctors and nurses know that it is usual to wait for a few days, even for urgent appointments and test results, and that a minor delay is unlikely to influence the eventual outcome. The suspense of not knowing – and even worse, of having information withheld because protocol requires the senior doctor to sanction the pronouncement of the diagnosis – unintentionally increases parental suffering at a time when they most need support.

> A mother was referred for psychotherapy a year after her daughter's death from a brain tumour. She looked gaunt with exhaustion, her eyes ringed by black circles, although she was otherwise smart and composed, and apparently functioning with her normal competence. She described how she visited her daughter's grave daily at the nearby church, taking fresh flowers and finding some comfort in feeling that she was close to her. She could not bear to spend time alone in the house, which was full of memories of her daughter's illness. She particularly hated the living room, where the child had been nursed in the final stages. It was clear that she was still overwhelmed by the intensity of her grief, but there was no denial of the death or undue idealization of her daughter. The sister played with the toys in her room, there were photographs around but not in excess, and she was mentioned

normally in conversation. Why then was it so difficult for her to let go of her dead daughter? When she slept, she dreamed of her bloated body and distorted face in the final terrible stages of her illness. She could not recall her as the sunny lovely child she had been before disaster struck, could not visualize her when she looked normal.

She was then able to use her once-weekly hour of brief focal psychotherapy to express some of her anger at the unfairness of it all. Why had this happened to them, normal devoted happy family that they were, when so many people did not love their children, when unwanted and abnormal children survived? Why was medical science unable to cure her daughter? She could not express anger directly at the doctors who had been so kind, understanding, and devoted in caring for her child. One day she came in to her session, furious because a very old man dying of advanced cancer, who lived nearby, had been sent into hospital for more treatment. 'The doctors should have made him comfortable and let him die in peace,' she protested, at last able to acknowledge her anger towards the professionals who could not save her daughter. As she went through all the painful details of her daughter's illness, death, and funeral, it became clear that the most difficult issue for her was her guilt and grief at having been asleep, and thus having missed the actual moment of her daughter's dying. She had been in a coma for several days, and both parents had been with the child constantly; yet she could not forgive herself for having fallen asleep and having 'abandoned her' at the final moments. If she let go of the last memories of her when she was alive, she feared she would have nothing left of this special daughter.

The mother agreed to bring a snapshot, taken shortly before she became ill, which helped her to share her 'healthy daughter' with the therapist, and recall her sense of fun and happy occasions. She was able to block her ruminating memories of the dying child, which always preoccupied her at bedtime, and to substitute a pleasant memory as she looked at the smiling photograph. The bad dreams ceased, and her daughter appeared reassuringly in a dream, together with her late grandfather – both looking well and happy. The mother began to sleep better and stopped visiting the grave daily. She no longer felt compelled to tell people who did not know them that they had lost a daughter. After ten sessions she discontinued therapy and was able to continue with the normal process of mourning, after confronting the tyranny of her grief with the help of the therapist.

A mother's bond with her firstborn seems to be especially strong, possibly because the child has been the exclusive subject of maternal pride and love before the arrival of younger siblings, and because all first experiences tend to be particularly memorable. The death of any child leaves an irreplaceable gap, but it often seems as if the lost child of a family has had special qualities – not being the cleverest or most talented, but being possessed of particular kindness, humour, or wisdom that may have been prominent during their illness and be a particular cause of pride and sadness for the bereaved parents. Children so often show amazing courage and grace as death approaches.

Sometimes the death of her child is accompanied by a series of other blows, which tax a mother to her limit.

> A couple came along together at the obstetrician's suggestion, after a miscarriage late in pregnancy. When their second child was 3 months old, their treasured first son began to develop alarming signs and symptoms which led to his death fifteen months later. The husband was particularly angry 'at the waste of it all', but they were close, and supported each other in mourning their dead son.
>
> They were coping well with life despite other misfortunes until the wife had two late miscarriages. These further blows to their hopes stirred up all their feelings about their son's death, and felt like a punishment – confirmation that they were unfit to be parents. Until then, the wife had never doubted her capacity to have babies, but she had not been able to protect her firstborn from disaster, and now her womb was breeding death. She was nearing 40 and felt that time was running out. She was angry with some of the hospital staff for their insensitivity to her plight. The couple attended a group for bereaved parents, which enabled her husband to expose his sadness to others in a new way. She relived her grief and explored her dilemma in individual therapy, eventually feeling able to risk a further pregnancy. Happily a new son was born six years after the death of their precious first child, and at Christmas, when he was 6 months old, the therapist received a photograph of 'the most beautiful baby in the world'. His fond mother wrote that he was 'the image of David.... It's lovely to see the resemblance and sad at the same time. John still includes David in his conversation, as we do.'

The relevance of a past family tragedy to long-term problems is often not recognized, particularly since many years may elapse between the tragic event and help being sought for family distress. Marital breakdown is likely after the death of a child, when the stress and depression has been too great for a couple to bear and one partner has sought comfort elsewhere. A child may unite a couple in their affection for him, and after his death there may seem nothing left in the relationship. If the child was the issue of a previous marriage, the maternal bond may be particularly strong, and a woman may think that her husband does not – indeed cannot – share her feelings of grief. If they have had children of their marriage to whom he is particularly loving, she may come to resent both them and him. Family rifts can develop when grandparents or other close relatives avoid mentioning the painful subject of the dead child, appearing insensitive in order to avoid their own sorrow. A cousin of similar age evokes memories, comparisons, and fantasies of how the dead child would have developed. Sometimes a mother will feel that her mission in life is to keep the dead child's memory alive, and that it would be a form of betrayal to enjoy her other children or allow herself to be close to them.

Because death in childhood is so tragic and incomprehensible, friends often withdraw from contact, both during a terminal illness and after a death. Such abandonment cannot be forgiven, for support and companionship is greatly needed at such a time. Siblings may be shunned and even excluded from invitations to play with schoolfriends, if *their* mothers are unable to cope with the prospect of the death. When words fail, actions are readily interpreted. The gift of flowers, or a cake left on the doorstep, is experienced as a heart-warming gesture; avoidance and silence as rejection.

For some women, grief at the death of their precious child may be exacerbated by other life experiences – previous, simultaneous, and subsequent – so that each of the blows that might have been coped with singly becomes part of a savage sequence that overwhelms their resources. Sadly, other aspects of their life and relationships may have been irremediably damaged by the time they are forced to seek help.

A dead child cannot be replaced, and no other child can be a substitute for one that has been loved and lost. It is important for other children of a family, including those who never knew the child who died, that the reality and the brief life can be acknowledged and remembered openly. Otherwise the lost child becomes a family ghost, idealized or dreaded, shrouded in mystery, with the potential for too much fantasy to develop around the little knowledge available. A dead child will leave a big gap in a family, but a hasty attempt to substitute for him by adoption, fostering, or having a replacement baby is unlikely to be successful. The substitute will inevitably fall short of the idealized lost child in every way, and may serve merely to increase the sense of loss and disappointment. But when there has been a satisfactory resolution of mourning, a loving family may feel that they have love to spare which can be extended to another child – of their own, or chosen – without denying the importance of the one they have lost. Loving another child for himself may paradoxically keep the memory of their dead child more alive.

Further reading

Kubler-Ross, E. (1983) *On Children and Death*, New York: Macmillan.

Useful addresses

The Compassionate Friends,
5 Lower Clifton Hill,
Bristol, BS8 1BT

The Association for the Study of Infant Death,
(5th Floor),
4 Grosvenor Place,
London, SW1
(Support for bereaved parents)

Chapter thirteen

Motherhood disappointed

The imperfect child

> In nature there's no blemish but the mind;
> None can be call'd deformed but the unkind.
>
> William Shakespeare.
> Twelfth Night

'Is my baby perfect?' This is the first question that every mother asks on the birth of her child. The secret dread of every woman during pregnancy is that she will give birth to an imperfect child. Some of this fear may be rational, related to the knowledge of risk factors such as maternal age and the statistical probability of bearing an abnormal child; some of it wholly irrational, stemming from feelings about her own imperfections and inadequacies, which may cause her to produce a deformed or deficient child. Despite these nagging anxieties, every mother has the built-in expectation that a perfect child will be hers by right, and increasing attention to antenatal care and prenatal screening has contributed to the universal fantasy that all developmental pitfalls can be avoided and that, having prepared for a healthy pregnancy and birth, a perfect baby will result.

The birth of an imperfect child is a major crisis for a family, raising powerful and primitive feelings (Solnit and Stark, 1961). The realization that all is not well may be immediate, or may only emerge over a period of time, when normal developmental milestones are not achieved. Withholding information from parents reinforces their fears and fantasies. If they are not even to be trusted with the diagnosis, how can they hope to cope with the difficulties of caring for their handicapped child?

Many mothers have described the terrible silence that surrounded the recognition on the part of staff present that they had given birth to an abnormal child, and the extra burden that this placed on them at a time of great emotional stress. A young pupil midwife described the situation as she first encountered it:

> The labour had been progressing normally and everything was just

> fine. We told her to push because the baby was ready to come, and as we delivered it, it was obvious that something was very wrong because a lot of the organs were outside the baby's body, like a great growth. Everybody went very quiet, and the sister in charge sent for the doctor, who took the baby away. Nobody said anything to the mother or explained what was happening. I felt very upset because I had never seen a baby like this before, and afterwards I went away and cried. I kept thinking of the mother and how she must be feeling.

The loss of the ideal child that the mother has carried in her womb is in many ways like a bereavement. (Drotar *et al.*, 1975) The first reaction is likely to be one of shock and denial, with an inability to comprehend the full implications of having a child that is 'different'. This may be accompanied by a sense of overwhelming disappointment, with feelings of personal failure, guilt, and self-blame, alternating with periods of unrealistic hope, and thoughts that it must be a mistake or cannot possibly be as bad as it appears.

Sometimes at this stage there is intense rage and a wish to disown the child, which may lead to a refusal to see or hold him, an avoidance of telling friends or relatives, or of discussing future plans, and occasionally, a refusal to have any contact with the child, so that alternative arrangements for care have to be made. It is unusual for a situation to go this far, but a degree of rejection, particularly if there is revulsion associated with the child's abnormality, is common. This requires sympathetic and skilled handling on the part of the nursing and medical staff in order to encourage a mother to have contact with her child, to hold him and care for him (D'Arcy, 1968). Even a confident and experienced mother may feel apprehensive about handling or feeding an abnormal child, fearing that she will harm him and that he will be especially vulnerable. In part, this may reflect her own hatred towards him, an unconscious wish to damage and destroy this imperfect extension of herself. In part, it may also accurately reflect some of the difficulties encountered in caring for an abnormal child.

An alternative parental response to an abnormal child is to be strongly protective towards him, to a degree that may be unwarranted. This may interfere with all other aspects of normal living, leading to the exclusion and neglect of other 'healthy' children and to the exclusion of other potential helpers, such as grandparents, from sharing the care of the handicapped child. Some parents accept the child but reject the handicap. A range of mixed feelings are experienced during the early days after discovering that a child is handicapped, but a feeling of uncertainty about the child, about the future, and about how they will cope, is universal.

Maternal bonding usually occurs in the early days and weeks after birth, associated with the mother's early preoccupation with her baby. But the shock of having an abnormal child, the consequence of surgical intervention or intensive medical care, of nursing in an incubator or special unit, with inevitable interruption of normal contact between mother and child and possibly a prolonged period of separation, all contribute to the difficulties that a mother may experience in bonding to him.

The early phase of shock and denial gives way to sadness and depression. The loss of the hoped-for perfect child must be mourned and this is essential if adjustment is to be made and acceptance reached. Disappointment must be faced, not only by the mother, but by the father too, and relationships sometimes founder if partners cannot share their disappointment, concern, and feelings of responsibility for their abnormal child, but are separated by the difficulties that the situation creates. There is a loss of normal hopes and expectations, not only for the child, but also for the family. Grandparents, particularly, will be affected, and may be wrapped up in their own grief, or find it difficult to talk openly about what they feel or to offer support. Older siblings may have looked forward to the birth with great excitement and may have difficulty in understanding why there is such confusion and sadness in the family. They may perceive themselves as somehow to blame for this misfortune, particularly if they have secretly longed to have their mother's attention for themselves, and were resentful or murderous towards the child growing inside her, pushing them off her ever-smaller lap. If parents become depressed or overwhelmingly preoccupied with the abnormal child, siblings may experience a sense of abandonment, thinking themselves punished for they know not what.

Once over the initial shock of discovering that she has given birth to an abnormal child, a woman requires the opportunity to talk about her situation, and to obtain advice and information to help her know what to expect and to plan for the future. Expert and sensitive genetic counselling will be important at this stage, since there may be great anxiety about whether it would be safe to risk a further pregnancy and a desire to know what chance there would be of having another abnormal child. Recognition of a link between the abnormality and the inheritance from one of the parents may be a great burden for that parent to bear, and may arouse resentment and shame in the partner.

> A young woman had worked as a nursery nurse until her first son was born. She hoped to have a large family and although she was bitterly disappointed when their second child was abnormal, she thought that she had all the necessary skills to cope, and looked forward to having other healthy children. Genetic counselling

revealed that the child was suffering from a serious inherited condition and only then was it realized that her husband had a mild form of the disease. The discovery that he had unwittingly passed on this inherited condition to his son was a terrible additional burden for him to bear, and was made worse by his wife's failure to acknowledge his emotions and the reality of the grave situation. He decided that he could not risk having any more children. His wife was angry about this, considering that her right to have further children had been taken away from her. She invested considerable energy in pursuing a programme of remedial activity for her handicapped child, and persisted in her claims that he was responding to her, although he was clearly deteriorating.

The impact on family life of this damaged child increased month by month. The older brother became very quiet and withdrawn, inhibited in his behaviour and unable to demand any normal attention for himself. His mother was totally preoccupied in caring for the younger child, and his father withdrew into depression, struggling to cope with the demands of his job and his family. He felt a failure, and his helplessness and hopelessness was increased by the conviction that he was a 'substandard model'.

Family therapy was offered but after two sessions the mother refused to attend, saying that it interfered with the timetable for her son's remedial exercises. She was not prepared to face the reality of the family distress that she *could* do something about, for this would have required her to give up her preoccupation with her damaged child and her fantasy that she could make him normal.

Advances in medical science and modern technology have resulted in the survival of many children who formerly would have perished at birth or in infancy and would certainly not have survived into adulthood. The life of a handicapped child may at best bring great joy and satisfaction to his family and all who know him, but at worst may be a source of family disruption and an intolerable burden, a life sentence from which there appears to be no relief. Any form of handicap requires adjustment of expectations and hopes for both child and family. The nature and severity of the handicap, the child's position in the family, their capacity to accept him for what he is and to make the most of his positive attributes, and their emotional, physical, and material resources will all influence the family's response.

A handicapped child who feels secure, supported, loved, and encouraged by his immediate family will be able to face the outside world. Handicaps may be viewed as a challenge, and every obstacle overcome may be a triumph and a cause for celebration. Handicap in one area may lead to the development of a particular strength in others.

A child who lacks mobility on land may develop particular strength and skill in water.

Many women find no difficulty in caring for a physically handicapped child, viewing this as an extension of a mother's normal caring role. A woman may take special delight in caring for her child with a selfless devotion, knowing that she is needed, and being rewarded by that very fact. Her husband, however, may find the constant burden of parental attention and the failure to develop independence much more difficult, particularly having to share his wife's attention and affection with the handicapped child, who remains a permanent and demanding intruder within their relationship.

> When their second child was born suffering from Down's syndrome and a heart defect, a young couple decided that he would be their 'extra child', and were relieved and delighted when their apparently healthy third child was born. This youngest child at first seemed to be developing normally, but when he did not walk they spent many anxious months visiting specialists, and waiting for the results of tests, which showed that he was suffering from a rare neurological disorder. The husband's job required him to move to another part of the country but his wife did not accompany him because she could not manage without her local support network. He was forced to move away, returning home at weekends; she became increasingly involved with her children and her local friends and, since she coped so well with family demands on her own, eventually felt that she had no need of her husband. He was grief-stricken by their subsequent divorce, feeling that he had been ousted from the marriage by the demands of his handicapped children. His own needs of family life had always had to take second place and now he was left with nothing.

A woman may find it much easier to cope with limited function in a child than with extreme and gross deformity (Johns, 1971). A child who looks ugly or abnormal, especially a daughter, will be experienced as a damaged reflection of herself. Great store is set, in our culture, on physical appearance as a measure of worth, particularly in girls, whereas boys attain status and admiration for physical prowess and cleverness.

Mental handicap provides a special problem, whether it arises from birth injury, genetic factors, or from causes as yet unknown. Sometimes a severely handicapped child looks normal at birth, but it gradually becomes clear that normal development is not proceeding, and that the child will not be capable of achieving an independent existence. Some women take comfort from the fact that their child will remain 'a special child who never grows up', encouraging his dependency and preventing him from developing any independent life skills.

Her guilt at producing a flawed child and her need to make amends may lead a woman to sacrifice herself to his care, to the exclusion of independent interests, social life, and friends. She may try to look after her child entirely alone, feeling that statutory provisions and institutional care are not good enough for him. She may invest her energy in promoting his interests through self-help groups, considering that other parents have more to offer in the way of understanding and encouragement than most well-meaning professionals.

Disability developing in previously healthy children

When a previously healthy and normal child becomes disabled, a family will have to face both their own and their child's feelings and difficulties in adjusting to the changed capabilities and expectations, with inevitable consequences for family relationships. Sometimes the damage and deterioration of personality associated with major handicap, resulting for example from severe head injury sustained in a road traffic accident, will leave the victim so changed that he is unrecognizable as the person he was. Not only will his family have lost their loved child, but the burden of caring for him will be a perpetual reminder of their loss, and may be made worse if he has no capacity to express appreciation of their devotion. Such burdens of care have traditionally fallen on women as daughters, mothers, and wives – an extension of their nurturing role. Such sacrifice may be freely undertaken, but the cost can be overwhelming, leading to breakdown of the marital relationship, of health, and of personal satisfaction in spheres outside the home. In spite of this, the rewards may sometimes be a sufficient recompense, particularly if a mother identifies strongly with her child and derives personal satisfaction from the child's success.

> A daughter was confined to a wheelchair by a progressive disabling disease from her late teens. Her mother was her constant companion, chauffeur, and helpmeet, gaining personal fulfilment from her daughter's academic success and activities. When her daughter suddenly deteriorated and died, the mother's life seemed to die with her. She would sit weeping at the emptiness; so complete had been her identification with her daughter that she had no interest in life without her.

Caring for a handicapped child may involve chronic sorrow – a grief that cannot be buried.

> A mother's first baby was brain-damaged following routine immunization. Elderly childless relatives took over her care for

twenty years before she was returned to her mother, who found it almost impossible to give her any physical care and attention. She had given unstintingly to her younger children and to many foster children, but she could not reconcile the severely handicapped non-communicating woman with the beautiful baby of whom she had been so proud, and she became deeply depressed. She could have coped with her death, but her survival was a constant source of grief.

Often the early care of a handicapped child is relatively straightforward once the initial shock and grief has been coped with. Parents are likely to be young and fit, and the physical burdens of coping are lighter. A small child can be lifted, carried, and held, and if disruptive and unruly, can be restrained easily. As the child grows, so the problems increase. Attendance at special units for care, education, or training may offer welcome respite from the 24-hour task of caring for the handicapped child, but will impose their own rigid timetable. Holidays, periods of illness, and the absolute necessity to be available to her child at all times when he is not actually in the care of professionals may seem even more of a burden than caring for him continuously. There may be feelings of competitiveness with other caregivers, and a particular need for a mother to prove herself to be competent and satisfactory. The presence of the handicapped child may limit the activities that she can undertake with her other children and restrict them in inviting friends to the home. Similarly, it may be difficult to take a holiday, to maintain contact with friends and relatives, to travel on public transport or to use other public facilities. Families who live in small close communities usually find it is easier for them to gain acceptance and realistic help when needed than families living in towns, where ignorance is more likely to lead to prejudice and fear.

Handicapped children are increasingly cared for in the community rather than being looked after in large institutions. Many parents prefer to keep their child within the family home, however severe the handicap, because they believe that individual attention and the stimulus of ordinary family life will enable the child to develop more normally. The burden that this involves is frequently underestimated, and marital breakdown is common. Other children may be overshadowed by the demands of the handicapped sibling, and may find it difficult to develop their own personalities. Parents may fail to recognize the individual needs of their normal children for care and attention, and expect them to be endlessly tolerant and loving towards their less fortunate sibling. Some families resolve difficulties by sending their normal children away to an institution – boarding school – so that their attention can be devoted to the handicapped child. This may be experienced as a rejection or as a liberation, depending on individual personalities and circumstances.

The handicapped child growing up

As the handicapped child grows up, so the difficulties increase. The physical exhaustion, the drain on emotional and material resources, and the particular difficulties of puberty, adolescence, and emerging adulthood may be particularly threatening. Sexuality can be a problem for women to deal with in their normal well-adjusted offspring; in a handicapped child it may rouse powerful emotions and serious difficulties of management. Mental handicap may be accompanied by a degree of disinhibition that is socially inappropriate and embarrassing. Burgeoning sexual feelings may be displayed in public. A girl may be unable to cope with her own menstruation, and may have difficulties with personal hygiene. Sexual precocity and uninhibited behaviour are likely to lead to sexual activity with attendant risks of pregnancy and exploitation. The emergence of adult sexuality may emphasize the fact that the child, though physically mature, lacks the capacity for autonomy that true adulthood requires. It may become more difficult for a mother to be close to her child and to carry out intimate caring functions, partly through embarrassment and partly through fear. Her own vulnerability may be touched upon and she may be haunted by the fear of the sexually mature child reproducing another damaged child in turn.

This may also be the time when parents begin to be preoccupied with the future of their child. 'What will happen when we can't look after our child any more?' Family life may be moving into the next phase with other children growing up, leaving home, perhaps marrying and producing families of their own. The 'perpetual child' may remain in the family home, or may live in some sheltered situation, but is likely to remain the primary concern and preoccupation of his parents. He may meet a real need for them to have someone to care for.

> A patient had had a very sad life, moving from an unhappy childhood with a brutal stepfather into a difficult marriage with a brutal husband. She became depressed and was admitted to a mental hospital, where she was diagnosed as having an 'inadequate personality', unable to cope with the demands of family life. In fact she was ill-treated and humiliated by her husband's affairs and sexual exploitation, but felt unable to talk about them. She eventually divorced him, shortly after the birth of their youngest child who suffered from Down's syndrome. All her life she had been looking for someone to love who would not abandon her, and she felt that her youngest child would fulfil this need, since he

would not become independent and leave home as her older children would.

One day she found her youngest son dead in his room, having accidentally asphyxiated himself whilst playing. Two years later, her deepening depression led to a further hospital admission, and she was referred for psychotherapy. It was clear that she had never been able to grieve the death of this son whom she had expected would be hers to cherish always. In therapy, she began to remember all the loving things that had made him so special for her. His childlike simplicity had made him grateful and loving, and she missed him sorely. She then became free to express her anger at her abandonment by her grown-up children, longing for them to pay her more attention rather than being wrapped up in their own families. As she became more confident, she felt that she would like to work with mentally handicapped people, having had so much experience of caring for her own son: and she found a job in a small home. She began to feel that her son's all too short life had not been in vain, and that in looking after other handicapped people she was continuing, in a way, to care for him. Her depression became a thing of the past. She began to see that her handicapped child had represented a damaged part of herself that no-one else could care for, and that she could care for in him, when hitherto she had been unable to experience herself as having any value except in his need of her. She no longer makes unreasonable demands on her other children and is contented and fulfilled for the first time in her life.

A woman who has devoted her life to mothering a severely handicapped child may find it difficult to let the child go, in adolescence, to a residential school or training centre that offers a partial independence, since it leaves her own life very empty. There is none of the gradual separation and preparation for independence that is experienced as a normal child matures and prepares to leave the family home. The knowledge that the handicapped child will never be capable of full independence, nor of reciprocating the care and support that she has given for so many years, may contribute to her becoming depressed. Parents are often reluctant to look ahead to the time when their own increasing age or infirmity will make it impossible for them to continue caring for their child, but unexpected illness, or the need to look after their own aging parents may force them to face the hitherto avoided issue. Sometimes anger, which has been bottled up for years, spills over onto the family, and the bitterness drives away much needed love and support. The decision to let a child go into residential care under these circumstances may be seen as a final failure by a mother. When one parent feels that the child should leave the family home and the other wishes to keep him there, considerable friction may occur. What might seem obvious action to an outsider may be anything but obvious to the parents themselves.

Normal healthy brothers and sisters of a handicapped child may not only have problems during childhood, but also in adulthood. They may feel guilt at their own comparative good fortune, which is the more severe if they have disliked or feared the sibling and wished him dead. They may compensate for negative feelings by zealously promoting his interests to outsiders, but they may still be jealous of the constant parental attention paid to him, and feel the need to be both good and successful, deserving of parental pride. They may repeat the family pattern of distorted relationships when it is not appropriate, showing long-lasting disturbance and depression as adults, and having difficulties with their own normal children.

The eminent psychotherapist Dr Bruno Bettelheim is well known for his life's work with disturbed and handicapped young people. His compassionate care and his belief in their individual potential and worth has given hope to many who were previously regarded as hopeless and beyond help. He wrote:

> Children can learn to live with a disability. But they cannot live well without the conviction that their parents find them utterly lovable.... If the parents, knowing about his (the child's) defect, love him now, he can believe that others will love him in the future. With this conviction, he can live well today, and have faith about the years to come.
>
> (Bettelheim, 1972)

Parents can learn to live with a child's disabilities and imperfections, and most find that the love and care that they lavish on him brings its own reward. Nevertheless, the disappointment of having failed to produce and raise a normal healthy child is a burden not lightly borne; and at certain times in the family life cycle, the distress that this failure occasions may result in a mother needing professional help.

Further reading

Furneaux, B. (1988) *Special Parents*, Milton Keynes: Open University Press.
Scotson, L. (1985) *Doran: Child of Courage*, London: Pan Books.
Lansdown, R. (1980) *More than Sympathy*, London: Tavistock.

Useful addresses

MENCAP
Royal Society for Mentally Handicapped Children and Adults,
123 Golden Lane,
London, EC1Y 0RT.

Association for Spina Bifida and Hydrocephalus,
c/o 22 Upper Woburn Place,
London, WC1 0EP
Tel: 01 388 1382.

Chapter fourteen

Motherhood depressed

She left the room undusted, did not care
To hang a picture, even lay a book
On the small table. All her pain was there -
In absences. The furious window shook
With violent storms she had no power to share.

Elizabeth Jennings
A Depression

Depression is the most common cause of distress and ill-health in women. At the age of 16 girls are three times as likely to attempt suicide as boys, and later about one-third of young women aged between 16 and 35 years old become seriously depressed. Throughout the developed world, with the exception only of Finland and Norway, women are twice as likely to become depressed as men. Working-class women with a child under 6 years of age are, as a group, highly at risk of developing depression; young women who come from the most deprived childhood backgrounds are eight times more likely to suffer depression than young men from privileged backgrounds. Women consult general practitioners for mental-health problems more frequently than men, and are generally more likely to be admitted to psychiatric hospitals. Given this gloomy picture, the disinterested observer may well wonder why there has been so little research directed to elucidating the causes of depression in women, and – in view of its prevalence in women with young children – so little concern with the implications of depressed motherhood for normal healthy child development.

There is a well-established relationship between adverse life events and the development of psychiatric illness (Paykel, 1978). Brown and Harris (1978) in their major sociological study of depression among women in Camberwell identified four vulnerability factors that contribute to the development of depression only in the presence of a provoking agent. When provoked by a particular stress – an adverse event or major difficulty – the majority of women have the resilience to withstand breakdown; those women rendered vulnerable by the possession of one or more predisposing factors were likely to develop depression. The central experience in the development of depression is hopelessness; loss events can be viewed as the deprivation of sources of value or reward, and can lead to an inability to hold good feelings, which are the source of self-esteem. Brown and Harris believe that the generalization of hopelessness forms the central core of depressive disorder. If a woman's self-esteem and mastery are low before a major loss or disappointment, she is unlikely to imagine herself surviving adverse life events. This notion of self-esteem and a sense of mastery is similar to Bowlby's (1973) concept of self-reliance, which is built up through the security provided by reliable attachment figures, and to Melanie Klein's (1940) idea of the introjection of a good object (parent figure). Bowlby described the distress of a child separated from his attachment figure, which has three recognizable phases – protest, despair, and detachment. This is similar to the phases of adult mourning following death. Freud (1917) pointed out that the loss of an object of love can lead to depression, without it necessarily having been lost through death.

The four vulnerability factors identified by Brown and Harris (1978) as rendering women liable to depression by reducing their self-esteem were: loss of their mother before the age of 11 years; lack of an intimate and confiding marital relationship; lack of paid employment outside the home; and the presence of three or more dependent children under the age of 14. When self-esteem is high, loss will lead to appropriate grief and resolution; when self-esteem is low, loss leads to failure to work through grief and to hopelessness and depression. The type of past loss affected the severity of depression, but Brown and Harris found that if her mother *died* before a daughter was 11 years old, this predisposed her to psychotic depression; they suggest that death leads to a sense of abandonment and retarded hopelessness. Loss by *separation* leads to a neurotic depression, perhaps because the situation seems less permanent, but gives rise to a sense of rejection and protesting despair.

Given the unavoidable predisposition to depression that seems to be a legacy of early maternal loss, many other factors act as stressors in vulnerable women, giving rise to depression. Women who have married young, sometimes because they find themselves pregnant and feel they have no choice, are at risk of depression following the birth of a child. Mothers who are unsupported, lacking a caring partner, or who exist in impoverished circumstances clearly have fewer resources with which to cope with the inevitable demands of pregnancy and motherhood. Pregnancy and childbirth may be regarded as a normal transitional crisis, but for the mother who is unsupported, who has had a previous reproductive mishap, such as a stillbirth or perinatal death, or who has had grave doubts about whether she wants the child that she is carrying, or whether she will be capable of mothering it because of her own experiences in childhood and her continuing relationship with her own mother, these factors may well precipitate depression. Any major crisis during the course of pregnancy will increase the likelihood of depression developing, particularly if the woman experiences the death of an important family figure, such as a parent. The loss of one baby of a twin pregnancy is a particular source of distress that is often overlooked, since professionals and family tend to focus with extra pleasure on the surviving child. Even without any obvious adverse factors, some women become depressed by their changing body image during pregnancy, resenting the feeling of being out of control, of being invaded and taken over by the baby feeding off them.

Helene Deutsch (1924) observed that there are two types of pregnant women – the one who endures her pregnancy, and the one who blooms during pregnancy. For the former, the anticipatory period of motherhood may be characterized by marked depression, and great relief may be experienced at the victorious termination of pregnancy when the child is born. For the majority of women, however, the birth of their baby is characterized by a feeling of loss and emptiness, and for some mothers, the grief of losing the baby from inside them is a potent cause of depression, even though feeding may re-establish unity in the form of the nursing couple.

Only relatively recently has motherhood become a lonely condition, when responsibility for the sole care of another human being, the baby, may be experienced as overwhelming and burdensome in its isolation. If her own experience of being mothered has been inadequate to prepare her for the task of mothering her own child, if her life experiences have been such that her sense of self has been battered and her self-esteem lowered, and if her partner is unable to give the support she needs or is unwilling to meet her demands, which may seem overwhelming or unreasonable, a woman is most likely to become depressed, and to present in need of psychiatric help in the early period of motherhood. Separation from her baby in the first six weeks after birth, and inevitable partial separation at about two years, resulting from the child's developing autonomy and relationship with others, threaten the 'facilitator's' identity as mother and may lead to depression (Raphael-Leff, 1985; see Chapter 5). On the other hand, the crucial and vulnerable periods for the 'Regulator', when her concept of herself as a *person* is threatened, are the first six months of enforced togetherness, and again after the first year when the child is becoming adventurous and out of her control.

Postnatal depression

Depression following childbirth can be divided into three discrete types.

'Maternity blues' affect the majority of women and are often regarded as a normal experience in the first few days after delivery. About seven out of ten women find themselves inexplicably weepy and downhearted, even though they are delighted with their baby and may have had no bad experiences with the birth. This can be puzzling and distressing to the woman and her husband, unless they have been warned that it is natural. Reassurance that it is not serious, and that it usually reaches a peak at about the fourth day after birth, and steadily improves thereafter, is all the treatment that is required.

The most severe and worrying form of psychiatric disturbance following childbirth is the puerperal psychosis, which was described by Hippocrates. It is a rare but serious condition, complicating one in six hundred pregnancies and developing within ten days of childbirth. It typically occurs in a woman who has not previously suffered from mood swings, who has a normal personality, and has been well until she suddenly develops an anxious and rapidly variable mood, difficulty in sleeping, misperception, and gross thought disorder. She frequently hears voices (auditory hallucinations). Following this acute stage, the characteristic symptoms of depression often develop, with serious risk of suicide. The debate continues about the cause of this condition, and its relationship to other serious mental illnesses, but Hays and Douglass (1984) believe that it is a special disorder complicating pregnancy, and that it does not arise in patients with a strong family history of other psychotic disorders. Research findings increasingly suggest that women who develop a severe puerperal psychosis may do so in response to biochemical and hormonal changes associated with childbirth (Riley, 1979). The first breakdown may occur after any pregnancy, but the onset is most commonly associated with the first birth, and they will be at risk of developing a similar puerperal psychosis following subsequent pregnancies.

During the month following delivery, women are eighteen times more likely to be admitted to hospital than during any other month of the pregnancy (Paffenbarger, 1961), indicating the crisis that childbirth represents from a psychiatric viewpoint. Yet it has been little considered in the planning of psychiatric services for women, which do not take into account the needs of their dependent children, and the further problems that separation is likely to create for both mothers and their offspring.

The third form of psychological disturbance associated with childbirth is postpartum depression, which starts within two months of delivery and may be the first episode of depression that a woman has experienced, although three-quarters of the women experiencing it in the puerperium will get a further episode following subsequent deliveries. The relationship to recurrent affective disorder is not clear, since about two-thirds of women who suffer these do not experience postpartum depression. There is probably a greater vulnerability to depression in women who suffer from recurrent affective disorder who also develop postpartum depression (Garvey *et al.*, 1983). There is no doubt that individual personality traits, deficiencies in social support and social conditions, and stressful life events all contribute to its development.

Depression in mothers of young children

The prevalence of depression in mothers of young children is worryingly high (Wolkind, 1985). It affects 30–40 per cent of the population, and is often persistent, leading to some degree of handicap in everyday functioning, affecting interaction with the child or children of the family, the ability to cope domestically, and to function competently in family and social spheres. Andrea Pound and her co-workers (1988) found that three-quarters of a sample of mothers, which excluded those thought to be most vulnerable, had experienced at least one episode of depression arising in the context of a pregnancy, usually in the first three months after having a baby. They confirmed the views of other researchers that maternal depression is associated with marital conflict, difficult economic circumstances, poor housing, lack of a close confidante, lack of family or friends to support her, and an unsatisfactory childhood. Depression related to pregnancy seems more likely to give rise to disturbance in the children, which is exacerbated by recurrent depression in subsequent pregnancies. Pound and her colleagues found that the children of mothers with poor marital relationships, whose depression had lasted for more than two years, tended to show persistent and marked disturbance.

It is not clear whether maternal depression affects the child directly, or whether the depression reduces the mother's parenting capacity by diminishing her self-esteem and confidence in her ability to care for her child. The significance of genetic factors, which may also be involved in the development of mental disorder in the children of mentally ill parents, remains unclear (Rutter, 1966). However, observation has shown that maternal depression leads to changes in a child's behaviour; this is apparently a direct effect, and is noted when mothers are particularly low. Children of depressed mothers are mostly less active, more clinging, and may seek to comfort their mothers, taking care of them in a 'parental' fashion. They noted also that disorder in the child is highly related to exposure to hostility, whether this results from direct criticism and aggression from the depressed mother, or whether it results from marital discord.

Depressed mothers often struggle heroically to take care of their children and to love them, sometimes concealing their depression from medical attendants and other carers who might otherwise be able to offer them help. In others, the depression is severe and obvious, leading to a degree of sluggishness and inability to cope that should alert other people to its severity and need for treatment. A depressed mother will be less responsive to her baby's needs and signals, less accepting and warm towards him, and less co-operative and accessible. When the baby looks into her face, he sees not a joyous reflection of himself, but a flat lack of response, so that he feels valueless. He will not look at his mother or smile so often, or will only do so anxiously to ascertain if he might get a response this time. A profoundly depressed mother may be unable even to feed her child, and a young baby will be at particular risk. If she is irritable and tense, her baby's crying, or demands for food and comfort, or the need to change him may give rise to hostile feelings that frighten both her and her baby. He senses her hostility and becomes increasingly anxious, withdrawing from her. If the father or another significant figure – older sibling or grandparent – is warm and accessible, he will turn to them, which will increase his mother's sense of inadequacy and hopelessness and contribute to the vicious circle of depression.

In most depressed mothers, this interference in the mother–child relationship at a crucial stage in child development leads to later problems for the child, particularly with regard to learning difficulties, with problems of poor attention and concentration. Pound *et al.*, (1988) observed that the *quality* of the meshing in joint interaction was different between a depressed mother and her child and a non-depressed mother and her child. There is a lack of spontaneity and interest in the child's activities, leading to failures of cueing and response, so that active engagement between mother and child leading to a continuous and reciprocal exchange of information and response is unlikely. Depressed mothers did have periods of activity with their children, but were more likely to engage in physical activity such as tickling and playing than to promote reflective dialogue.

There are a number of projects around the country, such as SCOPE in Southampton, NEWPIN in Walworth, and HOMESTART in Leicester, which have been developed to combat the isolation of young mothers and their children, which is a particular feature of contemporary society. Not only does such isolation leave mothers unsupported in their misery and their difficulties, but it prevents children having healthy role models to counterbalance the pathological home situation that results from serious maternal depression.

Self-help groups, which bolster self-esteem and play down the sick role and dependency aspects, encourage individual strengths and resilience and are particularly valuable in counteracting the effects of isolation. Intensive therapy for either mother or child may further undermine their relationship, and psychotherapeutic skills are probably best employed on the mother–child relationship. Andrea Pound concludes that:

> Joint work with mothers and young children which helps each to understand and value the other, and to identify the aspects of interaction which are destructive of mutual harmony, is often more effective and economical. In any event, treatment needs to be early rather than late. Too often, professionals are not involved until much later, after years of unhappy mother–child relationship, years which can never be recaptured.
>
> (Pound *et al.*, 1988)

The work of Brown and Harris, Pound and her colleagues, Bowlby, Rutter, and others has not only confirmed the prevalence of depression in mothers of young children and identified some of the factors predisposing to its development, but has also demonstrated its strong association with disturbance in the child. Adverse circumstances will obviously make a young mother's task more difficult, and this theme is touched upon throughout the book.

There are, however, many young mothers who become depressed in the absence of apparent adversity; they have become mothers by choice, bearing the child of a loved and loving partner in relative financial security at a time in their lives when parenthood has seemed fitting, and has been achieved without problems. These young women often have great difficulty in acknowledging their depression, since on the face of it they have everything they wanted – including a healthy baby. But motherhood in practice often turns out to be quite different from what had been envisaged, and even adaptable flexible young women with accommodating babies whom they enjoy can find themselves prey to a general malaise and discontent, 'the problem without a name' (Friedan, 1963), which may lead on to frank depression.

If a baby is difficult – cries constantly, vomits feeds, demands constant attention, deprives the mother of sleep or any time for herself – then the 'blame' for mother's depression is easily put onto her child. If she feels rejected by a baby who is not 'cuddly' and withdraws from too-close contact, or if she feels threatened by the constant need for physical contact of a fretful child who will not otherwise settle, the blame can still be put on the baby. If her loving and attentive husband now seems to be so besotted with their infant that she feels displaced in his affections, or that her primary importance to the child is usurped when he is around because he is so *good* with the baby and they have such fun together, she may begin to resent both the drudgery inherent in the housewife/mother role, and her baby for trapping her in it. If her husband had previously take a major share in household chores, when both had full-time jobs outside the home, but has withdrawn from these 'because she is no longer working', so that she feels she has to mother him as well as their offspring, she may be able to focus her discontent on him. Simple tiredness and physical exhaustion may leave no energy for sex and other previously enjoyable pursuits.

But for many young women the problem is more subtle and more complicated. They have high standards and expectations of themselves and their performance as wife and mother is not exempt from this inner taskmaster. They will have worked outside the home and achieved a degree of self-value rewarded by a regular pay packet; the more enjoyable and personally satisfying, and the greater the financial and social acknowledgement of their worth, the more difficult it will be to give this up – and having done so, to maintain self-esteem without it.

Few young women these days have any real preparation for motherhood. They mainly come from small families and lack experience with babies and young children. Their lives will have been given structure by the institutional demands of education and the workplace. They have been used to the companionship of others, to adult interests and conversation, and to peer-group norms. They have usually had time and money to spend on themselves, and a degree of freedom unknown to previous generations. The advent of a baby changes everything. The couple becomes a family, and previously simple decisions – to go out for an evening, to visit friends – take on a new dimension. A wife may feel obliged to have regular contact with parents and in-laws who are proud to be grandparents – but who may offer little useful support, and may actually undermine her self-confidence as a mother. She may have been delighted to give up work, determined not to share the care of her child or to 'neglect' it by going to work outside the home. Or she may have been a 'regulator' mum, determined that she would not become a martyr to her child, and that she would continue to work outside the home. Sometimes a couple will, these days, opt for a reversal of roles, especially if the wife has a more remunerative job, and the husband will stay at home with the baby. Whatever the individual circumstances, motherhood is a major life transition and the identity adjustment required may lead to an unexpected crisis and energy-sapping depression. There is usually no simple solution – return to work, or give up work – and, just as the contributory factors may be many and diverse, so are the adjustments necessary to weather a transitional depression and to discover the appropriate individual solution for that particular life crisis.

The publication *Health and Prevention in Primary Care* (Royal College of General Practitioners, 1981) delineated seven areas that offered the family doctors the best opportunity for preventive care at the present time. Four of these areas (family planning; antenatal care; fostering the bonds between mother and child; helping the bereaved) have particular relevance to the prevention of maternal depression, both in avoiding its development and in aborting it in the early stages. An awareness of the significance of life events, such as loss of the mother at an early age – and the contribution of life factors such as unemployment, marital disharmony, poor living circumstances, and lack of support – in the development and maintenance of depression is a valuable aid to diagnosis and management. Nevertheless, the evidence suggests that general practitioners prefer to prescribe rather than to talk to their patients. Cartwright and Anderson concluded that two-thirds of patients came away from the general practitioner's surgery with a prescription:

> by 1977 the cost of drugs was more than one and half times the cost of general medical services ... as a society we pay less for the advice, listening and explaining, and the support that General Practitioners give their patients than for the pharmaceutical products which they prescribe.
>
> (Cartwright and Anderson, 1981)

Whilst social change in areas of welfare, housing, and the planning of services for mothers and children is doubtless necessary, changes in attitudes have an important part to play. There is much that doctors and other health-care workers can do to promote health and to prevent unnecessary physical and emotional illness if an improved quality of life is to be achieved, and the coming generation protected from the unwitting damage imposed by maternal depression.

Depression later in motherhood

Vulnerable women may well become depressed at later stages in their life. It is important to recognize that this does not necessarily reflect a tendency towards affective disorder, but is merely an expression of dissatisfaction that finds no other outlet. Men who have suffered violence and deprivation frequently exhibit violence themselves, and may turn to alcohol and drug use at an early age. Alcoholism is becoming more prevalent in women, in part because it is freely available in supermarkets, and in part, also, because young people start drinking at an early age, developing a taste and a tolerance for it. The abuse of alcohol often begins as a socially acceptable way of deadening feelings that are uncomfortable. The tranquillizing effect reduces anxiety, and may provide 'Dutch courage', so that shy and anxious people can face social situations that are otherwise uncomfortable for them. It may also provide some relief from intolerable distress and discomfort associated with difficult life circumstances and personal relationships and may be used as an antidote to depression rather than anxiety. However, alcohol use is a potent cause of depression, and continuing use of alcohol for symptom relief may lead to true physical dependence with all the serious consequences that this entails. This subject will not be dealt with in great detail here since there are a number of specialist publications that deal with the issues and treatment of alcoholism, which are similar in both men and women.

Women are vulnerable to depression at each transitional period of motherhood. A mother may become depressed when her child starts school, feeling that she has lost her exclusive role and being unable to tolerate the gap that this leaves in her life. A mother whose child seems to be constantly at odds with her, or who seems alien to her, may become deeply depressed, experiencing herself as a failure. She may be unable to tolerate the normal maternal ambivalence, and hate herself for having negative feelings towards her child, particularly if these reflect her experience with her own mother. A woman may become depressed following sterilization, or her husband's vasectomy, since this brings home the finality of the decision to end the creative reproductive period of her life. She may feel depressed if her child fails to succeed and gratify the designs that she has for him, or may feel excluded by a child's success that takes him away into areas that she cannot share. Particularly if the marital relationship is unrewarding, there may have been a heavy investment in the child, and a fantasy that the child would provide perfect companionship. So often one hears a mother say – and proudly – that she is her 'daughter's best friend, more like a sister'. Such abrogation of the normal maternal role and responsibilities impedes the emancipation of the daughter from her mother and may be accompanied by profound rivalry. If this is achieved notwithstanding, the mother is likely to become depressed.

A woman's status, self-esteem, and personal relationships may be entirely tied up with her children and her role as a mother; when children leave home, a mother can feel that the important and fulfilling phase of her life is over. She cannot tolerate the emptiness, and feels that grandchildren are the only thing that she has to look forward to. If these are not forthcoming, she may be plunged into profound depression. The time of children growing up and leaving home usually coincides with the menopause. As long ago as 1857 Tilt wrote that many women became 'fairly unhinged at the time of the menopause'. Research evidence is conflicting, but it seems likely that menopausal depression – or involutional melancholia as it was formerly known – is, like postnatal depression, multifactorial in origin. There are undoubtedly hormonal changes and alterations in body rhythm, but most women manage to survive this without psychological disturbance.

Guilt and depression

A form of maternal depression that we have seen on many occasions is easily overlooked. This is the depression of the mother who has abandoned her children, and who is overcome by guilt and grief at a later stage. Because of the time gap, the relevance to her lost maternal role is frequently unrecognized, and years of unsuccessful treatment may follow.

> A middle-aged woman was referred for an opinion, having had psychiatric treatment with frequent hospital admissions, including ECT, lithium, and a repertoire of drugs. The therapist noted her hysterectomy several years earlier, which the woman said she had had 'reluctantly'. The therapist observed that her womb had been the last link with her children. This produced a dramatic change in the patient, whose attention became engaged, having previously been passively hostile.
>
> She had borne five children to a harsh husband. They had been her 'entire life', but she felt that she would either kill herself or her husband if she stayed any longer in the intolerable marriage. She eventually left him and her children when the youngest was 5 years old.
>
> The first couple of years were taken up with her struggle to survive, and she did well in a demanding job. She found a kindly new partner, but this was when her depression began. In therapy she worked through her hitherto unresolved feelings about the loss of her children, and her guilt at abandoning them. She was able to stop all her medicines and achieve new health.

Women are prone to depression. They repeat the pattern of deprivation that they themselves have experienced if their lack of self-esteem leads them to believe that they have nothing to give their own child. Such a woman frequently leaves the care of the child to the mother who has been so neglectful and critical of her in childhood, fearing her envy, and believing that her own depression will damage her child beyond repair. If the marital relationship fails, she takes this as further confirmation of her worthlessness and inability to give good things to others. Sometimes this sense of worthlessness is such that she cannot tolerate it, and she projects all the feelings into her child, severely inhibiting his development and sense of identity as a result. We see profoundly disturbed women whose own mothering has failed, caught in this intergenerational trap.

> A young woman was referred for psychotherapy after her second child was born. She had been admitted to a Mother and Baby Unit after each birth because she could not experience maternal feelings for her babies, although she knew rationally how to respond and what she 'should' be feeling. She was desperate and angry, and said that she would continue to have babies until she could experience normal motherly feelings.
> She was herself an adopted child, and had rejected all her adoptive mother's overtures, never allowing her to be close or affectionate. She had experienced the abandonment of her natural mother as a betrayal, and was not able to allow herself to have affection for anyone, including her children and the therapist, since her isolation was the only way in which she could maintain her identification with her natural mother.

Maternal depression is a substantial cause of ill health with incalculable consequences for the children and for subsequent generations. Motherhood is not fun. It is hard work, responsible, relentless in its demands and commitment, and not always rewarding. It is a full-time job, all day and every day, with sleepless nights and times of frustration and anxiety. Children can be fractious, selfish, tyrannical, and exhausting. They are always most angelic and loveable when asleep. Depressed mothers may find their children irritating beyond endurance, and respond to childish misery by 'giving them something to cry for', or by threatening to leave them or to withdraw their love.

Maternal depression is more common in isolated women in poor circumstances, but may be a cause of prolonged misery and disability in mothers of all ages and in all circumstances. In our culture and society, unlike those of nonindustrial societies, women do not share child care, washing, cooking, or extended family activities. They are poorly rewarded for their major commitment, and the value that our society puts on motherhood is low. Although it is a demanding occupation, it is not regarded as work or given financial recognition; yet the surprise is that so many women desire it above all things.

Further reading

Alvarez, A. (1971) *The Savage God*, London: Penguin.
Gavron, H. (1966) *The Captive Wife*, London: Routledge & Kegan Paul.
Oakley, A. (1974) *Housewife*, London: Penguin Books.
Orbach, S. and Eichenbaum, L. (1987) *Bittersweet*, London: Arrow.

Pedder, J.R. (1982) 'Failure to Mourn, and Melancholia', *British Journal of Psychiatry* 141: 329–39.
Price, J. (1988) *Motherhood: What It Does To Your Mind*, London: Pandora.
Welburn, V. (1980) *Postnatal Depression*, London: Fontana.

Chapter fifteen

Perverse womanhood

Physical and psychological child abuse

> Honour thy father and thy mother.
>
> The Tenth Commandment

Perversion

Stoller (1975) defines perversion as 'the erotic form of hatred', and writes that it:

> is a fantasy, usually acted out, but occasionally restricted to a daydream (either self-produced or packaged by others, that is, pornography). It is a habitual preferred aberration necessary for one's full satisfaction, *primarily motivated by hostility*. By 'hostility' I mean a state in which one wishes to harm an object: that differentiates it from 'aggression', which often implies only forcefulness. The *hostility* in perversion takes form in a fantasy of revenge *hidden in the actions that make up the perversion*, and serves to convert childhood trauma to adult triumph. To create the greatest excitement, the perversion must also portray itself as an act of risk-taking. (Stoller, 1975; our italics)

While it is easy to classify male sexual perversions in this way, it is more difficult to categorize female perversions. The percentage of men attending the Portman Clinic, which has pioneered the psychotherapeutic treatment of sexual perversion in Britain, far exceeds the percentage of women. Perversions such as exhibitionism, fetishism, and paedophilia have been extensively studied in men, but women seem to use these means of expressing hostility less frequently, perhaps because they have other sexual outlets. We have already seen how women need relationships, whereas men prefer to put distance between themselves and others (Chapter 3) and perhaps this is why men, but not women, are able to gratify themselves with an object (fetishism).

Estela V. Welldon in her recent book (1988) on perversion in women, based on her experience at the Portman Clinic, suggests that women may engage in perverted behaviour as frequently as men, but that it is not recognized or is denied by society. She states that 'Whereas in men the act is aimed at an outside part-object, in women it is usually against themselves, either against their bodies or against objects which they see as their own creations: their babies'. Moreover, 'women frequently act as if their whole body were a sexual organ', attacking their own bodies as in 'anorexia, bulimia and self-mutilation'. This is not to say that women never express hatred by erotic means, but rather that they are likely to express it in ways that are easily available to them, which have not been viewed as sexual perversion. Clearly, a woman is as capable as a man of being motivated by hostility and wishing to harm another, but a systematic ritualization of such feelings, associated with sexual arousal and satisfaction, is most likely to be incorporated into prostitution.

A prostitute may experience contempt for her clients and enjoy her experience of power over them, humiliating them and gaining satisfaction in withholding satisfaction from them. This is not the golden-headed whore of popular male fantasy, a universal mother/mistress, dispensing comfort and excitement. Many women, however, embark on prostitution simply as a way of earning money, since this offers a more lucrative return for their exploitation than other menial work. Often such a woman will be supporting a child or using the money to buy drugs on which she has become dependent. She may have a stable marriage or partnership that she 'splits off' from her life of prostitution as if it were any other meaningless employment. Such prostitution does not give her 'full satisfaction primarily motivated by hostility'. A lesbian woman may engage in prostitution as a form of perversion, deriving triumphant satisfaction from her knowledge that she is using or abusing men, while withholding herself from them. But perversion, as defined by Stoller (1975) does not seem in any way to be part of a loving and tender lesbian relationship.

The particular systematic and ritualized form of shoplifting, which is almost entirely confined to women, has been considered to be a form of female perversion. It may certainly be associated with fantasies of revenge, and give rise to feelings of triumph, and entail risk-taking associated with excitement and release, not unlike that associated with sexual climax.

> A patient was referred for a medical report after being caught shoplifting. She had a 'poacher's pocket' inside her coat and had taken a number of small items, including packets of seeds, for which she had no use. She had plenty of money in her purse, and admitted that she 'stole for the sake of it', throwing away the items

later. She was married to a man well-known and respected in the local community, and lived a comfortable life of some elegance. They had a young child and there were older children from her previous marriage, from which her present husband had 'rescued' her. It emerged in therapy that her first marriage had been characterized by instability and excitement, veering from rags to riches, but often subjecting her to shame and betrayal. Similar characteristics of 'all or nothing' had marked her relationship with her powerful idealized mother, whose energies were largely devoted to her social life and sexual conquests after she was widowed when the patient was only 3 years old. In a secure and predictable relationship for the first time in her life, she felt stifled by the lack of excitement. She could not express her anger to her 'good husband and lovely children' who took her time and energy; and she began to crave the excitement of shoplifting, taking increasing risks of being detected, but unable consciously to acknowledge her wish to harm her husband and shock her mother.

Another patient's systematic stealing had evident features of perversion. She was referred when threatened with prosecution for hoarding quantities of goods from a local store that she visited daily in order to see and be near one of the staff about whom she was obsessed. She scavenged in dustbins for personal objects belonging to this woman. She herself ran a successful business and knew that her world would fall apart if prosecution resulted in her perverse behaviour being made public. Her obsession was related to her early relationship with her mother and the association of sexual arousal with physical violence. Although she consciously wished to avoid the punishment of prosecution and public shame, the addictive quality of her perversion and her unwillingness to give up the excitement and the risks prevented any real desire for change.

Motherhood as a perversion

Welldon (1988) also puts forward the view that, for some women, motherhood can be a form of perversion that has passed unnoticed because it has been assumed that mothers are loving, cherishing, and benign, that motherhood is incompatible with hostility, and that mothering is an asexual activity. Most mothers will readily challenge these assumptions, acknowledging the ambivalence of their feelings towards their children, the temptation to abuse maternal power and the sensuous feelings often experienced when giving birth, suckling a babe at the breast, or seeing or holding a beautiful child.

A woman who may be powerless in political, social, and financial spheres occupies a position of control in relation to her children and her home. Even a woman who feels powerless within her marriage and subsequent family life wields the power of life and death over her babies, who depend on her absolutely for food, security, and developing self-esteem. Her child is her helpless victim, utterly at her mercy, gratifying her need for domination, to be in total control; the *apparently* loving mother can therefore physically, sexually, or psychologically abuse her child. The sexual abuse of children has been described in Chapter 7.

The unconscious fantasy that the child is not a separate being, but represents a part of the mother herself or of some other person important to her – the child's father, a brother, her own mother – may lead to bizarre and dangerous behaviour by the mother. Many mothers punish by proxy, telling a naughty child to 'wait till Dad comes home'; then, when he does come, recounting all the child's misdeeds, so that the father, willingly or unwillingly, metes out the punishment at the mother's behest.

When a man or a woman consciously and calculatingly feigns physical illness, it is called malingering. If an adult secretly takes tablets or injects himself with alien substances, inflicts physical damage on himself, or contaminates the results of investigations in order to simulate illness, this is known as Munchausen's syndrome, and it occurs in both men and women. It usually indicates a degree of distress that the patient cannot otherwise express, as do many other forms of overt 'acting out' which are not veiled in secrecy. Cutting or scratching the skin, causing pain and drawing blood, is a powerful way for a woman to release tension from within the taut container of her body. It may afford her some temporary relief, and the experience of the pain inflicted on herself reassures her that she exists. Recourse to alcohol, drugs, food, binges, or overdoses are other desperate attempts to gain release from tension.

A more sinister form of disturbance is seen in 'Munchausen-by-proxy' when, in order to simulate illness, a mother performs any of these secret manoeuvres on her own child. This results in endless visits to the GP and the hospital, and countless further investigations,. When no abnormality is found, the puzzled doctors cannot understand how the child was ever ill. The mother seems throughout all this to be understandably alarmed about her child's health and dutifully appears to do everything the doctors ask of her. She seems to be pouring out love and concern for him, yet uses distorted and damaging methods to gain attention from doctors and other professionals. There must be some element of hostility expressed towards the self in Munchausen's syndrome proper, but in Munchausen-by-proxy this unconscious hostility is extended towards the child.

Physical abuse of children

The physical abuse of children has been discussed in classic papers by Kempe and Kempe (1978). They describe how parents, often themselves deprived or abused as children, view their child as unlovable or deliberately difficult. They attempt to 'teach' him good behaviour by harsh physical punishment and, when this fails, the cycle of personal failure, rejection of the child, and further punishment is perpetuated. Difficult social conditions such as cramped living quarters with inadequate toilet facilities and lack of money or of employment, are the soil for abuse. A depressed mother may find it easier to block her child from her consciousness than to cater for his demands, and so neglect him physically or emotionally. An impulsive mother, with an explosive temper, especially when demoralized by some intercurrent crisis such as a row with her husband or mother-in-law, may become unendurably frustrated and lash out at her child or throw him against the wall. She may have no-one to turn to and feel hopelessly isolated from the rest of the world. She is so in need herself of love and attention that she cannot see her baby as helpless and vulnerable, needing her care; nor see herself as having any worthwhile love to give. She sees her child as a persecuting monster, deliberately wearing her down, and the rest of the world as continuously critical of her failings as wife and mother. An early warning of trouble is when a mother roughly wipes her baby's mouth or bottom as though he has deliberately soiled himself or has regurgitated food to create more work for her.

It is useless to try to help her simply by re-educating her about her baby's actual needs. Her own needs must be catered for by some consistent and supportive counsellor before she can become mature enough to cater for her child's needs. Otherwise she will feel resentful and jealous of any attention offered to her child and be even harsher to him.

It is easier to understand impulsive violence towards a child. Most parents have been tempted at some time or other, though they may never have crossed the barrier between thought and action. It is difficult to understand *deliberate* cruelty to a child, such as burning with a cigarette or an iron. Here the wish to inflict pain indicates deep emotional disturbance; the oppressor usually splitting off the acts from consciousness and denying responsibility. Sadistic behaviour of this nature is not lacking in a masochistic component; when a mother mistreats her own child, she is harming a part of herself. As with the woman who cuts or scratches herself, a woman who deliberately damages her child may reassure herself that she exists, the child confirming her power by responding to the pain she inflicts.

Soul murder

There are many ways apart from physical or sexual abuse in which a mother, from her unassailable position of control over her chid, may demonstrate her power, and derive a satisfaction from it that may be denied her in other aspects of her life. The withholding of affection or encouragement, the infliction of harsh criticism and humiliation, merciless teasing, seductive behaviour, and inconsistent demands may seem relatively harmless compared with the degradation and terror caused by sexual abuse; or compared with systematic beating, burning with cigarette stubs, starvation; or death-threatening physical violence. But the psychological damage can be as serious. One woman patient said

> My father would punch me on the face, belt me with the buckled end, or lift me up out of a chair by my hair, but those things don't hurt me now; its the mental things he did – threatening to put me in a home, giving my two brothers a bar of chocolate and leaving me out. Those really hurt, and they hurt me now, when I think of them.

This malevolent and inhuman disrespect for the dignity of a child by a parent has been called 'soul murder'. The term was first used by Strindberg in 1887 in an article on Ibsen's *Rosmersholm* and he illustrated the theme in his play *The Father*, in which a wife subtly and progressively undermines her husband's belief that his beloved only daughter is actually his, and ultimately drives him to madness. Shengold, (1978) an analyst in the United States, has written extensively about soul murder, describing it as the deliberate attempt to destroy the capacity for joy or love in a person, and the interference with their sense of identity. He quotes Daniel Schreber, a 50-year-old judge confined in an asylum in 1903 because of schizophrenia, who in his memoirs described his maltreatment as a boy. His father ran a gymnasium for children and forced his son to wear various head and body harnesses to correct his posture, which look like instruments of torture from the illustrations in a book he wrote on the upbringing of children. It is not surprising that the son remembered the Kopfhalter (head together-tying machine) in his delusions as 'little devils who compressed my head as though in a vice'.

> A girl's parents had divorced and married new partners. She remembered being locked with her sisters in a bedroom whenever her mother went out at night, and panicked in the dark. She went to live with her father and stepmother. As a punishment he made her and her sister stand on one leg for what seemed like hours. Her stepmother sat her own baby on a potty and whipped his legs with wire. Her father said he was a white witch and went through

> various rituals that scared her. He put her 14-year-old sister into a trancelike sleep in bed and, later, when she became pregnant, he kicked her, giving her a miscarriage. She said 'I can't remember a time when I was happy or not scared.' She had feelings of blackness and badness inside her, and immense guilt. She behaved like someone who had been sexually abused but could not remember this definitely happening, only wondering whether her sister had been abused.

This case illustrates the sexual overtones that colour soul murder – the psychological abuse of children.

One father held a young girl upside down by her legs over a bridge while a train was running under it, and on another occasion held her outside the door of a moving car, threatening to drop her. Another father buried his daughter in sand up to her neck while on holiday at the seaside, taunting and humiliating her while she could not move. He later taunted and humiliated her when he abused her sexually. Yet another beat his daughter for trivial misdemeanours, counting the strokes out loud. He would offer to reduce the number of strokes if a schoolgirl friend was present at the punishment. At the end, when his daughter was struggling to control her tears he would ask her to come and give him a hug. She felt guilty that she did not love him enough to come, and years later still thought she had deserved the punishment (Hall, 1987a). Yet another father forced his wife and children to sit on the stairs for most of Christmas day, then burned their presents. He once made each child stand in the corner of the kitchen while he heated a chip pan, telling them he would pour the boiling oil over them, and how it would burn them.

In all these examples, the child is mystified as well as humiliated and tormented. Why is the parent behaving like that? Is he or she friend or foe? But parents *must* love you, as *you* must love your parents. They must be right – (after all, right for a small child is defined as what your parent approves of). Why then do they hurt you?

Alongside the hurt, there is the rage and frustration experienced by the child. This is normally too much for him to cope with, and he denies it. It smoulders in the unconscious, ready to spark out later in life when an opportune victim presents him/herself. The child may pick wings off flies or bully a younger chid. As Alice Miller (1983) recounts in her book *For your own good*, an adult may turn the rage inward on himself by drug abuse or overdose or other self damage, or even resort to child molestation.

Shengold (1979) states that the child's emotions are paralysed by his confusion and terror, so that he becomes an obedient automaton. He needs the idea of a good and loving parent to ameliorate the fear, and often almost delusionally believes that the parent is in fact good and loving. The only possible explanation, then, for the maltreatment is that he himself is bad and is punished 'for his own good'. Shengold believes that soul murder can be prevented from destroying the child's identity by the presence of a good, loving, and honest person, perhaps a nanny, a grandmother, or a teacher, who can be the yardstick by which good and bad, love and hate, truth and hypocrisy can be judged by the child.

Mild forms of soul murder occur all the time. Parents shout at children in supermarkets for touching the tins on the shelves. They slap them when they whine because they are tired. They box their ears when they cry because they are frightened. At a conscious level this is part of the philosophy 'Spare the rod and spoil the child'. Children are seen to be inherently sinful, and that sin must be beaten out of them. At an unconscious level, the parent is often seeing his own wickedness in the child, and is beating *that* out of him (and symbolically out of himself). But for soul murder to succeed in destroying a person's identity, it has to be repetitive and persistent over a long period of time. A totalitarian regime is necessary; one person has to have absolute power over the other, and to be able to enforce submission, as in a secret-police torture chamber or in the brainwashing practised during the Chinese Cultural Revolution.

There is a double evil in 'soul murder'. When a victim is cruelly abused without any good person in his environment to ameliorate the annihilation of his sense of self, he may identify with his persecutor and in turn abuse others. Primo Levi, in his book reflecting on the Holocaust, *The Drowned and the Saved* (1988), quotes Manzoni 'Provocators, oppressors, all those who in some way injure others, are guilty, not only of the evil they commit, but also of the perversion into which they lead the spirit of the offended.' After months in the concentration camps, Jews would beat other defenceless Jewish co-prisoners. This also happens with child victims. When a child bullies at school or molests an infant, one should wonder what is going on in the home. When a daughter has been sexually abused, however horrified at her own tribulation, she may in her turn grow up to abuse her child. This may in part occur as a result of her fear of adult sexuality; a child is a less threatening outlet for sexual urges. A patient who had suffered incest described how she often had thoughts of abusing young children by fondling their genitals, and had given way to them when she was babysitting. She said, 'my mind's in a muddle. I'm me, and I'm also my abuser.' Or she may abuse her own child. Or simply acquiesce in her husband's abuse of their child. This is indeed corruption by the original perpetrator – the sins of the fathers.... It is the way gross psychological damage in one generation is perpetuated in succeeding generations.

This chain of horrifying behaviour can be broken. The most

important factor is that the victim's distress should be understood, *really understood*, by some wise counsellor or therapist. In order for this to happen, the patient must share the actual events with the therapist rather than pretend they did not happen or split them off. The pain must be faced, with the support of the therapist. Sharing the experience brings relief. The rage and frustration must be expressed. The responsibility can then be placed on the perpetrator rather than on the victim, and the guilt can be diminished. Then some healing can take place.

So many common psychiatric symptoms have their origins in physical, psychological, or sexual abuse of children by parents – depression, alcoholism, drug-taking, pathological jealousy, agoraphobia, school phobia, obsessive–compulsive behaviour, and sexual dysfunction. If a careful history is obtained, with time for the patient to trust the doctor or therapist sufficiently enough to disclose the abuse, the facts will ultimately emerge and will explain the symptoms, despite her wish to bury the memory forever. Physical abuse is relatively easy for a patient to disclose, although many patients are unsure at first whether or not sexual abuse has actually taken place. But psychological abuse is extremely difficult for a patient to recognize. Often it is the therapist who is alerted to the possibility by some chance remark, and who elicits the full story by careful exploration. The patient can then see the distorted experience through the undistorted eyes of the therapist, and gradually resolve her mystification and confusion.

After one of us had published an account of soul murder (Hall, 1987a) the following letter was received:

> I appreciated your article on a personal level. What you are describing happened to me. As a young girl I was raped, beaten and continually mentally oppressed. I saw Mum carve her wrists and attempt suicide many many times. My father would return only to 'get his oats' or beat her up. This, he would say, was all my fault. His bad marriage, his failures, all the guilt was loaded on me. At the age of ten he left me to be responsible for my mentally ill, alcoholic mother and two younger brothers. I then lived in Children's Homes.
>
> When I was thirteen my parents re-united to start again. To me they carried on as before, the same patterns of behaviour. The responsibility was still mine. I decided the best thing to do was to survive this bit, and when I was old enough – get out. I survived by guarding my spirit with a 'glass jar'. I clung to the fact that he – they were all wrong about me. I knew that I was OK. Now I am not sure where this message came from but it is clear to me it is at the heart of my survival.
>
> I left home at eighteen and a half years old. I had failed at home,

at school – at everything it seemed. I struggled to recognize loving or anything positive about myself. As luck would have it, I was the lodger of a family who gave me space to be angry and unhappy and encouraged me. They gave me permission to hate my father, be angry with him and know they would still love me. They supported me in my struggle to gain my self respect and pass my A levels. I did it.

I began a degree and had nine months' individual counselling. I figured out my destructive behaviour patterns and learned how to change them. I clearly acknowledged my hate for my father, and the anger at him and my mother for letting me down badly. My Mum died and I used her death as a source of inspiration.

Today, I am clearly a person in my own right. I am in the process of learning to love the child part of myself which I have up to now been very angry with. It is only recently I have relieved her of the responsibility of my mother's life and death, some of the guilt, and begun to reclaim some of the parts of what I call a misplaced childhood.

Your article helps me appreciate the validity of my childhood, which is often swept aside in one sentence. I find it warming to know that anger and hate are acknowledged, that the oppression I grew up with is worth taking notice of when trying to understand why young people behave in an 'odd' manner.

I have wholly re-evaluated my childhood role in my parents life. I am now able to say 'I am worth loving', 'I am beautiful'. That psychological re-birth Shengold spoke of has happened to me. I am a remarkable human being.

It is sad to reflect that the ideal place for abuse to take place is within the home, and the ideal victim one's own child. We easily think of men being violent, but find it more difficult to envisage a mother as an abuser, or as a collaborator, or as an acquiescent witness. Yet women do exploit their unique opportunities of exerting power in a perversion of motherhood.

There should be an eleventh commandment – *Honour Thy Child.*

Further reading

Kempe, R.S. and Kempe, C.H. (1978) *Child Abuse*, London/Shepton Mallet, Somerset: Fontana/Open Books.

Miller, A. (1983) *For Your Own Good*, London: Faber and Faber.

Miller, A. (1984) *Thou Shalt Not Be Aware*, London and Sydney: Pluto Press.

Renvoise, J. (1978) *Children in Danger: the Causes and Prevention of Baby Battering*, London: Routledge & Kegan Paul.

Welldon, E.V. (1988) *Mother, Madonna, Whore: the Idealisation and Denigration of Motherhood*, London: Free Association Books.

Chapter sixteen

Bereft womanhood

Bereavement and widowhood

> And we forget because we must
> and not because we will.
>
> Matthew Arnold
> *Absence*

The death of a partner is one of the most stressful events that a person can experience. Especially after a long marriage, the loss of a spouse can turn the world upside down, so that everything suddenly seems unfamiliar and nothing makes sense. Being alone after a life time of being half of a couple can be terrifying. Life may be empty and hopeless, with little point in going on alone, or in doing things when there is no longer a beloved spouse to share them with.

The closer and more important the relationship, the more devastating the loss will be and the greater the effect of the bereavement on the life that is left. Readjustment after bereavement takes time. A wife whose husband dies does not immediately begin to experience or think of herself as a widow, but adjustment to the change from wife to widow is essential if normal life is to be resumed.

There is always a sense of unreality about death and dying. It is impossible to imagine ourselves dead, and it is difficult to imagine life without those people who are closest to us; to imagine them being dead and not there for us any more. We therefore do not usually think about death or talk about it, although it is an unavoidable part of life. Facing this unimaginable situation, a bereaved woman has to cope with unfamiliar feelings that are not only confusing, but may be powerful and distressing to herself and to others. If she does not know what to expect, reactions that are normal and an essential part of grief may be frightening, or thought to be abnormal, or embarrassing. For some women, it may be a point of pride to put a brave face on things and not let other people see how sad and lonely they are. Denying emotions, or bottling them up so that others will not be upset by expressions of grief is not always the most healthy way of coping after a bereavement, and can lead to problems later.

Not all the effects of bereavement are adverse in the long term. Many people come through the stress and find themselves stronger and more mature than they were before. A woman whose life has revolved around her husband and family, with neither thought nor time for personal activities, may in widowhood – once she has recovered from the initial shock and grief – discover hitherto unsuspected talents. She may create a new and rewarding life for herself that would never have happened had she not found herself alone.

Reactions to death and the process of mourning

The immediate reaction to news of death is usually one of stunned shock and disbelief, particularly if a death is sudden and unexpected, as when a husband dies in an accident, or has a heart attack at work. But even when the death occurs following illness and has been anticipated, it may be difficult to believe that it has actually happened. If a wife does not see him after death, the sense of disbelief and unreality is greater because the evidence of a lifeless body is not there to contradict her previous experience of her husband alive.

This state of shock usually lasts for several days. The numbness can be a help in managing to get through the routines that have to be coped with, such as registering the death and arranging the funeral. Then the numbness gives way to pangs of grief and sadness. The normal mourning process is a fluctuating state that can last for months and years before it is completely resolved.

Loss is always accompanied by a sense of profound anxiety. The world has suddenly changed and it is difficult to make sense of it. A wife is likely to pine and yearn for her lost husband. She may be unable to settle, constantly moving around the house as if searching for him, and she may sense his presence or hear his voice. She may be comforted if she experiences his presence in a reassuring dream, but her distress will be greater when she wakes expecting to find him in bed beside her, and is confronted by the empty space.

Sometimes a woman will experience overwhelming anger towards doctors or nurses who did not prevent the death, or towards relatives and friends for not doing enough, and even towards her husband for having abandoned her. She may be full of guilt, blaming herself for not having prevented it or for being responsible for it in some way; or she may think that her husband's death is a punishment for some past failing on her part.

A woman can become compulsively overactive, so that no time is available for thinking or feeling. This may keep grief at bay, but such avoidance is not healthy. It needs to be experienced; tears are better shed than choked back. It is easier in our society for women to show emotions than it is for men, who are expected to 'keep a stiff upper lip' in most circumstances, and who may therefore find it even more difficult to cope with the overwhelming sadness that they feel if their wife dies.

The pining and yearning are usually most prominent about two weeks after the death, giving way intermittently to sadness and depression. Finding her mood changing with bewildering rapidity, a woman may fear that she is going mad and losing her reason. The experience of bereavement is not reasonable – it is strange, terrible, and overwhelming at times, but at other times life goes on as usual. For this reason it is better to take up a normal routine again as soon as possible, so that the reality of work and ordinary activities helps to balance the sense of unreality associated with the loss and change. The sadness and depression is usually most severe about four to six weeks after the bereavement. But it is usually better to return to work and normal activities after about two weeks; it is important not to avoid other people, nor reminders of the loss.

As time passes, a woman begins to adjust to her bereavement. Superimposed on the chronic background misery of her loss, she is stopped short on occasions by pangs of grief, which may be physical and intense. A favourite tune, the scent of his tobacco, his clothes, a book – anything can trigger these pangs of grief, evoking memories of her husband and their life together; they may occur at any time, catching her unawares, sometimes even after many years. At such moments the tears may come, and the grief is as acute as if the loss were yesterday.

Slowly the woman begins to emancipate herself from the husband who has been the most important person in her life. She finds herself beginning to do things that she chooses to do, perhaps things that she would not have done with her husband. She is no longer so preoccupied with his memory, and for periods of time is able to forget her loss. She finds things to laugh at and to look forward to, but still feels her loneliness and incompleteness, as if she has suffered an amputation, or has lost one half of herself.

Gradually she begins to reconstruct the way in which she perceives herself and the world around her. Her identity changes from being half of a couple, a wife, to that of being a woman alone, a widow. This shift in perception and reconstruction of her identity takes time. Though it may have been satisfactorily completed, she may even, years later, experience a sense of dislocation, and forget that she is no longer married to the husband who died, that he will not be there to share some interesting piece of information.

A young widow, happily remarried to a widower for some years after her first husband's early death, told how she had driven past a house, and thought 'I must tell John that they are making alterations there', only later realizing with a sense of shock that John had been dead for ten years. Another widow wept as she told how, following her husband's sudden death, she had struggled to keep family life going for her growing children, and how she had not allowed herself to break down and cry. She often found herself getting five eggs out of the fridge for breakfast, when now they only needed four. Such episodes produced unbearable pangs of grief.

Recovery is accompanied by a return to normal mood, with a renewed zest for living. Sometimes the renewed appetite for life is accompanied by a hunger for food and a resurgence of sexual feelings, compensating for the prolonged abstinence of mourning. Women may need reassurance, fearing that this is abnormal or shameful.

As with most facets of human experience, the way in which people mourn and the time it takes is immensely variable. About 85 per cent of people experiencing the death of a major figure in their lives are likely to come through the mourning process without need of any professional help. The significance of the loss, the quality of the relationship which they have shared with the dead person, and their own personality and previous experience will influence both the intensity of the mourning and their capacity for maturing into a new autonomy. Life circumstances are obviously important, and the presence of supportive family and friends expressing concern and interest is very helpful. If other people do not allow the opportunity for expression of the natural feelings of distress, or exhort the bereaved to 'snap out of it', impatient that they have not got over the loss quickly, their difficulties may be increased.

A woman whose husband died of lung cancer described her experience of his death. Although he was desperately ill, his dying was never spoken of between them, and after his death her daughter's family moved into her house so that she would not be alone. They were so kind that they sent her abroad for a holiday 'to take her mind off it', and after she returned, her husband's death was not mentioned. Her granddaughter had to share her bedroom, so that she had no privacy to weep. Long-standing friends avoided mentioning her husband's name in conversation, and she felt as though they were wiping out forty years of her life, as though it had never existed.

The circumstances of the death also influence the course of mourning. Sudden death may pose particular problems of disbelief, especially if there have been severe injuries in an accident and the widow has been advised not to see the body. If she has witnessed or been involved in the accident, the whole experience may be a waking nightmare for her, so awful that she cannot talk about it with other people; she may fear sleep because she relives the experience in terrifying dreams. If she has been injured herself, she may have no recall of the event, which makes it even more difficult to deal with. If her husband has been killed or if he has committed suicide, she will have to bear the stress of inquest proceedings, and may also have an overwhelming rage for which she can find no outlet.

The quality of the marital relationship is an important factor in her grief. If the relationship was good, there will be good memories to treasure from the past, even though the sorrow may be greater because the marriage was so precious. If the relationship has been poor, she may have harboured ambivalent feelings towards her husband for many years, and her first feelings on learning of his death may be of relief. There may be little grief initially but as time passes intense despair may develop. It is now too late for the failures in the relationship to be repaired, and the widow may punish herself by prolonged grieving as a form of restitution.

Sometimes, following unexpected death, the grieving process is complicated by feelings of self-reproach and by a continuous sense of the presence of the dead spouse, with feelings of obligation to his memory that make it difficult for the normal process of emancipation to begin. In these circumstances a widow may continue to do everything exactly as her husband would have wished, and makes no move towards any independence.

Chronic grief is fully expressed from the outset, but it continues with an intensity that does not diminish with time and persists, often for many years. The marital relationship might have been intense and mutually dependent, and the widow may feel particularly helpless. She may visit the grave excessively, and resent any efforts made by relatives or friends to 'take her mind off things' or to encourage her to resume a normal life. A woman whose grief is excessive in intensity or duration, or which takes an abnormal form, needs skilled psychotherapeutic help to facilitate its resolution.

The experience of loss

Who will take away
Carry away sorrow,
Bear away grief?

. . .

Talon and beak
Pluck out the heart
And the nerves of pain
Tear away grief.

Kathleen Raine
Spell Against Sorrow

As women usually marry men older than themselves and have a greater life expectancy, it is usually women who are left alone. The likelihood of their remarriage is limited since widows greatly outnumber widowers; therefore the finality of the loss may be made worse by the knowledge that the loneliness and isolation that they experience have little hope of amelioration.

The loss of a life partner causes great suffering, even if the relationship has not been very loving, or has been downright hostile. The loss of the mutual identity built up through habit and familiarity, and of the experience of proximity to another person over many years is a great shock. Death is so final, the silence and emptiness are so encompassing, that the widow can feel alone and abandoned in a vast and threatening world. She may experience doubts about her identity that are not unlike those of adolescence, with a resurgence of insecurity and of uncertainty. She is astonished to find herself one person again, instead of being one half of a couple; and yet she is not a whole person, only a lacerated part-person. Amazingly, the everyday tasks of life continue, but she may only feel real if she is talking about her husband or is with her close family. With the outside world she sees herself as a mere shadow, looking on. Unless she has young children, there is no-one in the world for whom she matters most and who matters most to her. She will never again be of first importance to anyone. Getting through the hours and the days seems an overwhelming effort without her partner to share it with. There is no welcoming voice, no companionship, no-one with whom to share the joys, disappointments, and humour of the day. She will even miss his irritating habits. In the difficult lonely hours – the drink before supper, the solitary walk, at bedtime – she misses him desperately.

If she is now living alone, there will be the new experience of existing for herself only. It may seem a self-centred and pointless life. At first, there is the constant expectation that she will see him in bed beside her when she wakes, or coming towards her in the street, or returning from work at supper time. Gradually, she becomes more resigned to her solitariness, and to the permanence of his loss. The pangs of grief recur with each memory evoked, and each has to be separately mourned. Once mourned, it cannot again produce a pang of such intensity, though there seem to be an infinite number of others that do.

Anniversaries – of his birthday, of their wedding, and of the death – are particularly painful times, consciously or unconsciously, and sadness and grief increase in the days leading up to them.

Women whose grieving has become pathological are especially vulnerable at anniversary time and, if depression has become severe, may attempt suicide on the anniversary of his death. If a woman has engaged in psychotherapy for help with unresolved grief, anniversaries need to be borne in mind when termination of therapy is considered. The usual brief focal psychotherapy may need to be extended, or a couple of extra sessions offered at a later date so that the resurgence of feeling associated with the anniversary of the loss can be shared in therapy. The termination issues of psychotherapy are never more important than in the treatment of pathological grief. The ending must be kept in constant view, so that the feelings can be dealt with.

Widowhood – the doctor's role

Doctors are always involved when someone dies because they have to issue a death certificate. Breaking the bad news of death or serious illness requires great sensitivity. People remember vividly the way in which news is given to them, and they may go over it repeatedly through the rest of their lives. If bad news is broken clumsily or brusquely, their inevitable distress is greatly magnified, and they may be extremely angry.

> A woman described how she learned that her husband was suffering from advanced malignancy barely one hour after she had found her mother dead in bed. Her anxiety about her husband and the future inhibited her mourning for her mother. She recalled that she was entirely preoccupied during the funeral arrangements and the service with the thought that she would be going through the same experiences for her husband in the near future. He died only three months later, after a rapid deterioration, and she developed symptoms of morbid grief. She longed to join him in the coffin. She removed none of his belongings from their place, keeping his watch by the bedside and holding his unwashed pyjamas at night for comfort. She gazed out of the window constantly, waiting for him to appear, and talked to him endlessly. Her refusal to acknowledge the reality of his death protected her from the necessity to grieve it fully. Her sensible and supportive family were desperate, having colluded with her avoidance of the subject by stifling their own sorrow.

Relatives often ask doctors to prescribe something after a bereavement, to relieve distress. It is insulting to spouses who have lost their life partner to suggest that their grief can be cured by a few pills. An open acknowledgement of their grievous loss, their shock, and loneliness, is much more helpful. A sympathetic arm around the shoulders and the warmth of human contact may be more useful than words in conveying support and understanding. After long illness, or in old age, death may have been anticipated, but even though it has been expected, the moment when it occurs is shocking and final, and there can be no preparation for such an event. Untimely death may have the extra complication of leaving a woman to bring up children alone, and cheating her of the future that she had expected to share with her husband. Death in old age is a foretaste of mortality for the remaining partner, and there may be little hope of solace for the future. An older woman may never have spent any part of her life alone, having often grown up in a large family and moved into marriage without any period of independent existence. Retiring to a solitary bed can be the most potent trigger of grief. The loss of physical closeness to another person, as well as sexual contact, is deeply painful.

The doctor who is able sensitively to appreciate the normal process of mourning, the particular facets of grief that are likely to be most painful for his patient, and the risk factors predisposing each individual to abnormal grief, is well placed for preventive counselling. He may suggest that the widow comes to see him at the surgery so that he can review progress with her. He should enquire directly how things are going, and acknowledge the loneliness and difficulty that must have resulted from her bereavement. It is better to ask specifically about sleep, mood, and appetite. The normal phase of depression, which is a part of mourning, sometimes progresses to a severe clinical depression with biological features. If there is very poor sleep, antidepressant medication is likely to be more useful and appropriate than prescribing hypnotics, which will do nothing to improve the mood and may cause her to become dependent upon them. A small dose of tricyclic antidepressants taken before going to bed may have beneficial effects, by restoring sleep and thus enabling the woman to cope with the unfamiliar extra burdens that widowhood has imposed upon her, as well as the work of her grieving. This will not, however, obviate the need for her to *ventilate* her grief in order to facilitate and complete the mourning process.

It is important that the family doctor should not simply issue repeat prescriptions for any medication prescribed, but should take the opportunity to review the woman's progress after a major bereavement. If her grief appears excessive in its observance, is abnormally intense and prolonged, or takes bizarre forms such as refusal to acknowledge that her husband is dead, referral for psychiatric help should be considered. However, it is unrealistic to suppose that the grief that follows the death of a loved partner of many years can be put aside in a short time. The first anniversary of the death may well be a watershed, and though she may have shown no signs of recovering from the blow before the anniversary, subsequently she may be less preoccupied with the past and more able to look to her own future. Overt grieving that is prolonged beyond two years should give cause for concern. Doctors need to be alert not only to the 'anniversary reaction' with a resurgence of depression, but also to the widow who has not complained of undue distress hitherto, but who presents at the anniversary time with physical symptoms. The unwary doctor may set physical investigations in motion if he fails to check the real cause of distress underlying her symptoms. It is not uncommon for widows whose grieving is blocked or distorted in some way to adopt the symptoms of their dead loved one.

Sympathetic support, reassurance, and encouragement to face up to the pain of grieving, and yet to look to the future with hope is an important part of the doctor's task. Even a very limited opportunity to talk openly about her bereavement may facilitate mourning and prevent abnormal grief developing. The doctor can also direct a widow to self-help groups and other sources of comfort and counselling, and encourage her to use them.

Further reading

Kübler-Ross, E. (1969) *On Death and Dying*, Tavistock: London.

Parkes, C.M. (1987) *Bereavement: Studies of Grief in Adult Life*, London: Penguin Books.

Worden, W. (1982) *Grief Counselling and Grief Therapy*, London: Tavistock.

Useful address

CRUSE,
Cruse House,
126 Sheen Road,
Richmond,
Surrey, TW9 1UR.
(Support for the widowed and their families.)

Chapter seventeen

Pairing and parting

Divorce and second marriage

Love's not Time's fool, though rosy lips and cheeks
Within his bending sickle's compass come;
Love alters not with his brief hours and weeks
But bears it out even to the edge of doom.

Shakespeare
Sonnet 116

In marriage, or a longstanding relationship in which partners live together, the two separate identities become entwined and a mutual identity is built up. Ideally, the two partners fashion each other with mutual sensitivity and adjustment, forming rules of procedure and boundaries. The factors tending to prevent union are fear of intimacy and the reluctance to lose some personal identity or to forgo autonomy. Even without much closeness in the relationship, the habit of living together through the various daily milestones and family events inexorably cements even a seemingly unstable union, making it difficult for either partner to 'put asunder'.

As the idealism of the courting couple gives way to a more realistic perception of each other's characteristics, repeated mutual abrasions caused by the ill-fitting parts of the two personalities begin to round off the sharp corners. Contentious issues usually arise out of the conflicting set of assumptions each partner brings to the union, and these in turn are based on the family from which each comes. They are the more potent for being largely unconscious.

Nevertheless, despite the difference in expectations and the ensuing disappointments when they are not realized, most couples manage to settle down together. Shared joys and sadness and crises surmounted, especially if the couple have children, contribute a growing store of memories, good and bad. Each partner provides a useful focus for the anger that the inevitable difficulties of life produce in the other. In a stable relationship a mutual identity is to some extent built up, where each partner begins to think like the other, anticipating the other's needs or wishes. The most healthy relationships are those in which the pair are deeply involved with one another and are committed to one another, but keep part of themselves separate for other relationships and interests. There must be space in the relationship for each to develop and grow.

Until recently, most partnerships were ended by death, and divorce was relatively uncommon. The ravages of war, disease, and childbirth resulted in many people dying young, so that people either lost their partners during the childbearing years, or survived with their relationship intact until they died in old age. Nowadays, marital breakdown is a commoner cause than death for the ending of a relationship and for a younger woman to find herself alone.

Divorce

> Men are April when they woo, December
> when they wed: maids are May
> when they are maids, but the sky
> changes when they are wives.
>
> Shakespeare. *As you like it*

Loss from separation or divorce is very different from loss through death, even if the marriage was not all that good, for the widow, unlike the divorcee, is afforded a certain respect by society. If the relationship was good, she can also feel pride in the memories of her successful marriage. Divorce, in contrast, seems to be an implicit admission of her failure, either to keep her man, or to have made the right choice of husband in the first place. Humiliation is greater if he has found a new partner and she has not.

The wife who has hitherto considered that the marriage was satisfactory, may be taken by surprise at her husband's desertion. She will need time to overcome her sense of outrage in order to realize that things must have been wrong for some time and that in some way she must have contributed to the breakdown of their partnership. The wife who has been unhappy in the marriage may, on the other hand, be delighted at the parting, feeling free at last from the violence, alcoholism, jealousy, infidelity, or denigration, or from the frustration of not being loved and of not being able to share feelings. None the less the crisis of identity experienced in being single again, instead of being half of a couple, may be much the same for the divorcee as for the widow.

The wife becomes the ex-wife, losing the status and the life style that marriage afforded her. Even the empty bed may be a continuing source of distress.

A woman abandoned by her husband for his mistress, after a

lengthy affair when he was unable to decide between them, had been increasingly upset by the knowledge that he would come from the other woman's bed to hers, and that he was sexually intimate with them both. She had loved him and had comforted him in his dilemma, hoping that he would not leave. Eventually she found a new partner, but could never allow him to marry her or to sleep in the same bed, since her dread of a further abandonment was so great.

After many years of marital difficulty, which may include repeated infidelity, a woman may divorce her husband because the relationship falls short of what she desires. Her mixed hope and disappointment may make it difficult to go through with the divorce, and afterwards her ambivalence may continue. A woman remarked sadly, after her faithless but attractive and successful ex-husband had remarried, that a share of him had actually been so much better than not having him at all. Depression as divorce is contemplated, as it is finalized, and in the aftermath, is understandably common. A fresh crisis usually arises if her former partner remarries, regardless of the fact that she may herself have a new and more satisfying relationship. Looking back at such a time, the better memories of their life together, of shared family pleasures and early romance, are likely to predominate.

A particular misery for a woman alone is the feeling that others pity her. She has nobody for whom she can be special, no partner to admire or flatter her. A major source of irritation and distress is the discovery that other wives may regard her as dangerous and a threat to their own marriage, whilst men often regard her as 'easy meat', assuming that she is hungry for sexual contact. A date or invitation, or even a casual meeting, may be followed by the expectation of sex and a bed for the night.

Whereas a widow slowly acclimatizes herself to the loss and learns not to expect the presence of the partner, the divorcee knows he is alive, existing somewhere, in her fantasy giving good things to other people and not to her. Even if the woman has left her husband and has formed a new partnership, she may be bitter that *he* remains in their marital home and her resentment increases if he installs another woman there. She will probably have to contact him by letter or phone, or even meet him in order to make the endless arrangements about finance, legal proceedings, and care of, or access to the children. She cannot, therefore, put him totally out of her mind. She may dislike contact with him or she may unrealistically hope for a reconciliation. If she is afraid of her ex-partner's violence, she may dread his approach. The stress will be greater if he abandoned her and she is forced to split up the mutual furniture and possessions or even to sell the house. Building up the home and caring for it may have been the only part of the marriage that was rewarding for her, and she feels as if a knife is being turned in the wound.

Usually, but not always, the mother has custody of the children. Fear of losing them may keep a woman from leaving an abusive husband. Yet husbands often suffer a great deal at having to give up daily contact with their children, and the management of access can give rise to endless conflicts. Fathers turn up late, or keep the children too long. They give them expensive presents that the mother cannot afford. They may try to poison the children's minds with critical remarks about their mother, and the mother in her bitterness may reciprocate. They often fail to pay maintenance. The mother is left alone during the times of access with her sadness and resentment. Her jealousy of his new partner may reawaken old oedipal struggles and sibling rivalries, and she suffers as she thinks of his love for his new wife – and possibly his new child – and fears that *her* children may love their stepmother more than they love her.

Second marriage

Once the pain of loss of a partner has been worked through the woman may contemplate a new relationship, though she may be reluctant to risk marriage again. If a widow felt the previous one was good, it may seem a betrayal of the dead spouse. If it was bad, she may dread the recurrence of the same conflicts and pain. Some women precipitately embark on fresh relationships, driven by loneliness and a desire to be needed. The resurgence of passion and sexual feelings, perhaps dormant for many years, can lead a woman to embark on a relationship with a partner who is in most respects totally unsuited to her needs and her usual life style.

In a second marriage, each partner hopefully will have learned from his or her previous relationship, and understand more clearly the continuing need for sharing the self with the other throughout the marriage. There will probably be less idealism, less romantic love, and more emphasis on dependability and trustworthiness. The woman is often more assertive and the man more ready to share in the household chores. Their roles are likely to be more equal, with joint decision-making. 'You have to get married the first time in order to get it right the second' (Furstenberg and Spanier, 1987).

There are, however, many dangers that the first marriage did not have to contend with. There is even greater need for flexibility, particularly after loss by bereavement, because past loyalties to the lost spouse and to the children keep each partner rigidly sticking to old habits and customs. This time, the basic assumptions that each brings to the marriage will not only derive from parents but from the pattern of life shared with the previous spouses and from their respective children. Because the home means so much to a woman, and because in general she will care for the children while the husband is away for much of his time, she may be obsessed with thoughts of the previous wife and the way in which she managed the home. A woman who moves into her husband's home may long to alter the decorations or furniture or to remove all the photographs and personal belongings of his first wife. This may be perceived as an attack on her memory, threatening to spoil the new relationship.

She may prefer to cook the main meal in the evening instead of at midday as his first wife did. He may resent the fact that she expects him to be home straight from work instead of spending an hour at the pub with his mates, which his first wife never objected to. There is need for much adjustment, and this must be mutual, or one or the other partner will feel trapped and ill-used. As George Steiner put it, we have to 'learn to live as one another's guests' (Steiner, 1988).

After bereavement, each must be careful not to compare the present with the remembered perfection of the past, even by implication. Comparisons are always dangerous, especially sexual ones. A woman may secretly worry that she is less successful than the first wife at housekeeping, looking after the children, or in bed. If the new partners were divorced, their ex-spouses may be only too much alive, demanding or threatening or manipulating the pair by means of finances or the children.

> A second wife, who had not been married before, told of her distress during a group session. Her husband's first wife, who had custody of the two children, created endless trouble over them, making excuses to prevent him seeing them, demanding money over and above the agreed payments, and using the children against him and their stepmother. He loved his children and was deeply hurt, feeling responsible and guilty. At the same time, he loved his new wife. She knew he was being torn by the conflicts for which she felt responsible by having married him. She also knew that she longed for a child herself by him, but that he could not really face any more stress in his life. So she had kept her anguish to herself, until it poured out in the group. As a result of discussing it openly there and finding that others sympathized with her dilemma, she plucked up the courage to talk to him about it. She was surprised to find him so understanding. They made plans together and she became pregnant two years later, to their mutual delight.

The first spouse's attack on a partner is present in its most extreme form in the abduction of their child, perhaps even to another country.

Once hostility between the parents reaches this pitch the damage is devastating, and particularly to the child.

The presence of children in the home may be more disruptive than the grief and guilt associated with their loss. In a new relationship the couple need time to enjoy each other and to talk out the many difficulties between them that arise from the conflicts in their basic assumptions and from the unmet expectations – and if need be to have a blazing row. With children around, there is often no time for the bliss or the row. The couple are too exhausted by bedtime to enjoy each other or to talk constructively. Moreover, the children add a triangular dimension to any conflicts.

Young children of second marriages have already suffered deeply because of the break-up of their parents' marriage and the conflicts that led to it, or because of bereavement. They are insecure, hurt, and angry, and not at all sure they welcome the step-parent. *His* children may resent *her* for replacing their mother and for now being first in their father's affections; and for not doing things the way their mother always did them. *Her* children will do the same to *him*, particularly resenting him if he tries to discipline them. These difficulties are greater if the children are adolescent, and are sometimes eased if a new baby is born, despite the half-sibling's sadness at being displaced, and envy of the fact that the new baby belongs to both parents. Pre-adolescent children show their distress in broken sleep, irritability, or withdrawal, and in behaviour problems at home or at school. Teenagers act out by resenting discipline, joining peer groups that may be delinquent, or by withdrawing into their own rooms away from the rest of the family.

The second wife is likely to be at home more of the time, coping with these turbulent emotions, trying to run the house (often on little money), attempting to be a mother to children she is not at all sure she can really love, and at the same time trying to cope with her own truculent children. Then, when her husband returns from work in the evening, she has little energy left for him. She is torn between her own children and him, angry with him if he is at all firm with them, especially if she had had them to herself for some time between the marriages; yet angry with them if they are so unpleasant to him that she fears they will drive him away. She tries hard to be good to *his* children, perhaps judging that she is giving them more care than their mother did; but they reject her and she wonders if it is worth the effort. Both parents tire of having to be 'grown up' all the time, caring for their needy children and for the needy child in their partner, never really having their own needs satisfied.

None of these problems are insurmountable, but they do account for much of the distress in women that lies hidden under the surface in second marriages. Setting aside time for discussing the difficulties openly between the partners and with the whole family, however potentially embarrassing, will remove many misunderstandings, and allow solutions to be found. It is a great relief to children to understand an adult's feelings, and to see that the 'wicked stepmother' is really a person like themselves who can also be unhappy and feel rejected. When the family in a second marriage can overcome the inherent problems, their lives can be enriched by each other, true affection can develop, and they can face the outside world, sure of family support.

Further reading

Franks, H. (1988) *Remarriage: What makes It. What Breaks It*, London: Bodley Head.

Willans, A. (1983) *Divorce and Separation*, London: Sheldon Press.

Chapter eighteen

Single motherhood

Jane Knowles

The single-parent family is becoming increasingly common and the majority of such families are led by women. For some, this is a matter of choice, but for many it is the force of circumstance. Single-parent families are usually born out of the decay and collapse of a marriage, a time that is psychologically exhausting for all the participants. Occasionally they result from the death or imprisonment of the father, events that are, if anything, even more traumatic than divorce. Hence, for most single parents their earliest days of attempting to parent alone are coloured by anger, grief, and guilt because of the circumstances leading up to their parental isolation. Because the pattern of the divorce tends to mirror the pattern of the previous marriage, emotional difficulties and physical violence may continue long after the law says that a marriage is over, looming like a black cloud over the heads of single parents.

A small but increasingly significant group of women choose to mother alone. Some make this choice for politico-feminist reasons, wanting parenthood but being unwilling to cohabit with a man. Others have powerful reasons in their past for being unable to imagine themselves relating lovingly to men for any length of time. They may have witnessed violence and hatred in their parents' marriage, or may have suffered physical or sexual abuse from men whom they had a right to trust, such as their fathers, brothers, or husbands. Not surprisingly, such experiences tend to make issues of trust in further heterosexual relationships an emotional minefield. A number make comments such as 'I wanted a baby and had no intention of doing all the work and then being forced to share decision-making with a less-involved partner, who might well back away from any sense of responsibility if our decisions turned out to be wrong' and 'It's easier to cope alone. I can be a mother to my child and not have to worry about mothering my bloke too.'

It is probably difficult for any woman to be sure of her reasons for making the decision to parent alone. It may well reflect a deep-seated need to prove her independence. The decision allows her to dismiss the importance of men, perhaps making the father of the child feel as useless and excluded as she herself has felt in past relationships. Or it may represent a defence against acknowledging the physical merging of two persons that conception entails. Whatever the psychological motives for the decision, there is no reason to believe that it is in any way a more psychopathological decision than to have a child within a marriage; simply a less common one. Certainly women who make this decision seem to do so from a position of psychological strength and can begin the single-parent journey with inner resources and advantages that women who are thrown into the situation do not, at least initially, possess, finding themselves unprepared psychologically or financially. The beginning of single parenthood is often beset with overwhelming practical difficulties: Where to live? How to finance the new family? How to gain support and help? As one such mother said,

> I suddenly felt I had to sort out all the details of our future in a moment. There we were, in the middle of the night, and what next? I'd made the decision to go, there was no going back, but the reality of leaving seemed like an endless range of mountains which I could never hope to conquer.

In fact, like the majority of women in this position, she set about conquering the seemingly unconquerable with considerable skill and energy. Some months later she said:

> I felt so good just to have survived. I look at our flat and although it's little and we don't have much, we are together, and for the first time the children and I are peaceful and not afraid any more. That's not just because we are away from the fighting, it's because I've realized I'm stronger and more capable than I ever thought I could be on my own.

Many women fear coping alone with the practicalities of finance and housing more than they fear the unhappiness and violence of their marital homes. Overcoming that fear is a first major hurdle, but the reward for discovering that they can cope is the increasing self-confidence and self-esteem that go with the discovery. In the first months of single parenthood many women report that it is the quality of their relationships, particularly with women friends, that makes the difference. If they have a supportive group of friends who can share the practical and emotional burdens sympathetically, they are less likely to feel isolated and abandoned. A mother finding herself alone may feel bitter at being left with so much responsibility. At such a time she may be vulnerable to suggestions from husband or family that she should return to the marriage 'I went back three times', Sally, a young-looking mother of three said, 'and each time I felt at the end of what I could bear. I was alone and felt I was on a desert island. It was the loneliness I was trying to escape from, and not the marriage that I wanted to go back to.' Sadly, but not surprisingly, such reunited marriages often fail again, leaving the woman with the same practical problems to face once more.

Single-sex therapy groups, in their various forms, can often provide a haven of support at this crucial time. They allow women a safe and confidential forum in which to discuss their fears without feeling that they are about to be condemned or rejected. Many women find difficulty in discussing their feelings about single parenthood, because people tend to dwell upon the potential harm to the children, rather than to focus upon the psychological wellbeing of the mother. As a woman in her forties, left with four teenagers to support, said:

> All my life as a mother I was told, overtly or covertly, that the children had to come first and that my feelings came way down anyone's list of priorities. When I was on my own I needed to give myself a higher priority in order to survive and function effectively. And yet, even then most of my friends, even other mothers, were telling me to put the children first because they must be upset by their father's desertion. One night I just exploded when my neighbour made this thoughtless comment. Of course I knew all about putting the good of the children first. I had been an ace martyr for years. Of course I was anxious for their wellbeing; part of my own distress was about their unhappiness. But in the final resort it was me who was down on her knees, it was me who had been deserted, and it was me who had to find what I needed if we were all going to survive. Once I had explained it like that to myself I never looked back.
>
> She found the support and help she needed in a women's group during the first two years. In that environment she was encouraged to put herself first at times and not to feel guilty. It became obvious that the children started to cope more adequately as a response to their mother's adjustments. Simon, aged 15, said of his mother, 'I really respect her now. Although we all suffered, I'm not sure I'd have felt as good about having the mother I have without all this. I might never had known that she is a really gutsy woman.'

As the weeks of single parenthood pass, there is an increasing tendency for women to deny their own needs. The pressures on them are great. Their children are often disturbed by their own experience of the separation, and may have difficulty in sleeping or eating, or may be unhappy at school (particularly if a change of school has been part of the general upheaval). They may blame the mother for the loss of their father, whatever the reasons for the separation. She may have financial and housing difficulties. Despite all these pressures, she may feel that she has to 'keep things normal' for the children, denying all the problems and her sense of sadness, emptiness, and frustration by putting on a brave face in front of children, family, and friends.

> As a teenager left alone with a new baby commented bitterly: 'I said I was doing fine so often I almost conned myself too. People were so stupid that they believed me; if they'd opened their eyes for a moment, they'd have seen the red eyes, the bitten nails, and the fact that, when I laughed, it came out more like a scream.'
>
> Her misery was not caused simply by the unresponsiveness of her friends, but by her own denial of her needs. She was convinced that she did not deserve help and that, even if she asked for it, nobody would give her anything. Rather than face the expected repeated rejection, she fooled herself, as well as everyone else, that all was well. When she finally broke down, the anger and resentment that accompanied her denial poured out, alongside her need for love and support.
>
> A 36-year-old widow with 8-year-old twins, said of her own needs, 'I buried them along with Tony (her husband). I remember thinking at the funeral, well, that's it Susan, now there is nothing and no-one for you. In a funny kind of way it made me feel strong to think like that and it held the sadness at bay.' Two years later, one of the twins broke his arm whilst climbing in a tree in their garden. 'Suddenly,' she recounted, 'I screamed at him. He stood there with his arm hanging at a funny angle crying because it was hurting him so much and all I could do was scream and scream. I was so furious with Tony for leaving me to cope with all this. How is anyone meant to cope alone?

It is hard for a single mother to accept that the reason she finds it difficult to cope is not because she is a failure as a person but because she is really being asked to do too much.

> A 19-year-old, with two children living in a bedsit, explained 'I wouldn't dare say I wasn't coping, even to myself, in case the social worker came and took the kids away. I simply can't afford not to cope, even if I know the reality is different. I suppose that eventually I will have played the coping game so long that I will forget what it feels like inside of me. I'll get cut off and hard, like I've seen happen to other girls like me. It's not what I'd have chosen, but where's the choice?'

Denying needs does not make them go away. This last patient was right in thinking that becoming 'cut off' from feelings of despair, inadequacy, and loneliness is a way to cope, although it is usually only successful in the short term. Many women use drugs or alcohol in order to produce that cut-off state, but motherhood, being the unpredictable and uncontrollable experience that it is, often overwhelms the denial, for example if one of the children becomes sick or has an accident. In that acute crisis, the bottled-up feelings come rushing out. Even if a woman suppresses her needs, there will be a growing resentment as time goes by that others do not recognize them. This is often more difficult to deny than the initial need and becomes a problem in itself. Because of this she may angrily dismiss friendship although the lonely, frightened woman inside longs to accept it.

She may be unwilling to have casual sexual relationships, and yet is frightened of another committed involvement. Her sexual needs are another difficult area. A woman sometimes cannot afford to be seen to have a new sexual relationship. If she has to depend on social security payments, she will be frightened to begin another sexual relationship in case this is seen as 'living with another man', in which case her money might be decreased or stopped altogether. If she is in a battle for custody, her solicitor may advise her to guard against further relationships, just at the time when her need for sex and to be cared for may be at their strongest.

> A 22-year-old with a 4-year-old son said: 'I felt that I couldn't be an attractive woman any more. I used this as an explanation to myself of why I was suddenly alone. I was terrified that Paul (the father of her son) would gain custody. He seemed to be able to offer much more than me and I thought that I had to be whiter than white if a judge was going to decide in my favour. Inside of me I was crying out for a man to notice me, compliment me, and fancy me. I could have felt alive again, but I was so scared of the consequences that I sent out lots of negative messages. Then I'd tell myself that nobody fancied me and that nobody ever would again. It seemed like the greatest loss in the whole horrible divorce.'

For a woman in the process of emerging from a violent marriage, in which sex was at best a duty and at worst a nightmare, the sensation of becoming sexually aware can be disturbing. Her sexuality may have been denied for years or never awoken in the first place. In the breathing space of single mothering, away from the pressure of having to relate to a man, her needs begin to surface, and yet ways of expressing them are limited or absent.

> A woman was 41 when she had her first child, rapidly followed by two more. At the age of 47 she decided she could not live with her husband any longer and left with the children. She commented, 'I'd missed the sexual revolution first time round and now I think my

> body would quite like to take the plunge and be more experimental. I know this sounds daft but I'm not sure how I will feel about myself if I take a few chances. I'm not sure that the moral code I've lived with for so long can bend enough to accommodate my new needs.'

An increasing number of such women leave marriages because they have either discovered that they are homosexual or have decided to give up the pretence of heterosexuality that marriage allowed them. For such women, the beginning of single parenting may coincide with new discoveries about their sexual nature. But they will also have to face a number of problems, in particular the fear that the courts will reject them as the custodial parent because of their sexual orientation, especially if their children are boys. Such fears leave them uncertain about how honest and open to be about themselves, even with friends and families, and yet at the same time they are frustrated and angry that they are not able to tell of their discovery about themselves.

> This problem was well expressed by a lesbian woman with a 5-year-old daughter and a 2-year-old son. She explained, 'I feel alright about my boy now. I can take him with me, and my friends accept him as a baby rather than a little boy. But I can see that in the future I am going to be torn between letting him get on with growing up as a male, and being ashamed of that in some situations. Once he is five I can't take him down to the Women's Centre anymore and a lot of my social contact at weekends is down there. A lot of my friends won't have anything to do with men and so they are going to find it harder to visit me. I want to do what is fair for him and yet, now that I have found this new life and warm friends, I don't want to lose that either.

It is not only their sons but children generally that seem out of place to these mothers as they first enter the homosexual world. This may be just a reflection of the fact that the number of such women is still relatively small. If their numbers grow, being a lesbian mother may become more normal and acceptable in both the outside world of the courts and the inside world of feminist lesbianism.

The practical needs of single mothers are also often ignored and unmet. For women from conventional backgrounds and marriages there may be a range of tasks and activities such as decorating, gardening, household repairs, and car maintenance that have previously been male activities. Suddenly as a single mother these have to be faced alone. Most women cope with this by enlisting help or learning to do the tasks themselves. One commented:

> My mother was appalled to see me with a power drill putting up bookshelves. She cried and said that she had never expected to see her daughter reduced to that. It was strange really, because I felt rather good about being able to do it once I had finished, but I felt angry half way through when things weren't going quite right. I thought, 'Why am I having to do this? I suppose that's an inner echo of all that my mother ever taught me.

There are also the many practical tasks of parenting that now need to be undertaken alone. No longer can the bathtime ritual be shared. Instead, a tired mother at the end of the day has to do it all herself. Transport to school, homework, clearing up mess, and repairing damage – all now drain one adult's energy, rather than two. Some single mothers make comments like, 'I did it all even when I was married, now at least I get all the credit too!' But for many, the total ongoing practical burden can feel heavy and unrelenting, and with no respite or support, anger and resentment towards the children can easily set in. Arranging Christmas or birthdays can be the saddest part of single mothering. At such times, the sense of being alone becomes acute and the responsibility of creating the expected happiness and surprise single-handed seems impossible.

Another major area of difficulty is the intensity of her feelings of depression or anxiety, which are the longer-term consequences of her unmet needs and her growing resentment and frustration. The severity of women's distress is often underestimated by helping agencies. Even if they go and seek help, they may well be dismissed as neurotic, attention-seeking, or hysterical, or be given a range of tranquillizers that may merely reduce their abilities to cope even further. Many are fearful of seeking help, struggling on for months and even years with depression, poor sleep, lack of appetite, and lack of energy, rather than risking missing work and losing the only income that supports them and their children.

Depressed single mothers find it hard to manage even the simplest task of mothering, and feel increasingly guilty that they are failing their children. They are often markedly anxious about them, which may be a result of their anger at the burden of mothering, but is also directly linked to their feelings of guilt and their sense of not being 'good enough'. It is important to help them to accept that they cannot be expected to perform the role of both parents. In every situation there are limits to what the mother alone can hope to achieve. The strain of being both the caregiver and the disciplinarian, the comforter and the one who sometimes has to say no, is great. It is difficult to find the energy to discipline older children, who may become wild and get into trouble. The worry about failing to meet all her own high standards leaves the mother even more depleted and less able to cope. She is caught in a vicious circle of misery, which is only finally relieved when the children grow up.

Another problem area for a single mother is how to express her anger. If she is isolated from other adults, the children may be the only possible targets for it, which in its expression may range from irritability, through verbal abuse, to beatings and torture. Children who remind the mother of the absent spouse are especially likely to be the victims. They are often aware of the explosive quality in their mother, even if she is keeping her rage under control, and may become confused and cautious as a result. It is another problem that is best helped by close and supportive friends who can understand and appreciate her need to let go of the tight control of her anger somewhere safe and away from the children, whenever this is possible.

The most unfortunate single mothers are those who rush into further unhappy and violent new relationships because they fear being without a man to protect them. They tend to repeat the disasters of their first choice of husband in the second relationship unless they have given much thought to what went wrong the first time. This becomes particularly tragic in those reconstituted families in which the new stepfather begins to abuse the woman's daughters sexually.

Most single mothers have to live within severe financial constraints because their work is low-paid and menial. They may have no marketable skills because they had limited education and no training. They may have to take what employment they can get in order to fit in with school hours, and can therefore be cruelly exploited by their employers. Lack of money makes it difficult to find accommodation. All too often they end up in the run-down inner-city areas, where life is cheaper, more violent, and less pleasant for women alone.

Even for a woman who has a career, there are problems with child care that are increased if she is the only responsible parent. Her job may be sufficiently demanding without also having to meet her children's demands in the evenings, at weekends, and during holidays. Such a life is extremely rigorous and tends to leave her feeling that she is 'sailing close to the edge' all the time.

In the initial months, and up to four or five years of being a single parent, her social network, particularly of supportive female friends, is the greatest protection against being overwhelmed by all these problems. Thereafter, it is her ability to earn a reasonable living and to feel accepted as a full and participating adult in her working world, that makes the all-important contribution to her self-esteem and her ability to cope. It makes good practical sense, therefore, to encourage women who become single parents to retrain, qualify, or re-engage in careers as quickly as possible.

As in all other areas of female psychological experience, a woman's relationship with her own mother may be a vital factor in her struggle to cope with single motherhood. The absent unsupportive mother will leave the daughter feeling abandoned at a crucial time in her life. Many women prefer to think that they do not deserve help rather than getting angry with their inadequate mothers. Thus the absence of her mother's support may result in the daughter feeling unable to ask for help from anyone else. If she does become angry with her mother, she often feels guilty, especially if her mother is old or ill. At the opposite end of the spectrum is the mother who seeks to re-enfold her daughter in a childlike relationship, proceeding to mother both her daughter and her grandchildren. This may be an appropriate reaction for a day or two during maximum crisis, but it can rapidly become an undermining experience for the single mother if it continues. Such a mother may become critical of her daughter if she senses that her autonomy and sense of responsibility is beginning to re-emerge, thus thwarting the growth of those important areas of self. Often marriage has obscured the previously pathological nature of the mother–daughter relationship and this reappears during its break-up. In such situations the children can often be beneficial in pointing the way to new things. As one woman commented, 'I suddenly realized that the children were standing up to my mum and saying things I wouldn't dare to. But she didn't disintegrate after all, and I found the courage to follow their example.'

Many women, however, find their mothers a major source of support and help. Indeed, their relationship may well improve as the single mother develops her ability to cope alone, while her mother gains new respect for her daughter. Many women have said that their relationships with their fathers improved similarly.

Although single motherhood is beset by difficulties, with massive demands and little support, it is impressive how few women say that they would rather be back in the former relationship. This is reflected in divorce figures, now revealing that twice as many women as men file for divorce. Only twenty years ago those women might well have stayed in relationships that, by their own descriptions, were more psychologically difficult than all the problems of single motherhood. Recent changes in the divorce laws enable a woman to leave a marriage with reasonable certainty of maintaining custody of her children. However, despite the problems and pressures on this growing group of women, the vast majority manage to cope well and find that living through the experience enriches and strengthens them. Their burdens would be eased if the caring professionals could show them that they understand their plight and the distress it causes.

Further reading

Barker, D.I. and Allen, S. (eds) (1976) *Dependence and Exploitation in Work and Marriage*, London: Longman.

Dowling, C. (1982) *The Cinderella Complex – Women's Hidden Fear of Independence*, London: Fontana.

Eichenbaum, L. and Orbach, S. (1985) *Understanding Women*, London: Penguin Books.

Letts, P. (1983) *Double Struggle: Sex Discrimination and One-Parent Families*, London: National Council for One-Parent Families.

Norwood, R. (1985) *Women who Love too Much*, London: Arrow Books.

Price, J. (1988) *Motherhood, What it does to your Mind*, London: Pandora Press.

Weiss, R. (1979) *Going it Alone. The Family Life and Social Situation of the Single Parent*, New York: Basic Books.

Useful address

GINGERBREAD
Secretary, Ms. J. Kausmann,
35 Wellington Street,
London, WC2E 7BN.
Tel: 01 249 0953.

Chapter nineteen

Stepmotherhood

Gill Gorell-Barnes

Stepfamilies have openly existed for many hundreds of years, but whereas they used to be formed following the death of a spouse and remarriage, the majority are now created by divorce and remarriage. Figures fell dramatically between the two world wars, but the estimate of marriages broken by death or divorce within twenty years of marriage is now in the region of 30 per cent, whereas the calculated figure for 1826 was 36 per cent. Remarriage within two years was normal.

Evidence gathered from 23 nineteenth-century working-class autobiographies with significant memories of stepfamily life suggests that there were many tensions similar to those in stepfamily life today (Burchardt, 1987). Grief and the need to mourn, unexpected poverty, associated strains of drinking and family violence, and children's resentment against a substitute parent or a natural parent's rejection of a separated child are all features that can be found today. Many of the outcomes and memories of these stepfamilies are positive; drawing on grandparents as a resource, or the welcome of a stepmother who brings relief to a bereaved family. Further work has also revealed the bonding factor of half-siblings born to the new marriage.

The stepmother role

Women in stepfamilies experience complex patterns of relationships, which may be difficult, unexpected, and stressful. In order to differentiate a sense of self, a stepmother has to be clear about the tendrils of emotional demand in which she is entwined. It may well be the lack of shared awareness of this complexity of stepfamily life (and the lack of channels for addressing the stress that this creates), that brings many women in stepfamilies to the attention of child-guidance clinics or to agencies offering therapeutic help to adults.

Women are usually assigned responsibility for the nurturing of human relations within the family. In stepfamilies, they not only carry the responsibility for making this second set of family relationships work, but they also have to do this under the scrutiny of critical observers, such as that of the former wife, her parents, and her wider family of origin.

In remarriage, a number of aspects of the daily family pattern have to be reorganized to include new functions from stepparent or cohabitee, and a loss of other functions for members of the family follow. Stepfamilies differ in the time they take to re-form. In some cases, parents and children will have spent a long time together before the single parent remarries; in others they will have moved straight from one two-parent household to another. If a divorced woman has been alone with her children prior to remarriage, space will need to be created in the intimacy shared during the single-parent phase for the adult partners to develop an alliance. The woman may have to give up some of the autonomy, including financial autonomy, that she experienced as a single parent, in order to allow authority to her new partner. A woman who has not previously been a mother may have to learn the tasks of mothering or parenting without having had the opportunity first to bond with the partner for whose children she is now in part responsible. The struggle to achieve a *new* balance, which does not replicate old models of the division of nurture, authority, and financial responsibility, is one of which women are now becoming more conscious. The new marriage and the family exist always against the background of the former marriage and of the loyalties to prior family systems that preceded the marital break-up.

In entering a second relationship with a legacy of a failed first relationship behind them, many women will hope that in this second relationship the balance of the family will be better than their earlier experience. They may hope for a more equal sharing of emotional responsibility for family relationships from the husband, as well as a more equal financial responsibility based on their own contributions and those of their former husband. Few will realize the complexity of the job they are taking on. Carter (1981; 1988) has explored the problems associated with the stepmother's central position. She has encouraged women to challenge the idea that they have to maintain traditional gender roles in the stepfamily situation. She stresses the unrealistic expectations placed on stepmothers to create happiness, erase guilt and unhappiness, and smooth angry interactions between husband and former spouse, as well as between children and their out-of-house parent. She emphasizes the value of permeable boundaries and open lines of communication between stepfamilies and ex-spouses, children and grandparents; the importance of spouses supporting one another in their responsibility for their own children, and the separation of family finance that acknowledges the contribution both of a former spouse and of the woman's own income, each partner perhaps managing different aspects of the family budget.

Most step-families will have to deal with children as part-time members of more than one household, which leads to many complexities of daily management. Movement between households constantly raises issues of divided loyalties, different expectations, and different requirements of behaviour. Small negotiations over access arrangements or the bearing of messages from one parent to another may be forums for much larger issues to be negotiated. Parents also need to face their own feelings about the resilience children may show in handling the differences in management of two households. They have to contain their curiosity over how life is managed in the home of a former spouse, and the pain of wondering how for part of the time their children manage so well without them.

The loyalty between the parents and the children precedes the formation of the couple. This often creates a powerful intergenerational alliance that may be difficult for a new couple to manage when either partner feels pulled in the direction of supporting a child in an argument against the other person. The dilemmas caused by this intergenerational alliance and the need for the children to adjust their position in relation to the new adult alliance may require constant negotiation. A fuller discussion of this may be found in Gorell-Barnes, (1984). As one mother cogently described the change that had to be made:

> I suppose honestly before I met Ted, we were on our own, and obviously Cliff would be a bit protective of me because he was the man of the house, wasn't he, and to be fair, ever since he was small, I've always spoken to him more as an adult than a child. He's been included in everything and if adults were in the room, he'd be included, he wouldn't be sent to bed, and so I suppose he's a little in advance of his years. He really has to drop down a step.

There may be doubt (or uncertainty) about which couple or parent is the primary reference point for decisions about a child. While large decisions may lead to stepfamily thought about how matters are to be handled, smaller situations may receive less attention. For example, to have a visiting child look constantly to her father for confirmation that she should do what her stepmother asks her to do can build up a tension that connects the stepmother to the child's own out-of-house mother in a way that becomes too powerful, giving too much weight to a relationship based on competition for authority over a child. A stepmother may feel frozen or clipped by the constraint of a family system that 'requires' that she does *not* assert herself in small ways. For a woman, the demand to be an equally good or better mother than a prior spouse from whom a separation has taken place is both a challenge, a seduction, and a danger; since to be better than someone who is loved but lost, and still held very dear by the children, is a very precarious position in which she is unlikely to get backing from any other family member.

Grandparents

A further complication may be created by alliances with grandparents, who may maintain loyalty to the previous marriage after the parents themselves have decided that the marriage is over. In many ways, grandparents may subtly undermine the position of a new woman in the family who is seen as disrupting a previously stable system in which their position as the older generation was securely established. Death, rather than divorce, may compound the fear that access to the next generation will be blocked at the point where a new mother is seen to be taking over the place of a deceased parent.

> A couple who had married following the death of the father's former wife sought consultation about the stepmother's right to become attached to the children (then under 18 months and 3 years old) in view of the grandparents' deep attachment to them. The grandparents had cared for the children following their mother's death. Some discussion of how their relationship with their grandchildren kept their daughter alive for them also revealed the new couple's anxiety about the grandparents' anger at the new couple getting together before they (the grandparents) were ready to 'sanction a new marriage'. Inevitably, the grandparents saw this as displacing the memory of their dead daughter for her children. The couple needed time to consider whether they or the grandparents had primacy in deciding on the children's future pattern of attachment. The second wife throughout showed extreme delicacy in relation to the grandparents' views, but needed permission from her husband to assume the primary maternal role in relation to very young children of whom she was very fond and who were attached to her.

The position of a newly married or cohabitating couple may therefore be potentially threatened both by the generation that precedes it and by the generation that follows it. The effort to organize a routine pattern of life in which reliable habits can be anticipated from the family members, with attendant peace of mind, can be exhausting and time-consuming. While it is essential that the couple find time for themselves, they very rarely have the opportunity to do this. Women who have never previously experienced jealousy of a relationship between parent and child may find themselves profoundly jealous of the intimacy between a new partner and a daughter (as may men between a mother and her son), and of course the jealousy and hurt may be profound if the relationship becomes pathological, as in stepfather/stepdaughter incest.

The illusion that there will be immediate bonding between stepparents and children also causes problems. Relationships can only develop as part of the process of sharing and creating new patterns of life together over time. The creation of such patterns also needs to take into account the fact that children often hang on to the fantasy of their parents coming together again, long after a new partnership is established. A recognition of this wish, and some clear statements by parents that this is not going to happen, can bring relief to children who are getting stuck in their inability to make use of the new relationships offered within the second family. The arrival of a new baby often acts both as a provoker of crisis and a catalyst in focusing on and resolving these issues (Burchardt, 1987).

In stepfamily life, two kinds of change have to take place simultaneously – external change and internal change. The interactions of the new family have to develop their own shape in relation to sets of loyalties to previous relationships, as well as to a set of current relationships. The original internalized structure of the family as a whole is often not experienced as lost until a spouse finds himself up against serious difficulties in the second partnership or family structure. The pain caused by this second sense of failure or letdown may make the partners wonder why they separated from their former spouses and broke up their original families. Comprehension of the power of prior ways of thinking, feeling, and believing can help women to understand how to facilitate adaption to the new situations in the life of the family. To be able to say: 'I know in your family you used to do it this way but let's sit down and think about how we are going to do it in this family here', can create a new focus of energy and attention that allows a juxtaposition of past and present in a facilitating way. Women may have to talk through with their own children and with their spouse's children the pain of loss for that part of the self that was constituted in the original family, and thus to find a way in which this self can develop free from some of the constraints that characterized the original family pattern. Such a freedom depends on a recognition of the loss and its accommodation in the joint processes of living together in the second family, with all the possibilities that has to offer.

The dilemma of centrality is familiar to many stepmothers, as illustrated by the following example.

> Linda, the stepmother, had married Bob, following each of their divorces. Linda had two children, Rachel and John by her first marriage and Bob had two, Siobhan and Kathleen by his. When

Linda and Bob first lived together, they only had to care for Linda's children of whom she had custody. However, three years later, following the unexpected death of Bob's former wife, Didi, in an air crash, the two girls came to live with Bob and Linda. The family were finding Siobhan's failure to take her school work seriously sufficiently problematic to consult for help. The following extract was chosen to show how the problem (school failure) connects to Siobhan's chosen representation of her dead mother in the stepfamily, where she feels there is no overt way her mother can be remembered and made part of everyday life. This in turn relates to Bob and Didi's previous inability ever to work out their parenting plans for the girls following their divorce. They had followed the conflicted co-parent model (Lund, 1987) after their divorce, and Linda had acted as a mediator. The extract follows Siobhan's growing awareness that she is keeping the memory of her mother alive by acting like her mother in putting 'fun before work'. The discussion has been about whether photos of Didi could be included in a family photoboard in the kitchen.

Siobhan: I guess I act in this way because they're all so serious and hardworking. My mum liked to have fun. I like to remember her.

Therapist: In what way do you think it would be a problem Didi becoming more of the family memory, instead of her photo being shut away in a drawer in your desk in your room and you having to fail school all the time?

Linda: It would be difficult all of a sudden for the girls to put her picture up where Bob could see it – it would be uncomfortable.

Therapist: She's still a powerful memory for him, that would upset him?

Siobhan: Yes she was, but she was really a fun lady.

Linda: I guess that the memories you have are going to be different from the memories Daddy has. The two of them could never get along. I had to manage all the negotiations between them.

Therapist: These memories are a part of all your lives in a different way, but they are part of the girls' growing up and their identity – do they need to be kept so secret?

Siobhan: I don't mind keeping it for myself; no offence, but I mean – I still don't feel this is my family. If I were with my grandmother in Glasgow, I could still have the photos up.

Therapist: Is this a problem for you – are you going to cruise for

	the next five years, or are you going to join *this* family at some point?
Siobhan:	I don't know: I mean we have fun – but – I also think a lot about Rachel and John too – this must be difficult for them.
Rachel:	(burst out crying and shouts) I feel so upset, I don't think this is fair at all – it's like the two of you are just rejecting us totally – we can't do anything correct – you say we're not your family and we've all been trying so hard to be that.
Siobhan:	We didn't say you hadn't been trying.
Rachel:	I feel that Mum feels really rejected as if she hasn't achieved anything.
Siobhan:	I didn't say anything against her. (Linda is weeping)
Therapist:	(to father) How do you feel when you have these two women weeping (indicating Linda and Rachel) and the other two women your daughters, saying they are not going to be part of the family?
Bob:	(slowly and thoughtfully) It's pretty difficult – I think I see it a little bit differently – I sometimes wonder if Linda works too hard – if she could step back – and maybe let the girls sort it out more themselves – maybe she doesn't have to take it all on.

This new perception by the man in the family came as a revelation to his wife, who needed his permission not to work so hard to be the good mother for all four children as well as making up to her two stepdaughters for their mother's loss. The recognition by Bob of the importance of Didi's memory to his daughters in spite of his own angry memories of her, led to new negotiations initiated within the session. Siobhan and Kathleen were to make time to meet their father on their own as his daughters to talk about their dead mother. Siobhan was put in charge of organizing a young-person's rota for household tasks, which was to be agreed with Linda and designed to give her time off; and so that Linda was not left feeling displaced, she was put in charge of ensuring that the emotional work in the family was done. This included her spending time with Bob every evening discussing his ideas on how things were going in their new family.

It will be seen that in this chapter the position of the stepmother and her centrality is taken as a fundamental dilemma for women in stepfamily life. Therapy addressed to women who are stepmothers needs to take this key position and all its complexities into account and to focus on the reorganization of the pattern within the stepfamily, and between the stepfamily and other aspects of the wider family system of which it is a part.

Further reading

Carter, E.A. and McGoldrick, M. (1981) *The Family Life Cycle*, London and New York: Gardner Press.

Gorell-Barnes, G. (1984) 'Stepfamilies' in *Working with Families*, London: MacMillan/BASW, Chapter 6.

Maddox, B. (1975) *Step-parenting: Living with Other People's Children*, London: Unwin Paperbacks.

Raphael, K. (1986) *A Step-parent's Handbook*, London: Sheldon Press.

Visher, B. and Visher, J.S. (1988) *Old Loyalties, New Ties: Therapeutic Strategies with Stepfamilies*, New York: Brunner/Mazel.

Useful address

STEPFAMILY (National Association of Stepfamilies),
162 Tenison Road,
Cambridge, CB1 2DP.
Tel: 0223 460312/3.

Chapter twenty

Femininity assaulted

Hysterectomy, gynaecological malignancy and mastectomy

> Beauty is momentary in the mind –
> The fitful tracing of a portal;
> But in the flesh it is immortal.
>
> Wallace Stevens (1879-1955)

A woman's identity, her perception of herself as a woman, her femininity, and her self-confidence are closely bound up with her body image. The reflection she sees in her mirror will be less important than the view that other important people in her life reflect back to her. If she feels good, she is also likely to appear attractive to others; if she feels attractive, she is also likely to feel good. From our earliest days we benefit from experiencing the approval and admiration of others – first of our mothers, then of our fathers, and then of the wider world. Such enhancement of a woman's self-esteem is important throughout her life.

Things that adversely affect a woman's appearance are likely to create a degree of distress that is disproportionate to the importance or severity of the blemish in health terms, but reflects its psychological significance for her. Adolescents, particularly, may become preoccupied with their appearance, worrying about a few spots or the shape of their nose, experiencing their breasts as too small or too large, and feeling their whole identity threatened by a casual remark construed as critical. But with maturity most women come to terms with their imperfections, acknowledging them as part of their own uniqueness and knowing that real beauty has more to do with personality and a capacity for loving than with perfection of physical features. However, the increase in confidence and wellbeing often noted to follow successful cosmetic surgery – be it for harelip, birthmark, protruding ears, or unattractive nose – confirms the importance attached to appearance (Edgerton *et al*, 1960).

> A sophisticated and glamorous businesswoman in her mid-thirties was referred with depression and relationship problems. She was

elaborately coiffured and made-up, and was contemplating further plastic surgery. Having already had her nose remodelled three times and her breasts revised twice, she expressed her lack of self-acceptance and inner dissatisfaction by attempting to change her external appearance and to conceal her (inner) flaws. Her depression lifted as she found herself accepted in the therapy group which she attended for eighteen months. Following treatment, she gave up her pursuit of physical perfection and began to ask for what she *really* wanted, with a consequent improvement in her relationship with her partner.

A constant preoccupation with some blemish, which appears unremarkable or, indeed, invisible to the observer, may herald serious mental illness (Hay, 1983). Doctors should beware of unhappy people who constantly seek to remodel their appearance, since it is unlikely to help their inner dissatisfaction with themselves. The similarity with eating disorders is clear, and such problems may co-exist.

A teenage girl began to find it difficult to eat. She was obsessed with odd spots and blemishes on her face and body, and picked at them constantly, gouging with her nails so that she scarred herself badly. Plastic surgery in her twenties to improve her disfigured face was complicated by infection, and worse scarring (keloid) resulted. Although she was still picking holes in herself, prolonged surgery and skin-grafting followed, during the course of which she finally asked for psychotherapeutic help. She wrote 'My messing with my skin went almost hand in hand with dieting. Obviously I was not very happy about myself. I can think of many contributory factors in relation to my difficulties but realize there must be more to it; I have continued all these years to be self-destructive and do not want to carry on like this. I really do need help.'

As a woman grows older, she needs to accept the inevitable changes wrought by aging. Her skin loses its elasticity and becomes wrinkled, her hair becomes grey, her body contours change, her vision and hearing may deteriorate so that she needs spectacles or a hearing aid, joint problems may limit her mobility. Most women accept the aging process and the gradual loss of their youthful attractions. The benefits of maturity may outweigh the inevitable losses, and if she has a partner, also growing older, who accepts her as she is, sheer physical attributes will be of little importance to her. If she is alone and looking for a new relationship, physical appearance and deterioration may be feared and experienced as a handicap.

For many women, however, illness strikes in middle or later life and may bring problems, either in itself, or resulting from its treatment, which savagely assault their feminine identity. Anything that alters a woman's appearance will diminish her 'marketplace value' (Meyers, 1965) and disadvantage her in competition with others. A cerebrovascular episode may leave her with facial asymmetry, even if she escapes serious paralysis and physical disability. An accident may leave her scarred, commonly on face and hands, the parts that, because they show, were therefore unprotected from flying glass or hot liquid. Malignant disease of mouth, face, or head may require extensive and disfiguring surgery – the enucleation of an eye, the removal of half the jaw. Both the curious stare and the averted gaze of the passer-by cause distress.

Self-confidence is related to appearance, and we look for approval in the gaze of others. Extensive surgery that leaves relatively minor surface scars may be more easily accepted than relatively minor surgery that involves disfigurement and mutilation, particularly of the face and head, and of the breast and genitalia. The symbolic meaning of the operation for the woman depends on the significance of the bodily part or organ concerned and on the value that she attaches to it (Lindemann, 1941; 1958).

Every patient who is facing an operation reacts in a particular and individual way, depending on personality and previous life experience. The severity of the condition, the nature and pathology of the illness and the possible consequences for body image and function will all affect the patient's reaction. Unconscious factors play a basic role in the development of anxiety during the pre-operative phase and, when anaesthesia is necessary, death fears may emerge. Partial or full removal of an organ may be connected with fears of childhood punishment. On becoming a patient, a normally mature and responsible woman surrenders her autonomy and her right to self-determination, and becomes a relatively powerless child in the hands of powerful professional 'parent figures' who may take responsibility for life and death decisions without open consultation, and who indeed may deliberately withhold information from her.

The uterus and breasts contribute to a woman's sexual identity. They are related to the concepts of femininity, sexuality, procreation, and motherhood and are necessary parts of a woman's body image. The Greek word *hyster* is now familiar to us for its etymological association with both hysterectomy and hysteria – an indication that the uterus was associated with the psyche. The old English word 'womb' means belly or stomach or deep cavity. As the organ from which all higher mammals are delivered to a separate and independent existence, it is uniquely female. Primitive cultures have left us abundant evidence of womb worship. Reproduction ensured survival of the species; fertility rites were of prime importance. But today, overpopulation is recognized as the major problem and with it, the need to control reproductive capacity. The uterus has been reduced in significance to an organ with functions of menstruation and pregnancy – which may be convenient for some, inconvenient for others, at various times. Yet the psychological importance of the uterus and the consequences of its removal have meaning because the uterus is central to a woman's sense of wholeness and wellbeing.

Many women deeply regret losing the possibility of choice of which hysterectomy deprives them – the opportunity to have a baby if they want one, even though that prospect may be unlikely. They value the meaning and reassurance of their menstrual periods, a sign of their womanliness.

> A gifted artist of 40 sought psychotherapy for disabling depression. In her late teens she had had regular hormone treatment because menstruation was not established, and had been told that she might never conceive. She had been overjoyed to find herself pregnant, feeling fulfilled and creative in a very special way. After the birth of her babies she had haemorrhaged excessively. Eventually at 36, because of severe dysfunctional uterine bleeding, she had been advised to have a hysterectomy. She described her sense of profound loss and desolation, the recognition that something precious had gone for ever, and her feeling of being left somehow asexual and indeterminate, cheated of her birthright. She became deeply depressed.

Conflicting evidence has resulted from research into the psychological consequences of hysterectomy (Sloan, 1978). Younger women are more easily able to accept hysterectomy for the treatment of *serious* disease. It is more likely to be followed by depression if there has been previous psychiatric disturbance, or if marital relationships are strained. If the symptoms for which hysterectomy is recommended are severe, the operation is likely to be welcomed, and health improves post-operatively. There is comparatively little in the literature about the psychological effects of treatment of gynaecological malignancies and about the effects of gynaecological surgery generally, considering that hysterectomy is the most commonly performed major operation for women of reproductive age in Europe and America. The operation is done twice as frequently in America and Australia as in Britain, which may reflect the higher number of gynaecologists per head of population. When health-insurance benefits provided by a union in one American state were changed so that hysterectomy for some indications did not attract full benefits, the rate fell dramatically and was maintained at the lower level. It rose again immediately the insurance benefits were restored. In 1974, Bunker and Brown calculated that 33 per cent of women in the USA had had a hysterectomy by the age of 65; this rose to 50 per cent for physicians' wives! In the USA an estimated 700,000 hysterectomies are done each year. If this rate continues, *half* the female population could be expected to lose their wombs by the age of 65.

Hysterectomy is sometimes advocated on 'prophylactic' grounds for relatively mild problems, on the basis that after child-bearing is complete, the uterus becomes a useless bleeding potentially cancerous organ best removed. Meyers (1965) pointed out that the prophylactic removal of the prostate in men, an operation analogous in many respects to hysterectomy, has not found enthusiastic advocacy. He suggested that perhaps surgeons, largely male, have more respect for the integrity of masculine anatomy.

> A 55-year-old woman was referred with a ten-year history of depression that had been treated at times with antidepressants and tranquillizers. The therapist discovered that her depression had been precipitated by a hysterectomy. She described her terrible shock and panic at being told by her doctor that she 'ought to have a hysterectomy', and the feeling that something precious and central to her whole existence was being threatened. Because she was so depressed afterwards, she sought a private appointment with the gynaecologist 15 months later. He told her that there were no after-effects from hysterectomy. The uterus was simply a baby carriage for which she had no more use. It was better removed.

Genital cancer presents a double threat to a woman; first, a threat to her physical survival, which is obvious, and dealt with by an impressive battery of surgical techniques, magical rays, and powerful drugs, and second, a threat to her sense of self, her identity as a woman, her body image, and her personal and cultural roles. These threatening aspects may be *invisible* to everyone else (Krant, 1981). The problem is sizeable. About 13,000 new cases of genital cancer are registered in Britain each year. Happily, relatively few will be in women under 25 years of age, bur carcinoma of the cervix and of the ovary have a significant incidence during the next decade – the years when most women are occupied with child-bearing and rearing young children – and then will rise dramatically during the years surrounding the menopause, after which there is some levelling out.

The majority of these women will have radical treatment if their condition is operable. They will lose their uterus, ovaries, and appendages at operation – and thus their capacity to bear children; they will lose their regular menstrual flow, and experience an abrupt menopause with the attendant discomfort of hot flushes, disturbed sleep and appetite, and emotional upheaval. Many will have radiotherapy or chemotherapy in addition – treatments that some women find very unpleasant and which have, until recently, been characterized by unpleasant unwanted effects including nausea, vomiting, and hair loss.

Some women will ask for, or be told, their diagnosis and likely prognosis and be invited to share in the decision-making process – that is, to exert some choice or influence in treatment. Most will not be given the opportunity for open discussion, and the word *cancer* will not be used. Most of them will know why they are having all this treatment, and the reaction of others, including informed spouses, to their illness may distress and confuse them. A secret within a close relationship may be alienating and isolating. Staff who cannot be trusted and seen to be truthful cannot expect to have their reassurance believed when they are genuinely optimistic and encouraging. Regular appointments for progress checks will always provoke anxiety, followed by relief if reassurance is given. Even the simplest routine test, such as a blood check for anaemia, will have sinister implications until the 'good result' is relayed to the patient, and x-rays and scans may be seen as evidence that the doctor has 'found something suspicious'. Some women are reassured by regular check-ups and take them as a hopeful measure, feeling the doctor cares about them. Others prefer to forget about this frightening episode in their lives, and do not want to consider their state of health unless forced to do so, regarding check-ups as an unnecessary intrusion.

> A woman of 67 was referred with continuous nausea that developed after she had had several fits. Extensive investigations had revealed no cause for either fits or nausea. She was clearly clinically depressed. Twelve years previously she had undergone a Wertheim's hysterectomy for advanced cancer of the cervix and against all expectations had remained disease-free. She had seen her surgeon for annual consultations until his death five years earlier. She had never been *told* that she had cancer, and her fears that the fits might have been caused by brain tumours were 'laughed away' by all her attendants. She initially responded well to ventilation of her feelings and fears and a small dose of antidepressants, and she ceased to be 'sick with fear'. She used individual psychotherapy to express her anger and terror of dying of cancer, later working through the loss of her womb, which had been her only link with two sons who had perished at birth.

Cancer of genital organs brings out repressed conflicts arising from earlier psychosexual development, as well as real or fantasized guilt over sexual transgressions in the past. Cancer may be seen as a punishment for this guilt and shame. Many women, and especially younger patients, fear the postoperative effects that radical surgery will have on their love life, but it is only recently that attention has been paid to this vitally important area. The meaning of sexuality for cancer patients is as variable as for the rest of the population. However, there has been a growing awareness that intimacy, closeness, and sexual activity are linked. Sexual intimacy is one of the most rewarding and sought-after experiences life has to offer; its importance is not diminished by the unfortunate experience of developing cancer (Derogatis and Kourlesis, 1981). Despite much evidence to the contrary, many people, including doctors, still believe that there is a dramatic decline in libido when an individual reaches the age of 55, progressing to an essential asexuality by the time they reach pensionable age. However, the most frequent deterrent to satisfying sex for older women is the absence of an interested partner. Becoming ill often does not alter the importance of sexuality to elderly patients. Focus on cure or amelioration of the cancer relegates the patient's sexual functioning to a low priority in the eyes of the treating specialist, *regardless* of how important it is to the patient. Interviews with women undergoing radical pelvic surgery for cancer have revealed their intense fears about what their life will be like after surgery. They are concerned about their body image and attractiveness, about their sexual functioning postoperatively, and about the survival and stability of their marriages.

A retrospective study of 46 women who underwent surgery for pelvic genital cancer classified patients into three groups according to the type of surgery (Sewell and Edwards, 1980). It was predicted that the more severe the surgery, the greater would be the influence on the patients – emotionally, psychologically, socially, and sexually. The researchers found to their surprise that personality factors and social-adjustment measures were clearly related to each other, but not to body image or sexual functioning. The women responded to the crisis with psychological defences that enabled them to re-establish a sense of psychological wellbeing in a relatively short period of time (six months). However, there was a significant change in body image, sexuality, and interpersonal relationships as a result of surgery in all three patient groups. A longstanding relationship with a partner was less likely to deteriorate. Thirty per cent reported a marked deterioration in their relationship as a result of surgery, and five relationships terminated completely.

Mastectomy

> The finest bosom in nature is not
> so fine as what imagination forms.
>
> Gregory
> *A Father's Legacy to his Daughters (1809)*

Breast cancer is the commonest cancer in women, accounting for one-fifth of all female cancer deaths. One woman in twelve develops breast cancer, and 25,000 women in Britain develop the disease every year. Because there is so much publicity about the disease, every woman who discovers a breast lump fears that she has cancer. Nine out of ten breast lumps prove to be benign but, unlike surgery performed on internal organs where the degree of both disease and surgical excision will be concealed, the extent of breast surgery is obvious, and any extensive surgery will quite clearly have been performed for one reason only – breast cancer.

Recently, limited excision of the tumour with the breast tissue immediately surrounding it (lumpectomy) associated with chemotherapy and radiotherapy has become the new trend in the surgical approach to breast cancer. But mastectomy is still a very common operation, and much of the fear of breast cancer is due to every woman's dread of mastectomy, which involves the loss of a valued part, a symbol of femininity and sexuality, which reduces a woman's attractiveness. She has to cope not only with this blow to her femininity, but also with the constant reminder of her potentially life-threatening disease, which is forced upon her every time she looks at herself. This constant reminder is also a burden for her partner, who will have to cope with his own sense of loss at her disfigurement, and his fear that she will die. Most women faced with mastectomy would choose to have immediate surgical reconstruction to avoid the sense of mutilation, even if advised that the risk of recurrent disease is slightly increased. Morale and general sense of wellbeing is greatly improved by later cosmetic surgery in both apparently well-adjusted and coping women and those with marked postmastectomy morbidity (Maguire, 1976).

Many women have consulted us following mastectomy. Some of them have died of their disease, but most of them have survived. Some have known that their disease was advanced by the time that they consulted us, and others have come because they lived in a state of constant fear that their disease would overcome them, in spite of all evidence and reassurance to the contrary. The disturbance to their image of themselves has been considerable. Many of them have been unable to look at themselves or to touch their scars, and take care never to be seen without clothing by their husbands or their families. They avoid looking at themselves in the bath or washing the scarred area, and may remove mirrors from the bathroom.

> One woman, who had previously survived severe life-threatening illness and much abuse, described her experience thus: 'You know how they used to stone witches? I feel like that, as if they are piling on the stones. I have put a notice on my bedroom door to remind me, because sometimes I forget and think I am normal.' She had

pinned up a notice saying 'Don't forget, you are not normal, you are mutilated.'

A patient was referred from the breast clinic thirteen years after her mastectomy. An ample woman, she wore a tee shirt printed with 'Fruit of the Loom' and luscious fruits over her false bosom. She had never had any opportunity to talk about the meaning of her surgery and her grief at having lost her breast. Her own needs had always been subservient to those of the rest of her family, and her husband's heart surgery one year after her mastectomy had totally overshadowed her own illness. She described how another woman had consoled her by saying, 'never mind, your one breast is more than most women have with two', but she observed sadly that 'even a couple of fried eggs are better than a false breast, if they are your own'.

Very young women who suffer a mastectomy fear not only for their own lives, but for the effect that their disease will have on their partner and their children. They fear that their husbands will leave them, and if their partners exhibit any distaste for their scarred body, find themselves unwilling to engage in sexual activity. One woman never forgave her husband for saying that it 'turned him off'.

Sometimes one session to ventilate her feelings about the things that have happened to her will be sufficient for a woman to go on to make a good recovery. For others, brief focal therapy is required. Regular weekly sessions – usually between six and twelve hours in total – are used to explore the anxieties, feelings, and fantasies associated with the discovery of the cancer and its treatment, which remains the central focus of the psychotherapy. Diversion into other aspects of past and present life experience is generally avoided by the therapist's encouragement to focus selectively upon it. If there are long-standing problems with relationships, or general life difficulties, the breast cancer may simply serve as the focus that brings them for treatment, but it will not necessarily be the central issue of therapy.

Many women make major life changes following a mastectomy, perhaps giving up a stressful job, or deciding to leave an unrewarding marriage. If a woman is young, with dependent children, she may feel unable to make changes despite wishing to do so, because she fears a recurrence of her disease.

A young woman with two small children left a convalescent ward shortly after having a mastectomy. Her husband, a difficult man who drank and often abused her, beat her that night, calling her 'a boobless bitch'. She was too frightened of him to assert herself against his violence, and too frightened of her disease to risk leaving home with her children. She was able to use brief therapy

> to express her feelings without fear of being brutalized, and her depression lifted. She discontinued therapy as it became clear that her real wishes would lead her to a choice she dared not contemplate.

Women with nubile daughters often feel envious of their developing figures, and this increases their misery.

> A strikingly attractive woman with an easy smile, proud of her body and her physical agility, engaged regularly in sporting pursuits. She was referred after reconstructive surgery had failed, leaving her with a result that was cosmetically far worse than the initial mastectomy. She insisted on undressing at interview to demonstrate the ugly body that she could not bear to look at herself. She had not felt able to share this with friends or family, and feared the effect that it might have on her teenage daughter who was developing a womanly figure, and for whom she felt the need to be a successful feminine model. The woman was angry at the way in which, at her follow-up appointment, the doctor had sat her on a stool and eyed her critically, appraising her figure. When she asked if she could put on her blouse, he had replied that he was 'not looking at her as a woman'. She had found this to be offensive because he confirmed her own feelings about herself, that she was indeed no longer fit to be looked at as a woman, but as a freak or specimen.
>
> Her easy smile concealed deep rage and bleak despair that she should have been left to face the world in this mutilated way. When another patient had asked her whether reconstructive surgery was worth having, she had replied that it certainly had not been so for her. She felt that this had incurred the surgeon's wrath and that if she returned for further surgery to correct the deformities, he would punish her by deliberately permitting further disaster. These fantasies were too painful and shameful to articulate, and her relief at the acknowledgement of this possibility during psychotherapy was immense. Her disabling symptoms immediately abated, and after only three sessions of therapy she decided that she would approach the surgeon again, having previously been filled with panic and being unable to go into hospital when summoned.

The importance of feeling in control of her treatment, and of participating actively in decisions about her own body and her own future is important in sustaining a woman's morale. The disease seems even more frightening if she feels out of control.

> An intelligent woman in her fifties was referred for a consultation a year after mastectomy. She was used to making decisions and

being in control of her life. Following previous removal of a benign breast tumour, she had attended for annual check-up, when a sinister lump was noted. A mastectomy was performed the following day, which had not given her time to adjust to the prospect, nor to make any plans. An important family celebration had to be cancelled, and she was angry at this interruption in her life and at the mutilation. She felt unready to contemplate her own death, but found it difficult to share her fear with anyone else. She sought counselling help, but was dismayed to find that the counsellors had not suffered from cancer themselves. She was deeply resentful that she had not been permitted to share in the decision-making about the management of her breast cancer.

Sometimes women seek psychotherapeutic help when they have advanced disease.

A young woman with a small child was referred for psychotherapy immediately after a mastectomy for almost inoperable tumour. She had rejoiced in her sexuality and her womanly figure, and was panic-stricken at the discovery that she had cancer. As her disease progressed inexorably, she used therapy with an intensity increased by her knowledge of the short time left to her. She confronted death, which held so much terror for her. She confronted her sexuality and the implication of the loss of the breast of which she had been so proud. She confronted her previous life experiences, and was able to work with the feelings of guilt and fantasies of retribution that the disease brought in its wake. She died only five months after her mastectomy. Her death was inevitable, but she triumphed because she was ready to meet it.

The major issue, common to all who develop cancer, is that the diagnosis confronts the universal illusion of immortality. The only two major points in life beyond personal control are conception and death. Between these two points we are able to exercise will and choice and we may properly expect to be in control of our daily lives. When a woman is well, normal life expectancy is taken for granted. With the diagnosis of cancer, the automatic entitlement – the normal life expectancy – is lost. Normal grief requires the acceptance of personal mortality; a recognition that suffering and death can be mitigated, but that death is our ultimate fate.

There are several common concerns that women with cancer bring to psychotherapy, including anxiety about their mortality, awareness of their vulnerability, anger about mutilation, and dread of alienation. They also bring all their unique life experiences, both past and present, but they bring them with a degree of urgency that is not characteristic of most patients who come for psychotherapy. Old issues are brought into immediate and urgent focus when the woman realizes the importance of the present as the only time that she can be sure of having. Most of us live our lives with many discontents, and put off making changes because we feel that there will be plenty of time to do so in the future. When the future is under threat, such hazy and distant concerns may be perceived with a fresh urgency and immediate attention may be required for issues that have actually been present and neglected for many years, including difficulties in relationships with parents and partners. The psychotherapist with an interest in working in this field requires flexibility and sensitivity. The degree of help required varies from a single exploratory consultation or crisis intervention, through brief focal work, to long-term psychotherapy over many years. In some cases, psychotherapy has to continue through the vicissitudes of the disease right up until death.

When life may be endangered, it is the proper concern of doctors to protect their patients' health, and a woman facing life-threatening illness will usually want to co-operate with the treatment that will offer the best chance of survival, however painful and distressing in the short term. It is usual medical practice for a diseased organ to be removed. However, it is important that doctors should be aware of the meaning that certain organs have for their women patients, and the significance of certain treatment procedures.

Serious morbidity may follow treatment that has been planned to prolong life, without full consideration of the individual cost to the woman in immediate suffering, general morale, and quality of life. If she is included in discussion about possible courses of treatment open to her, and encouraged to share responsibility for the decision, she will be better able to give informed consent, and to choose the course that is best for her and for her family – a truly healthy course in the context of her particular life experience.

Further reading

Robinson, N. and Swash, I. (1977) *Mastectomy. A Patients Guide to Coping with Breast Surgery*, Wellingborough, Northants: Thorsons.

Useful addresses

The Breast Care and Mastectomy Association
26a Harrison Street,
London, W.1
Tel: 01 837 0908.

Let's Face It – Network for the facially disfigured,
Christine Piff,
10 Wood End,
Crowthorne,
Berks, RG11 6DQ.
Tel: 0344 774405.

Hysterectomy Support Group (and leaflets available),
Judy Vaughan,
Central co-ordinator,
'Rivendell',
Warren Way,
Lower Heswall,
Wirral, L60 9HV.
Tel: 051 342 3167.

Hysterectomy leaflets also available:
'The Change of Life'
Health Education Council,
78 New Oxford Street,
London, WC1A 1AH.
'Hysterectomy'
Woman and Home Magazine,
King's Reach Tower,
Stamford Street,
London, SE1 9LS.

Coda
Distress comprehended

> My art is to intensify the expression of things so that their heart and innermost meaning is vividly made visible.
>
> Thomas Hardy.

The aim of this book has been to enable the innermost meaning to be made visible both to the woman in distress and to her professional helper. We have not attempted a comprehensive guide to all the ills for which women seek help, but have confined ourselves to those of which we have considerable experience because we see them over and over again in our practice. We hope that by sharing this experience we shall encourage colleagues to look more closely at the problems women bring to them.

From these chapters it can be seen that the way to help a woman with physical or mental symptoms due to emotional causes is by understanding her predicament in terms of her image of herself as a woman, particularly in terms of her reproductive function, and by tracing her story back to the key events that precipitated her distress. These frequently pass unnoticed by professional workers.

A patient's childhood is seldom explored. Even in a psychiatric history, the enquiry may be perfunctory, concerned only with minor symptoms of childhood distress – such as nailbiting, temper tantrums, nightmares, or sleepwalking. Enquiry about parental illness, particularly mental illness, or of any separations from the parents would be more useful. Even more pertinent might be sensitive questioning about experience of abuse as a child, whether physical, psychological, or sexual. This could be especially helpful for disturbed adolescents with records of suicidal attempts, delinquent behaviour, or alcohol or drug abuse.

If a woman is uncooperative or is upset by chest, vaginal, or rectal examinations, or responds to them in unexpected ways, doctors should ponder why. Is there a reason for it, a meaning for her behaviour? She may have been sexually abused, or have been treated roughly by a thoughtless partner. Unless the doctor is aware of this possibility, he unwittingly recreates for her the original situation of her abuse. Bizarre or apparently inexplicable symptoms such as self-injury and other 'acting out' behaviour, or menstrual and eating disorders can become understandable to the baffled professional helper if they are viewed from the point of view of a girl's identity, her image of herself as a woman.

Other symptoms may be comprehended as the expression of a woman's distress at finding herself childless through increasing age, barrenness, or losing a child. Or they may represent her distress at the loss of a sibling, a loved grandparent, or of a spouse or partner. Doctors should wonder whether there has been, in her past, an incompletely mourned termination or stillbirth or a bereavement. The discovery of any one of these events in her history is well worth further enquiry in order to find out if it is the source of her present problems. Such events as sterilization, stillbirth, or mastectomy are often either not enquired about at all, or are dismissed as fairly common life events; their deep significance for the woman is not appreciated.

The causes of a woman's distress may be traced not only to her past, but to adverse factors in her present environment. She may be overwhelmed by the identity problems and social adjustments she has to make because of her lesbianism. She may be submerged beneath the burdens of being a single parent, or a stepmother, or of having a handicapped child, all of which may lead to depression and a lowering of her capacity to cope.

Busy doctors faced with the varied physical and mental symptoms of a woman's distress often overlook these everyday causes just because they are so familiar, and because they know they cannot change her circumstances or her environment. They may think, often rightly, that she has brought many of her problems on herself, and wish to spend as little time as possible in considering them and in trying to help her. They are then experiencing the same despair and impotence that she herself is feeling. They may also be overwhelmed, as she is, by the sheer number of different life traumas to which she is subject; and select only one or two of them for exploration, possibly neglecting others, which may be contributing more to her distress.

The prescription of minor tranquillizers has, in the past been the panacea for all such situations; it is easy and quick and painless – for the doctor. Now, with the increasing realization of the dangers of disinhibition and of addiction, this panacea is no longer so acceptable, which makes comprehension of the underlying reasons for the distress all the more imperative.

When a woman patient comes for help with symptoms that seem to have no coherence, and for which no obvious physical cause can be found, she should not just be dismissed as a nuisance – a neurotic, a hysteric, or a 'heart sink patient' (O'Dowd, 1988) – with 'functional' or emotional symptoms. Why have they erupted at this moment in her life? Why in this way? What underlying stresses have caused them? What distress is she communicating through these symptoms? The professional carers, and sometimes the patient too, may well regard the outpouring of grief, rage, or despair as embarrassing, time-consuming, or even distasteful; indeed, unworthy of anyone's attention. On the contrary, it is precisely when such outward expression of the patient's deepest feelings are listened to attentively and really valued that healing and recovery can occur. And it is this profound respect for the patient and her sense of self that lies at the heart of psychotherapy.

For once the factors responsible have been fully explored and recognized by doctor and patient, the emotions relating to the trauma can be worked through, so that the symptoms arising from the defences against the painful emotions can disappear. The memory of the traumas will remain, but the emotional intensity will fade, leaving the woman free to make more healthy and fulfilling relationships, to mature and to become truly creative.

We hope that this book, by increasing the understanding of professionals caring for women, will have provided some signposts and illuminated the pathways by which women in distress can be helped back to mental and physical health.

Bibliography

Bargate, V. (1978) *No Mama No*, London: Jonathan Cape.

Bell, A.P. and Weinberg, M.S. (1978) *Homosexualities. A Study of Diversity Among Men and Women*, London: Mitchell Beazley.

Bettelheim, B. (1972) 'How do you help a child who has a physical handicap?' *Ladies Home Journal*, 89 (34).

Bourne, S. and Lewis, E. (1984) 'Pregnancy after stillbirth or neonatal death. Psychological risks and management', *Lancet* ii: 31–33.

Bowlby, J. (1969) *Attachment and Loss, Volume 1: Attachment*, London: Hogarth Press.

Bowlby, J. (1973) *Attachment and Loss, Volume 2: Separation: Anxiety and Anger*, London: Hogarth Press.

Bridenthal, R. and Koonz, C. (1977) *Becoming Visible: Women in European History*, Boston, Mass.: Houghton Mifflin Company.

Brown, G.W. and Harris, T. (1978) *Social Origins of Depression: A Study of Psychiatric Disorder in Women*, London: Tavistock.

Bruch, H. (1978) *The Golden Cage*, Shepton Mallett, Somerset: Open Books.

Bruch, H. (1985) 'Four decades of eating disorders', in D. Garner and P.E. Garfunkel (eds) *Handbook of Psychotherapy for Anorexia Nervosa and Bulimia*, New York: The Guilford Press.

Bunker, J.P. and Brown, B.W.J. (1974) 'The physician's patient as an informed consumer of surgical services', *New England Journal of Medicine* 290 (19): 1091–8.

Burchardt, N. (1987) Structure and relationships in stepfamilies in early twentieth century Britain, working paper, Stepfamily Research Project, Paul Thompson, Gill Gorell-Barnes, Natasha Burchardt, Tony Lot (forthcoming).

Calam, R. and Slade, P. (1987) 'Eating disorders and sexual experience', paper given to the conference of the British Psychological Society, January.

Carter, E.A. (1981) 'Reconstituted Families', in E.A. Carter and M. McGoldrick (eds) *The Family Life Cycle*, London and New York: Gardner Press, Chapter 12.

Carter, B. (1988) 'Forming a remarried family', in B. Carter and M. McGoldrick (eds) *The Changing Family Life Cycle*, New York: Gardner Press, Chapter 17.

Cartwright A. and Anderson, R. (1981) *General practice revisited: a second study of patients and their doctors*, London: Tavistock.

Chodorow, N. (1978) *The Reproduction of Mothering*, Berkeley, Cal. and London: University of California Press.

Dally, A. (1976) *Mothers: Their Power and Influence*, London: Weidenfeld & Nicolson.

D'Arcy, E. (1968) 'Congenital defects: mothers' reactions to first information', *British Medical Journal* 3: 796.

de Beauvoir, S. (1953; 1972) *The Second Sex*, London: Jonathan Cape, London: Penguin Books.

Derogatis, L.R. and Kourlesis, S.M. (1981) 'An approach to evaluation of sexual problems in the cancer patient', *CA. A Cancer Journal for Clinicians* 31 (1): 46–50.

Deutsch, H. (1924) 'The psychology of woman in relation to the functions of reproduction', *International Journal of Psycho-Analysis* VI: 405.

Dinnerstein, D. (1976) *The Rocking of the Cradle and the Ruling of the World*, London: Women's Press Ltd.

Drotar, D., Baskiewioz, A., Irvin, N., Kennel, J.H., and Klaus, M.H. (1975) 'The adaptation of parents to the birth of a child with a congenital abnormality', *Medical Journal of Australia* 1: 523.

Duby, G. (1981) *The Knight, the Lady and the Priest*, London: Penguin Books.

Edgerton, M., Jacobson, W., and Meyer, E. (1960) 'Surgical/psychiatric study of patients seeking plastic (cosmetic) surgery: 98 consecutive patients with minimal deformity', *British Journal of Plastic Surgery* 13: 136–45.

Erikson, E.H. (1959) *Identity and The Life Cycle. Psychological Issues*, Vol. 1, No.1, New York: International University Press.

Fraser, A. (1984) *The Weaker Vessel*, London: Methuen.

Freud, S. (1897) *Letter 69 to Wilhelm Fleiss*, Standard edn, vol. 1, London: Hogarth Press.

Freud, S. (1917) *Mourning and Melancholia*, standard edn, vol. 14, London: Hogarth Press.

Freud, S. (1924) 'The Dissolution of the Oedipus Complex' in *On Sexuality* (1977) London: Pelican Freud Library, Vol. 7.

Freud, S. (1931) 'Female Sexuality', in *On Sexuality*, (1977) London: Pelican Freud Library, Vol. 7.

Friedan, B. (1963; 1982) *The Feminine Mystique*, Pelican Books: London.

Furstenberg, F. and Spanier, G. (1987) *Recycling the Family. Remarriage after Divorce*, London: Sage Publications.

Garvey, M.J., Tuason, V.B., Lumrey, A.E., and Hoffman, N.G. (1983) 'Occurrence of depression in the post-partum state', *Journal of Affective Disorders*, 5(2): 97–101.

Gilligan, C. (1982) *In a Different Voice* Cambridge, Mass. and London: Harvard University Press.

Golombok, S., Spencer, A., and Rutter, M. (1983) 'Children in lesbian and single-parent households: psychosexual and psychiatric appraisal', *Journal of Child Psychology and Psychiatry and Allied Disciplines* 24: 551-72.

Gorell Barnes, G. (1984) 'Step-families', in *Working with families*, London: Macmillan/BASW.

Hall, Z.M. (1987a) 'Soul Murder', *Changes* 5 (5): 303–6, January.

Hall, Z.M. (1987b) 'Group therapy for the victims of child sexual abuse', paper given to the winter quarterly meeting of the Royal College of Psychiatrists, London.

Hay, G. (1983) 'Paranoia and dysmorphophobia', *British Journal of Psychiatry* 142: 309.

Hays, P. and Douglass, A. (1984) 'A comparison of puerperal psychosis and the schizophreniform variants of manic-depression', *Acta psychiatrica R.I.C.A. Scandinavia* 69 (3): 177–81.

Johns, N. (1971) 'Family reactions to the birth of a child with a congenital abnormality', *Medical Journal of Australia* 1: 277.

Josselson, R. (1987) *Finding Herself: Pathways to Identity Development in Women*, San Francisco and London: Jossey Bass.

Kafka, F. (1977) *The Trial*, London: Pan Books.

Kempe, R.S., and Kempe, C.H. (1978) *Child Abuse*, London/Shepton Mallett, Somerset: Fontana/Open Books.

Klaus, M.H. and Kennell, J. (1976) *Parent–Infant Bonding*, St. Louis.: Mosby.

Klein, M. (1940) 'Mourning and its relation to manic-depressive states', in E. Jones, (ed) *Contributions to Psycho-Analysis*, London: Hogarth Press.

Klein, M. (1957) *Envy and Gratitude*, London: Tavistock.

Kohut, H. (1978) 'Remarks about the formation of the self' in P. Ornstein (ed.) *The Search for the Self*, New York: International Universities Press.

Krant, M.J. (1981) 'Psychosocial impact of Gynaecological cancer', *Cancer* 48: 608–12.

Laing, R.D. (1970) *Knots*, London: Tavistock.

Levi, P. (1988) *The Drowned and the Saved*, London: Michael Joseph.

Lewis, E. (1976) 'The management of stillbirth: coping with an unreality, *Lancet* ii: 619–20.

Lindemann, E. (1941) 'Observations on psychiatric sequelae to surgical operations in women', *American Journal of Psychiatry* 98: 132–37.

Lindemann, E. (1958) 'Observations on women after operations', *American Journal of Psychiatry* 98: 132.

Lorca, F.G. (1984) *Casa de Bernarda Alba*, H. Ramsden (ed.), Manchester: Manchester University Press.

Lund, M. (1987) 'The non-custodial father: common challenges in parenting after divorce', in C. Lewis and M.O'Brien (eds) *Reassessing Fatherhood: New Observations on Fathers and the Modern Family*, London, Beverly Hills, and New Delhi: Sage.

Maguire, P. (1976) 'The psychological and social sequelae of mastectomy', in J.C. Howels (ed.) *Modern Perspectives in Psychiatric Aspects of Surgery* New York: Brunner/Mazels, pp.390–421.

Mahler, M. (1967) 'On human symbiosis and the vicissitudes of individuation', *Journal of the American Psychoanalytic Association* 15: 740–63.

Marks, I. (1978) 'Rehearsal relief of a nightmare', *British Journal of Psychiatry* 133: 461–5.

Menning, B.E. (1975) 'The infertile couple, a plea for advocacy', *Child Welfare* 54: 545.

Meyers, T.J. (1965) *The Psychologic Effects of Gynecic Surgery*, Seattle: Pacific Medicine and Surgery.
Miller, A. (1983) *For Your Own Good*, London: Faber & Faber.
Miller, A. (1984) *Thou Shalt Not Be Aware*, London and Sydney: Pluto Press.
Morrow Lindbergh, A. (1985) *A Gift from the Sea*, London: Hogarth Press (originally published in 1955).
Nicholson, N. (1973) *Portrait of a Marriage*, London: Futura.
Nijs, P. and Rouffa, L. (1975) '*AID couples: psychological and psychopathological evaluation*, Andrologia 7: 187.
O'Dowd, T.C. (1988) 'Five years of heartsink patients in general practice'. *British Medical Journal* 297: 528–30.
Orbach, S. (1978) *Fat is a Feminist Issue* London: Virago.
Paffenbarger, Jr. R.S. (1961) 'The picture puzzle of the post-partum psychoses', *Journal of Chronic Diseases*, 13: 161–73.
Paykel, E.S. (1978) 'Contribution of life events to causation of psychiatric illness', *Psychological Medicine* 8: 245.
Pound, A., Puckering, C., Cox, T., and Mills, M. (1988) 'The impact of maternal depression on young children', *British Journal of Psychotherapy* 4 (3): 240–52.
Raphael-Leff, J. (1980) 'Psychotherapy with pregnant women', in B. Plum (ed.) *Psychological Aspects of Pregnancy, Birthing and Bonding*, New York and London: Human Sciences Press.
Raphael-Leff, J. (1985) 'Facilitators and regulators: vulnerability to postnatal disturbance', *Journal of Psychosomatic Obstetrics and Gynecology* 4 151–68.
Riley, D. (1979) 'Puerperal psychiatric illness: psychogenic or biochemical', proceedings of the Fifth World Congress of the International College of Psychosomatic Medicine.
Royal College of General Practitioners (1981) *Health and Prevention in Primary Care*, London: Royal College of General Practitioners.
Rutter, M. (1966) *Children of Sick Parents*, Oxford: Oxford University Press.
Sewell, H.M., and Edwards, E.W. (1980) 'Pelvic genital cancer: body image and sexuality', *Frontiers in Radiation Therapy and Oncology* 14: 35–41.
Shengold, L. (1978) 'Assault on a child's individuality: a kind of soul murder', *Psychoanalysis Quarterly* 4 (3): 419–24.
Shengold, L. (1979) 'Child abuse and deprivation: soul murder', *Journal of the American Psychoanalytic Association*, 27 (3): 533–59.
Shuttle, P., and Redgrove, P. (1978) *The Wise Wound*, London: Paladin Books.
Simmons, R.G. (1987) 'Self-esteem in adolescence', in T. Honness and K. Yardley (eds) London and New York: Routledge & Kegan Paul.
Sloan, D. (1978) 'The emotional and psychosexual aspects of hysterectomy', *American Journal of Obstetrics and Gynecology* 131 (6): 598–605.
Sloan, G. and Leichner, P. (1986) 'Is there a relationship between sexual abuse or incest and eating disorders?' *Canadian Journal of Psychiatry* 31 565–60.
Solnit, A.J. and Stark, M.H. (1961) 'Mourning and the birth of a defective child', *Psychoanalytic Study of the Child* 16: 523.
Steiner, G. (1988) *The Times*, 14 May.

Stoller, R.S. (1968) *Sex and Gender*, London: Karnac Books.
Stoller, R.S. (1975) *Perversion. The Erotic Form of Hatred*, London and New York: Karnac Books.
Tilt, E.J. (1857) *The Change of Life in Health and Disease*, 2nd edn, London: Churchill.
Trouse, M.A. (1981) 'Extra postpartum contact: an assessment of its intervention and its effects', in V.L. Smeriglio (ed.) *Newborns and Parents: Parent–Infant Contact and Newborn Sensory Stimulation*, New York: Lawrence Erlbaum.
Warner, M. (1981) *Joan of Arc: The image of female heroism*, London: Weidenfeld and Nicolson.
Welldon, E.V. (1988) *Mother, Madonna, Whore: The Idealization and Denigration of Motherhood*, London: Free Association Books.
Wiehe, V.R. (1976a) 'Psychological reactions to infertility', *Psychological Reports* 38: 863.
Wiehe, V.R. (1976b) 'Psychological reactions to infertility: implications for nursing in resolving feelings of disappointment and inadequacy', *The Journal of Obstetric and Gynaecologic Nursing*, 28 July.
Winnicott, D. (1960) 'Ego Distortion in Terms of True and False Self', in *The Maturational Processes and the Facilitating Environment* (1979), London: Hogarth Press.
Winnicott, D. (1971) *Playing and Reality*, London: Tavistock.
Wolkind, S. (1985) 'The first years: pre-school children and their families in the inner city', in *Recent Research in Developmental Psychopathology* J.E. Stevenson (ed.) *Journal of Child Psychology and Psychiatry, Supplement no.4*.

Index